Praises

"In this bracing and profound study of the Book of Revelation, Msgr. A. Robert Nusca swims into the deep waters of Scripture and the world, finding in them God's call to a sacrificial hope for the Church. Engaging a rich set of testimony from the tradition, as well as a biting cultural critique of our present postmodern era, Nusca explores Revelation's intricate imagery as a window onto contemporary Christian ecclesial witness. He does not offer us a predictive code for the Bible's final book but a path that leads us in, through, and toward God in Christ, in an Augustinian journey between 'two worlds' of rebellion and redemption. The Book of Revelation, Nusca shows, is a mirror of the truth, but also the mirror of a real struggle, one of enormous, infinite cost that takes us through the postmodern assaults on our spirits to the divine end of our life with God. This is necessary reading for every Christian leader today."

—EPHRAIM RADNER
Professor of Historical Theology
Wycliffe College, Toronto

"Few people would think of seeking the face of Jesus in the Apocalypse, with all its bizarre imagery. The Gospels provide a more transparent image of Christ. The Book of Revelation, however, was not written to scare people but to encourage and console believers who found themselves in the storm of history, over which the Risen Christ, King of history, walks. Msgr. A. Robert Nusca presents three facets of Jesus' person: Glorified Angel, Lamb of God, and

Divine Warrior. The author illustrates the meaning and import of these three images with a careful and well-documented exegesis, to present the reader with some facets of the Risen Christ which might have hitherto escaped him, thus enriching his faith in Jesus. Nusca goes on to add also a fourth face: that face reflected in the faith and conduct of Christians, with both its splendor and deformities. The author concludes by transporting John's Christological message into our postmodern society to show the relevance of Revelation in each successive period of Church history. The book is very readable and will contribute to both personal faith and pastoral practice."

—PROSPER CARDINAL GRECH, OSA
Co-Founder, Institutum Patristicum Augustinianum

"A remarkable tour through the least read and most misunderstood book of the New Testament: informative and challenging; deeply learned yet entirely accessible; an inspiring, emboldening contribution to the New Evangelization."

—GEORGE WEIGEL
Distinguished Senior Fellow and
William E. Simon Chair in Catholic Studies
Ethics and Public Policy Center

"This is an inspired book which is clearly the product of not only deep and wide learning but also profound and prayerful contemplation. Msgr. Nusca guides his readers through the bewildering and sometimes bizarre language and imagery of the Book of Revelation to a recognition of how they can participate, even now in the midst of our wounded postmodern world, in the new creation that has come about through the crucified and exalted Christ.

This is biblical scholarship at its finest and most spiritually potent form!"

—KHALED ANATOLIOS
Professor of Theology
University of Notre Dame

"I am grateful to Msgr. A. Robert Nusca for highlighting a rich and attractive perspective on the Book of Revelation: the portrait of Christ that emerges from it. In Msgr. Nusca's accessible style, a scriptural book that may appear remote is revealed as charged with life and valuable for our spiritual lives today."

—TIMOTHY M. GALLAGHER, O.M.V.
Author, The Discernment of Spirits:
An Ignatian Guide for Everyday Living

"Monsignor A. Robert Nusca's *The Christ of the Apocalypse* makes a significant contribution to eschatological literature. His focus is on the coherence of the message of the Book of Revelation and its relevance for the contemporary Christian in giving an integrated vision of life. Revelation has always proved a controversial part of the New Testament corpus, but for Nusca the overlooked portrait of Christ is what most draws his attention under the themes of Glorified Angel, Lamb of God, and Divine Warrior. Nusca's analysis of the book in the first part of the work is complemented by his exploration of the contemporary relevance in the latter part of the work. Worthy of note are the following: the emphasis he gives to a transcendent God-centered perspective; the call to patient endurance of suffering; the important spiritual struggle as the human person endeavors to live truly the *imago Dei* in which he is made. There is a powerful critique of contemporary society in its lack of transcendence and unwillingness to own a Jewish-Christian heritage. Nusca has a helpful focus on the mystery of the transformation of the human person which resonates with much contemporary systematic theology. He sees the warnings to the seven Churches as being relevant also to the self-delusion and spiritual apathy that can abound in our contemporary scenario. His denunciation of private mysticism and his advocacy of the need for dynamic public witness by lives radiant with grace and holiness are a siren call to conversion, renewal and deeper purification. Above all, Nusca helps his readers to see that the Book of Revelation can assist a deeper entry into the mystery of God and the mystery of divine grace operative in the cross of Christ. Surely this is at the heart of St John's purpose in writing it."

—Sr. Gill Goulding, C.J.
Professor of Systematic Theology,
Regis College, Toronto

"Msgr. A. Robert Nusca is a specialist on the Book of Revelation, and this new work puts into fresh focus an aspect often overlooked in this apocalyptic book: John's presentation of the person of Jesus Christ. Without overlooking the dramatic and apocalyptic images in the Book of Revelation, Msgr. Nusca leads the reader through the presentation of several key epithets for Christ, which point to a coherent and relevant understanding of the human person for our contemporary world. Masterfully written by someone who obviously has presented the Book of Revelation in various pastoral and theological settings. Highly recommended reading for theology and spirituality."

—Michael Kolarcik, S.J.
Rector, Pontifical Biblical Institute

The Christ

OF THE

Apocalypse

The Christ

OF THE

Apocalypse

CONTEMPLATING THE FACES OF JESUS
IN THE BOOK OF REVELATION

Msgr. A. Robert Nusca

EMMAUS
ROAD
PUBLISHING

Steubenville, Ohio
www.EmmausRoad.org

Emmaus Road Publishing
1468 Parkview Circle
Steubenville, Ohio 43952

Library of Congress Cataloging-in-Publication Data

Names: Nusca, A. Robert, author.

Title: The Christ of the Apocalypse : contemplating the faces of Jesus in the Book of Revelation / Msgr. A. Robert Nusca.

Description: Steubenville : Emmaus Road, 2018.

Identifiers: LCCN 2017037500 (print) | LCCN 2017041057 (ebook) | ISBN 9781945125775 (ebook) | ISBN 9781945125751 (hardcover) | ISBN 9781945125768 (pbk.)

Subjects: LCSH: Bible. Revelation--Criticism, interpretation, etc. | Jesus Christ.

Classification: LCC BS2825.52 (ebook) | LCC BS2825.52 .N79 2017 (print) | DDC 228/.06--dc23

LC record available at https://lccn.loc.gov/2017037500

Cover image: *Angels at Mamre (Holy Trinity)* (15th-century) by Andrei Rublev, Tretyakov Gallery, Moscow, Russia.

Cover design and layout by Margaret Ryland

TABLE OF CONTENTS

Foreword

The Book of Revelation, or Apocalypse, has long intrigued the Christian people. It is filled with stunning and enigmatic imagery, and with scenes of judgment and glory. Too often the strangeness of the imagery and unawareness of its original context and purpose have led to it being used as a kind of inkblot, onto which the reader can project his or her own imaginings, and so the sacred text has been misused to give divine authority to whatever political or religious project the interpreter favors.

But the Apocalypse is a marvellous book through which the contemporary reader can share in a vision of the glory of God, and especially of the Lord Jesus, and so be challenged to be faithful to a life of Christian discipleship in a world which, now as at the time when the Apocalypse was first proclaimed to the early Christians, is hostile to Christ and to His disciples. Now, as in the first century, Christians face martyrdom, and those who are not called to die for Christ are called to live for Christ in a world which in many ways rejects the Gospel. More than ever, we need the apocalyptic vision, to have our own vision of reality clarified, and to be strengthened in our evangelical witness.

In *The Christ of the Apocalypse,* Monsignor Nusca offers

us a profound reflection upon the Christology of the Apocalypse, and upon the way in which meditation upon the various images of Jesus in the book can help the contemporary Christian to be a faithful disciple in a hostile world. Drawing upon the resources of modern interpretation and upon the rich tradition of the Fathers of the Church and of the spiritual teachers of our faith, he sets the text of the Book of Revelation within the context of the whole of Sacred Scripture, and within the context of life in a fallen world.

No book of Scripture is to be read passively, and that is certainly true of the Book of Revelation: it demands of us active engagement and, like an icon in the tradition of Eastern Christianity, invites us to enter into an encounter with the Lord which will change our life.

With deep learning and spiritual insight, Monsignor Nusca helps us to encounter Christ in the Apocalypse, and with pastoral sensitivity and cultural awareness he leads us to apply to our own situation as modern Christians the spiritual wisdom of the Seer of Patmos. *The Christ of the Apocalypse* is a book to be read and reread with great spiritual profit, so that in reading the Book of Revelation we may become fully engaged in our difficult but glorious mission as faithful disciples of Christ, the Lamb who was slain but who rules the universe in majesty.

—HIS EMINENCE THOMAS CARDINAL COLLINS
Archbishop of Toronto

Preface

Many people who read the Book of Revelation experience some degree of perplexity when faced with language and symbolism that seem so far removed from the realities of our postmodern world. The struggle often begins with some experience of incoherence occasioned by the book's intense apocalyptic imagery. The story's either/or rhetoric as well as its language of violence are among other reasons why the contemporary reader might be led to abandon the effort to derive some meaning from this masterpiece of early Christian literature.

In the following reflections—which trace their origins to a series of spiritual conferences given in Canada and the U.S.A.—I would like to underscore precisely the underlying *coherence* of the Book of Revelation's message, as well as to situate its meaning and relevance within the larger context of the structures, theology, and spirituality of contemporary Christianity. In the process, I hope to assist the reader in arriving at some appreciation of the inherent order and consistency of the book's God- and Christ-centered universe. Below the surface of the narrative's clashing apocalyptic visions of heavenly worship and approaching judgment, there emerges an integrated vision of life. As one order passes away and a new one comes into being, heaven and earth are called to unite their voices in the "new song" of praise to God the Almighty and to the Lamb (Rev 5:9–14).

To arrive at this goal, I would like to begin by following the experience of St. John as recorded in the text itself. This I propose to do in two ways. First, in chapters 1 through 4, I would like to sound the depths of the book's complex portrait of Jesus Christ too often overlooked amid the dramatic scenes of approaching judgment. Here, I employ what is essentially the language of contemporary biblical exegesis in highlighting relevant details of the text. The second, larger part of this book, steps back from the text with the aim of achieving an enhanced perspective on the overarching message and meaning of this prophetic book in relation to the life of the Christian today. Here, I would like to slow the pace considerably by providing greater detail concerning the spiritual depths of a message which is "ever ancient and ever new," in the words of St. Augustine. It is within the context of the cultural and spiritual realities of the contemporary postmodern world that I propose to offer some reflections in chapters 5 and 6. The endnotes provided are, admittedly, somewhat more abundant than those often found in books that presuppose—as this book does—no previous specialized knowledge of Sacred Scripture. For this reason they may be more of interest to some readers (including students) than others. What I would like to pursue centrally in the pages ahead is the unfolding of the reader's experience of the visions of Christ in the text itself and of their larger meaning and message for us today.

In Memoriam:
JOHANNES CLEMENS NIX

Πάντα ῥεῖ . . .
"Everything flows . . ."
                    —Heraclitus of Ephesus

Acknowledgments

I would like express my heartfelt gratitude to many people who have played a role in bringing this book to completion. Sincerest thanks to Cardinal Thomas Collins, Archbishop of Toronto, for writing the Foreword and for his gracious encouragement and support. I am grateful to Fr. Ugo Vanni, S.J., for his very insightful comments in the early stages of the project. Also, I am deeply indebted to Fr. Jean-Pierre Ruiz for his sage advice at various stages in the preparation of the manuscript.

I owe an enormous debt of gratitude to Fr. Robert Barringer, C.S.B., the former Dean of Studies at St. Augustine's Seminary of Toronto for his friendship, enthusiasm, and encouragement. I am most grateful to him for having edited the original manuscript for content and length, with a view to making the book more accessible to a wider audience. Sincerest thanks as well to Janine Langan and to Sr. Mechtilde O'Mara, C.S.J.—both Professors Emerita of the University of St. Michael's College—for their very insightful comments, support, and encouragement throughout. Many thanks to Fr. John Elmer Abad, a patristics scholar and lecturer at St. Augustine's Seminary, for his insights and advice.

Sincerest thanks to Scott Hahn for his enthusiastic

support and for offering to publish the book. I am most grateful to Chris Erickson and Melissa Girard for all of their efforts throughout the editorial process, and to the entire staff of Emmaus Road Publishing. Sincerest thanks as well to those who have taken time to read the book and offer their words of endorsement.

Many thanks as well to: Fr. Michael Patella, O.S.B., Fr. Yvan Mathieu, Fr. Andrea Spatafora, Fr. James K. Farge, C.S.B., and Prof. John Kloppenborg; to the faculty, seminarians, and staff of St. Augustine's Seminary of Toronto & Serra House; Fr. Hansoo Park, Fr. Fred Chung, Bishop Wayne Kirkpatrick, Fr. Edwin Gonsalves, Fr. Louis Malo, Fr. Tom Lynch, Bishop Attila Mikloshazy, S.J., Fr. Walter Werbylo, C.S.B., Fr. Peter Marr, Fr. John-Mark Missio, Fr. Devin Roza, Mr. Patrick Jordan, Dr. Josephine Lombardi, Dr. Patricia Murphy, Theresa Kelly, Sheila Connolly, and Maryam Rezai-Atrie. A word of thanks as well to the Franciscan Sisters of the Eucharist, the Religious Sisters of Mercy of Alma, and the Sisters of Life.

Much gratitude as well to the auxiliary bishops, priests, and deacons of the Archdiocese of Toronto; to Fr. Michael Busch and the Staff of St. Michael's Cathedral; Msgr. John Borean, Fr. Constantine Siarapis, Fr. Pier Giorgio Di Cicco, Fr. David Reilander, and the late Fr. John Affleck for his unwavering support and enthusiasm.

Finally, I express my sincerest gratitude to Angeli San Juan, Jennifer Ramos, Cathy Carroll, Catherine Pawluch, Martha and Haley Dilazzaro, Hermy Villasenor, John Artibello, Dr. Don Roncevic, Nicola Suppa, Dominic Mesiano, Ron Caravaggio, the parishioners of Holy Rosary Church and All Saints Parish, and to my immediate family for their spiritual support and prayers.

CHAPTER ONE

The Faces of Jesus in the New Testament

The extraordinary images that fill the story world of the Apocalypse of John sparkle, simmer, and seethe with an electric, otherworldly glow that has helped to account for its perennial allure since it first appeared toward the end of the first century. Its influence reaches far beyond the realms of theological and religious reflection into the worlds of literature, music, and the plastic arts and extends in our own time into the fragmentary, ephemeral, twittering, virtual reality of cyberspace. The highly symbolic nature and cosmic scope of the visions described in the book have yielded a colossal array of conflicting interpretations. Even a casual study of the history of the book's interpretation reveals that controversy has been its steady companion from the time of the ecstatic utterances of the second-century prophet Montanus to the Branch Davidians in the tragic events that unfolded at Waco, Texas, in 1993. Indeed, G. K. Chesterton once said that even though St. John "saw many strange monsters in his vision, he saw no creature so wild as one of his own commentators."[1] Given the book's unwavering capacity through the centuries for eliciting some description of exaggerated response in its readers, it is not without reason that one commentator refers it to as "the paradise of fanatics and sectarians."[2]

The Apocalypse certainly contains many haunting images of death and destruction on a cosmic scale, as the images of locusts, frogs, hail, earthquakes, and falling stars recall the plagues described in the Book of Exodus (and those reprised by the sage in the Wisdom of Solomon 11:2–19:22). In the narratives which focus on judgment, these plagues are unleashed by the Lamb before God's throne (Rev 5:6), as He opens the mysterious scroll that is sealed with seven seals (beginning in 6:1). The book's portrayal of the dark side in the battle between good and evil features a cast of infernal characters that includes the unholy trinity—or at least triad—of Satan (12:3ff.), the "beast rising out of the sea" (or "Antichrist" in 13:1), the "beast rising out of the earth" (or false prophet in 13:11), and the armies—both visible and invisible—that are allied with them. The story relates a succession of images that have captivated the imaginations of successive genera- tions of readers, including: the Four Horsemen (6:2ff.), the Number of the Beast (13:18), the battle of Armageddon (16:16), the "lake of fire that burns with sulfur" (19:20, 20:10), the thousand-year reign (20:2–6), and the second death (20:14, 21:8) reserved for God's enemies.

The basic facts about this Apocalypse (from which the literary genre of apocalypse takes its name) have too often gone unnoticed: That it is an Apocalypse of Jesus Christ (1:1), and that the story world is throughout a God- and Christ-centered one, and the Seer's visions permit the reader to look with him through the open door to heaven (4:1ff.) onto a shimmering, celestial world that resounds with the songs of angels. Far beyond predictions of the end of the world, John invites the community that listens to his prophetic message not only to gaze in awe and wonder upon the world described beyond the opened door, but to enter with him through that door and to stand alongside the angels in the praise and worship of God and of the Lamb. While many powerful and captivating images emerge as the book's narrative unfolds, the audience is presented with a rich and multi-faceted portrait of Jesus Christ, the Son of God, who stands—alongside God—at the very center of this enigmatic last book of the Bible.

The figure of Jesus Christ that emerges from among the many powerful apocalyptic visions described in Revelation's story world is a complex and profoundly theological one that speaks directly to the life situation of John's audience in late first-century Asia Minor. The book's literary genre (apocalypse), its use of language, and the vast array of symbols that fill its story world are, admittedly, quite distinctive in contrast with the Gospels. Unlike the accounts of the appearances of the Risen Lord to the disciples handed down in the Gospels, Revelation's images of Christ are the fruit of the author's own Spirit-inspired apocalyptic visions and his theological reflection several decades after the events described by the evangelists. While the author writes as an early Christian prophet (22:6, 9) and understands his work to be a book of prophecy (1:3; 22:10, 18–19), his Apocalypse—just like the other writings of the New Testament—presents a coherent, theological reflection on the person and the mystery of Jesus Christ, the Son of God (Mk 1:1; Jn 20:31) to nourish the faith life of the communities of believers to whom his book is addressed (1:4).

Although John's portrait of Christ is extraordinary in its apocalyptic tenor and tones, what he is striving to accomplish is entirely consistent with the aims of the other sacred writers of the New Testament. Indeed, from the Gospel of Matthew to the Book of Revelation, the New Testament contains a variety of portraits of Jesus Christ. They have been shaped by history and tradition by a variety of theological concerns and specific pastoral issues. They have been preserved and handed on by living communities of faith, guided by the refining fire of the Holy Spirit in prayer and worship. The Faces of Christ in the New Testament have succeeded in speaking through the centuries to the hearts of spiritual seekers in every age and have the power to continue to speak to us today. It would be helpful to consider briefly the outlines of these different Faces.

The Face of Jesus in the Gospel According to St. Matthew

From the outset, St. Matthew places the context of his portrait of Jesus within the broader narrative of Jewish salvation history (Mt 1:1–17), drawing deeply from the wellsprings of the Old Testament. In the First Gospel's compelling figure of Christ, God has brought to fulfill-ment the hopes and aspirations of His holy people. The Gospel's narrative reflects both continuity and discontinu-ity with Israel's story of salvation, as Matthew's Jesus has come "not to abolish . . . but to fulfill" the law and the prophets (Mt 5:17). In the First Gospel Jesus is "Christ" (from the Hebrew *messiah,* or "anointed one").[3] He is Son of God,[4] Son of Abraham,[5] Son of Man,[6] Lord,[7] Son of David,[8] Emmanuel or "God with us,"[9] and the Teacher[10] who proclaims the arrival of the Kingdom of Heaven as He extends to others God's healing powers. Moreover,

Matthew's Jesus is worshipped from the very outset by the Magi (2:2, 2:11), by the disciples during His earthly ministry (cf. 14:33), and within the context of the Resurrection narrative (28:9, 17). Adding to the spiritual depth and sophistication of this portrait are clear associations between Jesus and the Wisdom of God (11:19, 28–30).

Matthew presents impressive materials that are not found in the other Gospels. The image of Jesus standing before the crowds gathered around Him at the Mount of Beatitudes evokes the figure of Moses on Mount Sinai. In place of the Ten Commandments, Matthew's New Moses reveals the Beatitudes of the Kingdom of Heaven (5:1–12) as He issues a resounding call to a higher righteousness (5:20). Jesus founds His Church upon the rock of Peter's faith (Mt 16:13–19), establishing in this way a community of believers who will continue His saving work until the end of time (28:20).

The Face of Jesus in the Gospel According to St. Mark

The shortest of the four Gospels, Mark gives us "the beginning of the gospel of Jesus Christ, the Son of God" (1:1; cf. 16:8). Cast in the more stark and somber tones of Jewish apocalyptic, Mark's spare and fast-paced narrative tells the story of the life and ministry of Jesus in terms of the spiritual battle that rages between the power of God and the forces of evil that oppose His will.[11] The narrative is dominated by the mystery of Christ's suffering and Cross. Jesus is the Son of God, but His identity is known, at first, only to the demons (1:24; cf. 5:7) and to Mark's readers (1:1; cf. Peter in 8:29). Mark's Jesus is a misunderstood Messiah, who is rejected, condemned as a common criminal (15:27), and isolated in His suffering and death (15:34), but who is raised from the dead on the third day by the invisible God whom He calls "Abba" (14:36). As scholars point out, Mark's narrative abounds with paradox, irony, and a powerful sense of reversal. For example, while those closest to Jesus are portrayed as struggling to perceive both His true identity as Son of God and the nature of His suffering messiahship, Mark describes a number of outsiders whose understanding of Jesus exceeds that of His closest followers—be it Jairus (5:22, 5:35–43), the unnamed woman (5:25–34), the Syrophoenician woman (7:25ff.), the so-called "strange" exorcist in 9:38 (cf. 9:18), Bartimaeus (10:46–52), the woman who anoints Jesus before His death (14:3–9), or the Roman centurion at the crucifixion (15:39).

Mark's Jesus is a great miracle worker and exorcist.[12] He is Christ[13] and Messiah,[14] Son of God,[15] Son of Man,[16] King,[17] and Lord.[18] He is Son of David,[19] Son of Mary,[20] Teacher,[21] Rabbi,[22] and a prophet[23] who is more powerful than John the Baptist. At the same time, the humanity of Jesus emerges as a subject of profound reflection:

> The sheer humanity of Mark's portraiture catches the eye of the most careless reader; and yet, it is but half seen if it is not perceived that this Man of Sorrows is also a Being of supernatural origin and dignity, since He is the Son of God.[24]

Here is the royal Son of God who was not fully recognized as such during His earthly ministry.[25] Mark's portrayal of the shortcomings of Peter and the disciples contrasts with Matthew's more positive account (16:17–19), as Jesus Himself appears to emerge as the model to be emulated by those who would strive to follow the will of the Father on the royal road of the Cross.[26] The Markan Jesus is truly the Messiah and Son of God. He is rejected, suffers, and dies, but is vindicated by His Father in heaven as He is raised from the dead on the third day. He will return again upon the clouds in power and glory as the eschatological Son of Man—that is, the One who will come in judgment at the close of the age (13:26).

Why does this portrait of Christ seem to speak so eloquently to so many of today's youth? What does this portrait say to a generation who have suffered the effects of divorce and the breakdown of the family? Do they identify with the tragic depiction of a Jesus who is rejected, in pain, cast aside, misunderstood by both loved ones and opponents alike, and betrayed by those closest to Him?

The Face of Jesus in the Gospel According to St. Luke

Luke extends the story of Jesus of Nazareth to a wider audience, "claiming a place for Christianity on the stage of world history."[27] Luke-Acts offers a comprehensive, orderly, two-volume account of Christianity's origins (Lk 1:1–4). The evangelist relates the story of Jesus to a predominantly Gentile public by employing an elegant literary style in which harsh or discordant elements have been toned down. Luke's joyful narrative begins and ends in the Temple of Jerusalem and is permeated by the incense of prayer and an atmosphere of worship (1:10; 24:52–53). Moreover, Luke accords a special emphasis to the prayer of Jesus.[28]

Luke's Jesus—whose genealogy is traced back to Adam (3:38)—is Savior,[29] Lord,[30] Christ,[31] Christ the Lord (2:11), Son of Man,[32] Teacher,[33] Prophet,[34] Son of David,[35] and Son of God.[36] The prophetic dimension of Luke's portrait of Jesus is apparent throughout and emphasizes His mission to the poor (4:18–19), the blind, the lame, lepers, and indeed, all those who remain outside of contemporary society's spheres of power, wealth, and social standing. Pope Francis has spoken often of the need for the Church to go forth beyond its own comfort zone, extending the love, mercy, and healing presence of Christ to the poor and suffering who dwell in the peripheries of our world today.

The brighter colors of Luke's Gospel are further enhanced by the way the Evangelist accentuates the role of the Holy Spirit from the very beginning of the story of Jesus of Nazareth, as well as in his emphasis on the universal mission to the Gentiles. In Luke-Acts, the reader is led on an inspiring, uplifting journey as God's offer of salvation—which will "dawn" upon the world "from on high" (Lk 1:78)—is brought beyond Jerusalem to Rome and extended to all nations.

The Face of Jesus in the Gospel According to St. John

In his portrayal of Jesus Christ as "Word of God Made Flesh," St. John adopts from the very outset a transcendent "from above" perspective (Jn 1:1ff.; cf. 3:3) which is indebted to Old Testament wisdom traditions. Absent are the genealogies and infancy narratives featured in Matthew and Luke. Rather, it is the Book of Proverbs, Sirach, and the Wisdom of Solomon which serve as the wellsprings of the Fourth Evangelist's account of the pre-history of the Word who was with God at the dawn of creation (1:1–18). The highly theological Johannine Jesus pronounces a series of magnificent "I Am" statements that recall God's revelation to Moses on Mount Sinai (Ex 3:14). In addition to titles found in the Synoptic Gospels—such as "Christ" and "Messiah" (cf. 1:41; 4:25)—the Jesus of the Fourth Gospel is the Bread of Life (6:35, 6:48), the living bread (6:51) that "came down from heaven." He is the Light of the World (8:12; 9:5), the Gateway to the sheepfold who brings "life to the full" (10:10); the Good Shepherd (10:11, 14), the Resurrection and the Life (11:25), the Way, the Truth, the Life (14:6), and the True Vine (15:1, 15:5).

When compared with the Synoptic Gospels, the earthly ministry of Jesus detailed in John extends over a longer period of time. Jesus' ministry takes place over the course of three Passovers (see 2:13–3:21, 6:4ff., 13:1–19:42), whereas the Synoptic Gospels only refer to one Passover (see Mk 14:1; Mt 26:2; and Lk 22:7). He works fewer—if more magnificent—miracles (referred to as "signs"), performs no exorcisms, characteristically speaks of "eternal life" rather than the "Kingdom of God" (cf. Jn 3:3, 5), does not preach the Sermon on the Mount, and does not teach His disciples the Our Father. He pronounces quite extensive—and at times repetitive—theological discourses that stand in contrast to the parables found in the Synoptic Gospels. The Johannine narrative presents a multi-layered portrait of a Jesus who is the central focus of a complex "two-level drama."[37] At one level, the Fourth Gospel relates traditions concerning Jesus of Nazareth, while at another level the Johannine Christ speaks directly to the life situation of John's faith community some decades later:

The result is a complex intermingling of two time periods and historical situations. The Johannine Christ is at once the traditional Jesus of the Christian community's heritage and the contemporary Christian missionary.[38]

Like the portraits of Jesus found in Matthew, Mark, and Luke, the Gospel of John reflects a very lofty understanding of Jesus Christ the Son of God. But the distinctiveness of this portrait is seen in the majestic stature of this Word-Made-Flesh, whose divinity is never in question: from the account of His pre-history (1:1–18), throughout His transit from—and back to—the Father through this passing world, during His arrest and crucifixion (18:6; 19:30), or in His post-Resurrection splendor and return to the Father. Only in the Fourth Gospel "is the term 'God' applied to all phases of the career of the Word: the pre-existent Word (1:1), the incarnate Word (1:18), and the risen Jesus (20:28)."[39] The Johannine Jesus reveals the face of the Father, for "Jesus and the Father are one" (10:30; 14:9–11).

The Faces of Jesus in the Book of Revelation

Popular approaches to the Book of Revelation have tended to overlook the remarkable portrait of Jesus Christ elaborated in this early Christian masterpiece, with the result that the Faces of Christ—along with visions of the open heaven that the narrative sets before us—risk being overshadowed by visions of approaching judgment. Admittedly, the author expresses himself through a richly interwoven network of "polyvalent"[40] symbols which are open to more than one interpretation. The vast range of responses that the book has elicited is commented upon by one scholar:

> Revelation's bizarre imagery, obscure references and mythopoeic discourse have engendered almost endless interpretations and help to account for its fascination for a wide range of people. But seldom is the gap between critical scholarship and popular perception wider than in the case of Revelation.[41]

Throughout its twenty-two chapters, the Book of Revelation presents a complex and coherent vision of an all-powerful, glorious, radiant, cosmic Christ. And the advanced portrait that emerges is in no way lacking in substance. Indeed, John has developed a very lofty portrait of Jesus Christ, one "that is unique among the writings of the New Testament."[42] As is the case in the four Gospels, Revelation's Jesus is in no way a conceptual abstraction like the gods of the Greek philosophers. He is Jesus Christ the living "Son of God" (Rev 2:18), the Son of Man (1:13, 14:14), Word of God (19:13), Lord (11:8), Root of David (5:5, 22:16) and much more. At the same time, titles and descriptive language elsewhere associated with Jesus and His earthly ministry in the New Testament—rabbi, teacher, prophet, Nazarene, servant, miracle worker, and exorcist—are not used by John.[43] The Jesus of the Apocalypse is a complex Spirit-inspired fusion that synthesizes pre-Christian images of a warrior God (Ex 15:3; with "a sharp, two-edged sword" [2:12], who "will rule all the nations with a rod of iron" [12:5]), and the glorious, luminescent, post-Resurrection Morning Star who promises those who remain faithful a share in His own divine life.[44] He is the "Alpha and the Omega, the first and the last, the beginning and the end" (22:13), indeed: "As a way of stating unambiguously that Jesus Christ belongs to the fullness of the eternal being of God, this surpasses anything in the New Testament."[45]

In the pages ahead, we shall reflect upon Revelation's captivating portrayal of Christ, the shining face (1:14) of the Living God, who continues to walk amid the modern-day seven Churches. This Morning Star stands in our midst bidding His faithful to bear witness uncompromisingly to the truth of the Gospel so as to win a place among the ranks of the angels and saints who worship God and the Lamb forever around the heavenly throne. What emerges is a complex portrait of Christ that is developed through several different, though complementary, images.

Jesus the Glorified Angel

First of all we encounter Jesus as a glorified, angelic being in the opening visions of the book (cf. 1:12–20). This angelic Jesus stands in the midst of the seven Churches as He speaks a message that is addressed to the heart of the universal Church. Here is the face of the risen and glorified Christ whose radiance overwhelms the prophet—so much so that he falls before the Lord in fear and trembling (cf. 1:17). In this first Face of Jesus we encounter an awe-inspiring, angelic Son of Man (1:12ff.), the "Living One" who was dead and is now alive forever and ever (1:18). At the same time, we encounter Him as the voice of a glorified angel who calls out to the prophet on the Lord's Day (1:10), commissioning him to address the congregations of the seven Churches of the Roman province of Asia Minor (1:11).

This Jesus—who is equal to God and is worthy to receive the praises of all creation alongside the "One seated upon the Throne" (4:2)—nonetheless appears in the form of an angel (scholars speak here of an "angelomorphic" Jesus[46]) and addresses the faithful in the midst of crisis. To communities threatened by persecution, plagued by division, lukewarm, and at risk of apostasy, the voice of Christ comforts, consoles, challenges, threatens, exhorts, and calls to conversion, while promising a share in His own glorious, transformed existence (2:26–28; 22:16) to those who prove victorious in giving faithful witness to the truth of the Gospel in the world in which they live. The angelic Jesus of the first three chapters of Revelation is presented as being very close to us, as He walks in the midst of His Church, calling out to the faithful to enter bravely—and without delay—into the vast spiritual struggle portrayed in the book, for "the time is near" (1:3).

Jesus the Lion/Lamb of God

At the heart of Revelation's story world, John describes elaborate visions of God's heavenly throne (cf. 4:1ff.). These visions are strongly reminiscent—with respect both to the details provided and in the numinous quality of the text—of the prophet Ezekiel's "throne-chariot" (*Merkavah*) mysticism (cf. Ezek chapters 1 and 10, as well as 1 Enoch 14). It is here within the innermost circle of God's celestial court and throne room that we next encounter Jesus as the Lamb of God in Revelation 5. Far from a meek little lamb, He is both the Lion of the Tribe of Judah (5:5) and the apocalyptic Lamb with "seven horns" and "seven eyes" who was slain for the life of the world (cf. 5:6, 9–10). This paradoxical Lamb represents the centerpiece of the book's apocalyptic reflections on Jesus Christ (cf. 5–22). Here is the cosmic Lord of time and history who has achieved total victory over the powers of sin and death by emptying Himself upon the Cross for the salvation of humanity.

Christ the King and Lord of the cosmos, the Judge of Heaven and Earth, opens the gates of heaven through His death on the Cross. This apocalyptic Lion/Lamb of God "takes away the sins of the world" (Jn 1:29) but also writes the names of the elect in the Book of life (Rev 3:5; 21:27). John's Lamb of God is the Lord of History, humanity's Savior and eschatological Judge, who will vanquish the forces—both invisible and visible—that oppose God's designs. Although John's audience is led on a tour of the celestial realms through an opened door in heaven, the image of the slain Lion/Lamb constantly confronts the reader with the mystery of Christ's suffering self-sacrifice on Mount Calvary.

John's is a God-centered and Christ-centered universe, one in which Jesus is praised alongside the Father by "every creature in heaven and on earth and under the earth" (5:13), as all creation joins together in song. In the telling of the story of the Book of Revelation, the faithful are invited to add their voices to the growing chorus of the heavenly hosts as the circles of praise expand outward to encompass the audience, whether ancient or postmodern. The Apocalypse here provides us with a powerful and coherent picture of "one Church of angels and human beings" united in their exalted praises of God and the Lamb.[47]

Jesus the Divine Warrior

Finally, we encounter Jesus in the Book of Revelation as the messianic Divine Warrior, the King of kings and Lord of lords (19:16; cf. 17:14), who is "clothed in a robe dipped in blood" (19:13) and accompanied by the "armies of heaven" (19:14). This messianic Face of Jesus leads the audience to contemplate the mystery of God's justice in a world where the "Kingdom of heaven suffers violence" (cf. Mt 11:12) at the hands of those intent upon building an earthly empire that has shut itself off completely from the mystery of God's divine transcendence. John's unveiling of the view through the door to heaven offers a powerful corrective to the spirit of the postmodern age and an unbridled autonomy that would build a world without God (cf. Gen 11:1–9).

Chapter 19 of the Book of Revelation focuses on the definitive arrival of God's justice at the end of time. Those who refuse to meet Jesus as merciful Lord and Lamb of God are destined to encounter Him as a Just Judge at the close of the age. As we shall have occasion to discuss in chapter 5, this ambiguous portrait of Christ invites measured and sober reflection. Is the blood on the Rider's robe His own (19:13; cf. 5:6, 5:9)? Or is it that of His opponents—the Beast, the kings of the earth, and their armies (19:19)? Has "the slaughtered Lamb turned slaughterer," or is this "the witness turned judge"?[48] Old Testament images of a vengeful, warrior God from which the prophet seems to have drawn the colors for this imposing portrait of Christ (cf. Gen 49:10–11; Dt 32:40–42; Jer 46:10) should not obscure the fact that no battle is described, for Christ's definitive victory over His opponents was achieved long ago, through His suffering, self-emptying and death at Calvary on Good Friday, and by His rising from the dead on Easter Sunday. In the Book of Revelation, the Christian achieves victory "by the blood of the Lamb and in no other way."[49] Other images emerge in the context of the Seer's meditation upon Christ the Divine Warrior. The messianic child in Revelation 12:4–5 as well as the angelic "One like the Son of Man" described in 14:14 figure in the discussion and add to the complexity of John's oscillating portrait of Jesus (cf. 10:1).

The Book of Revelation offers a succession of images of Jesus Christ: the glorified angel, the apocalyptic Lamb of God, and the Divine Warrior. Each has something to say to us about our life with God, as well as our relationship both to this passing world and to the world to come. Above all, each aims to draw us closer to Christ as we contemplate Him under the various facets of His Paschal mystery.

A Fourth Face

In addition to these three Faces of Christ, a fourth Face of a different kind will emerge for the reader's consideration. Here we consider the Face of Christ as it has come to be reflected, refracted, deformed, and misshapen in the face of a fallen and sinful humanity originally created in God's own image and likeness (Gen 1:26–27) and now called through the Spirit to be conformed to the image of Christ, the "first born among many" (cf. Rom 8:29). This takes us beyond theological and Christological reflections to a consideration of the book's lofty understanding of the meaning of Christian salvation (what theologians call "soteriology") and of the farthest reaches of human nature

in Christ, the New Adam.[50] The story of the arrival of a
new heaven and a new earth would not be complete then
without some consideration of the significance of paradise
regained for the human person who is created in God's
image and likeness. Indeed, as St. Bonaventure remarks:
"Into this heavenly Jerusalem no one enters unless it first
comes down into the heart by grace, as St. John beheld in
the Apocalypse."[51] The Book of Revelation envisions that
those who give a bold and courageous public witness to
the values of the Gospel will come to acquire a share in
Christ's own divine glory—beginning even in the present
life. Those who have borne the marks of Jesus' own suffering and rejection will also bear the marks of His glory.
Thus, John offers the reader a remarkable portrait of his
lofty hopes for the faithful and for their own transformation in Christ, both in this world and the next.

Endnotes

[1] G. K. Chesterton, *Orthodoxy* (London & New York: John Lane, 1922), 27.

[2] G. B. Caird, *The Revelation of St. John the Divine* (London: A & C Black, 1966), 2.

[3] Cf. 1 Sam 16:6; 24:6; Jer 30:9; Dan 9:25. See also Mt 1:1, 16–18, 2:4, 11:2, 16:16, 20, 22:42, 23:10, etc.

[4] Cf. Mt 3:17; 4:3, 6; 8:29; 11:25–27; 14:33; 16:16–17; 17:5; 26:39, 42, 63; 27:40, 43, and 54; see also the parables in 21:33–46 and 22:1–10.

[5] Mt 1:1.

[6] Cf. Mt 8:20; 9:6; 10:23; 11:19; 12:8, 32, 40; 13:37, 41; 16:13, 27–28; 17:9, 12, 22; 19:28; 20:18, 28; 24:27, 30, 37, 39, 44; 25:31; 26:2, 24, 45, and 64.

[7] See for instance Mt 8:2, 6, 25; 12:8; 14:28, 30; 15:22, 25, 27; 16:22; 17:4, 15; 18:21; 20:30, 31, 33; 21:3, 9; 24:42; and 26:22.

[8] Cf. Mt 1:1; 9:27; 12:23; 15:22; 20:30–31; 21:9 and 15.

[9] Mt 1:23.

[10] Cf. Mt 5:2; 7:29; 8:19; 9:11, 35; 11:1; 12:38; 13:54; 19:16; 22:24, 36; 23:8, 10; 26:18.

[11] Cf. John Painter, *Mark's Gospel: Worlds in Conflict* (New York: Routledge, 1997), 17.

[12] Cf. Mk 1:32–34; 3:7–12, and 6:53–56. See also 1:23–24 and 3:22–26.

[13] Cf. Mk 1:1 and 9:41.

[14] Cf. Mk 1:1; 8:29; 12:35; 13:21; 14:61; and 15:32.

[15] Cf. Mk 1:1; 3:11; 5:7; and 15:39. See also 1:24 (the "Holy one of God") and 14:61 (the "Son of the Blessed one").

[16] Cf. Mk 2:10, 28; 8:31, 38; 9:9, 12, 31; 10:33ff., 10:45; 13:26ff.; 14:21, 41, and 62.

[17] Cf. Mk 15:2, 9, 12, 18, 26, and 32.

[18] Cf. Mk 2:28; 7:28; 11:3; and 16:20. See also "the Lord Jesus" in 16:19.

[19] Cf. Mk 10:47–48.

[20] Mk 6:3.

[21] Cf. Mk 4:38; 5:35; 9:17, 38; 10:17, etc.

[22] Cf. Mk 9:5; 11:21; and 14:45. See also "Rabboni" ("my Teacher") in 10:51.

[23] Cf. Mk 6:4 and 6:15.

[24] Vincent Taylor, *The Gospel According to Mark*, 2nd ed. (1952; London: Macmillan, 1987), 121.

[25] Cf. Mk 1:11; 9:7; 10:47–48; 12:35–37; 15:39.

26 Larry W. Hurtado, "Following Jesus in the Gospel of Mark and Beyond," in *Patterns of Discipleship in the New Testament*, ed. Richard N. Longenecker (Grand Rapids: Eerdmans, 1996), 25ff.

27 I. Howard Marshall, *The Gospel of Luke: A Commentary on the Greek Text*, The New International Greek Testament Commentary (Grand Rapids: Eerdmans Publishing, 1978), 40.

28 See Lk 3:21; 5:15–16; 6:12; 9:18, 28; 10:21; and 11:1; the parables in 11:5–8; 18:1–8; as well as comments by Joel B. Green, *The Theology of the Gospel of Luke*, New Testament Theology (Cambridge, UK: Cambridge University Press, 1995), 58–60. Stephen C. Barton, *The Spirituality of the Gospels* (London: SPCK Publishing, 1992), 90–91.

29 Cf. 2:11.

30 Cf. 7:13, 19; 10:1, 39–42; 11:39; 12:42; 13:15; 17:5; 18:6; 19:8, 31, 34; 22:33, 38, 49, 61; 24:3 ("the Lord Jesus"), and 24:34.

31 Lk 2:26 ("the Lord's Messiah"), 3:15, 4:41, 9:20 ("the Christ of God"), 20:41, 22:67, 23:2, 35, 39; and 24:26.

32 Lk 5:24, 6:5, 6:22, 7:34, 9:22, 26, 44, 58; 11:30; 12:8, 10, 40; 17:22, 24, 26, 30; 18:8, 31; 19:10; 21:27, 36; 22:22, 48, 69; and 24:7.

33 Lk 3:12; 7:40; 8:49; 9:38; 10:25; 11:45; 12:13; 18:18; 19:39; 20:21, 28; 21:7; and 22:11.

34 Lk 4:16–20, 24; 7:16; 9:19; 13:33–34; and 24:19.

35 Lk 18:38–39; cf. 20:41.

36 Cf. Lk 1:32, 35; 3:22; and 9:35.

37 Cf. J. Louis Martyn, *History and Theology in the Fourth Gospel*, 3rd ed. (Louisville, KY: Westminster John Knox, 2003).

38 See Robert Kysar, *The Fourth Evangelist and His Gospel* (Minneapolis: Augsburg Fortress, 1975), 149.

39 Raymond Brown, *The Community of the Beloved Disciple* (New York: Paulist Press, 1979), 46.

40 M. Eugene Boring, *Revelation*, Interpretation Series (Louisville, KY: Westminster John Knox, 1989), 54ff.

41 Frederick J. Murphy, "The Book of Revelation," *Currents in Research: Biblical Studies* 2 (1994): 181.

42 Matthew E. Gordley, *Teaching Through Song in Antiquity: Didactic Hymnody among Greeks, Romans, Jews, and Christians*, Wissenschaftliche Untersuchungen zum Neuen Testament [hereafter WUNT], II, 302 (Tübingen: Mohr Siebeck, 2011), 344.

43 See comments in Ben Witherington, III, *Revelation*, (Cambridge, UK: Cambridge University Press, 2003), 28.

44 Ibid., 27.

45 Richard Bauckham, *The Theology of the Book of Revelation*, New Testament Theology (Cambridge, UK: Cambridge University Press, 1993), 56–57.

46 Bogdan G. Bucur, "Hierarchy, Prophecy, and the Angelomorphic Spirit: A Contribution to the Study of the Book of Revelation's *Wirkungsgeschichte,*" *Journal of Biblical Literature* 127, no. 1 (2008),175, note 6 and literature cited. "The virtue of this definition is that it signals the use of angelic *characteristics* in descriptions of God or humans, while not necessarily implying that the latter are angels *stricto sensu*" (175).

47 Andreas of Caesarea, *Hermēneia eis tēn Apokalypsin,* Patrologia Graeca, volume 106, col. 610.

48 Bauckham, *The Theology of the Book of Revelation,* 105.

49 Wilfrid Harrington, O.P., "Worthy is the Lamb," *Proceedings of the Irish Biblical Association,* 18 (1995): 67.

50 Concerning this expression, cf. Abraham Maslow, *The Farther Reaches of Human Nature* (New York: Penguin Compass, 1971).

51 St. Bonaventure, *The Journey of the Mind to God,* trans. Philotheus Boehner, O.F.M., ed. Stephen F. Brown (Indianapolis: Hackett Publishing, 1993), 24.

CHAPTER TWO

Jesus the Glorified Angel Walks amid the Churches

B eyond images of fire and falling stars, the Book of Revelation develops an elaborate portrait of a Christ with many Faces who stands at the center of life—on earth and in heaven—alongside God the Father Almighty in the power of the Holy Spirit. When taken together, John's visions convey to the Churches of Asia Minor a remarkable preview of God's world, where the heavenly throne of God and the Lamb stands at its very center. The story of this Apocalypse invites its audience not only to behold the symbolic universe that the text creates, but also to step with the author into that world of vision and to be transformed in the process.[1] John's aim is "not just to tell but to reveal" his Spirit-inspired visionary experience through the process of the community reading aloud and contemplating the text of the Apocalypse on the Lord's day (likely within a worship setting; 1:3, 10).[2] Whether the early Christian Eucharist may have been intended as the original setting (or what scholars refer to as the "theatre of reception") for the reading aloud of the book remains an intriguing possibility that is not without support among commentators.[3]

We should bear in mind that the first-century world

of the Christians in Asia Minor is in turmoil. It is a time of crisis. It is a dangerous time—not unlike our own— in which there are "wars and rumors of wars" (Mt 24:6). False prophets abound (2 Pet 2:1) and the poor languish in the margins of society. Dominated by an empire whose symbols and values stand in stark opposition to those of the Gospel, it is a world in which God is not accorded His proper place at the center of life and human relationships. St. John has been banished to an island for his witness to the word of God (1:9). Facing a terrible situation personally and concerned for the faithful to whom he addresses his work, he offers his audience a glimpse into heaven through a door that has been opened by the Spirit (4:1ff.). Not unlike Jacob at Bethel, who was shown a stairway extending up into heaven (cf. Gen 28:11–16; Jn 1:51), John not only sees visions of God, but draws his readers with him into that world of vision, beginning in chapter 4. In a time of crisis it is given to an early Christian prophet to "draw back a veil" for his Churches (hence the name Apocalypse, from the Greek *apocalypsis*, a "disclosure," an "unveiling," or "re-velation"). And as the curtain is lifted, not only is John permitted to see what he describes, but those to whom the book is addressed are invited to look over his shoulder through the open door. The community that listens to the reading aloud of the book (1:3)—"on the Lord's day" (1:10)—stands with the prophet at the "threshold of a new world,"[4] God's world—where "God triumphs over evil through the death of Jesus and the suffering of his followers."[5]

Understanding the Book's Symbolism: Seeing This World from the Standpoint of Heaven

This "Apocalypse of Jesus Christ" (1:1) has been written not only to offer hope in the midst of crisis, but to give its readers an opportunity to view their own everyday world from a different perspective—a transcendent, God-centered perspective. Thus, John's visions offer a place to stand above the sorrows, illusions, and confusion of this passing world, so as to provide clarity and perspective concerning their place in it.[6] The audience is offered a viewpoint of this passing world "from the standpoint of heaven."[7] The day-to-day world (whether ancient Rome or postmodern Toronto or New York) looks very different when "opened to transcendence"[8] and, thus, illuminated by the light of heaven. As such, the book does not merely reflect the first-century world of its author, it also "creates a world."[9]

In the interplay of opposing symbols within the Book of Revelation—images of heaven and earth, of the throne of God and the throne of Satan, of spiritual warfare between angels and devils, of the smoke of Babylon and the sparkling luster of the New Jerusalem—the faithful are offered a deeper insight concerning this passing world and their place in it. John's visions offer his audience "a place on which to stand" in "an expanded universe."[10] The book offers "a set of Christian prophetic counter-images," that inspire the reader "with alternative visions of how the world is and will be."[11] The division, indeed the "partitioning of humanity" into two diametrically opposed camps—the followers of God and the Lamb, and those allied with God's opponents—is all part of the book's art of persuasion,[12] even as it reflects the belief that one's eternal destiny is inextricably linked with the object of one's worship in the present life. Thus, the audience is urged to worship God, and God alone: "To hold firm, to recognize the beast behind the beauty of Greco-Roman culture" and "to remain faithful witnesses."[13]

Throughout, John wants to bring us to the realization that the powers of the empire have no claim to finality. The destiny of the world is in the hands of God and the Lamb, good will triumph, sin and evil will come to an end, and the old order will pass away as all things are made new in Christ (21:5). Then as now, the faithful are invited to choose Christ and so to prepare to enter a new world: one that is already in the process of arriving through the life of prayer and the Spirit. We too are led to consider our own attitudes toward the political, economic, social, and technological forces that shape the globalized postmodern, post-national world in which we live.

The First Face: Jesus Appears as a Glorified Angel

Following the opening prologue in Revelation 1:1–3 and the opening address of greeting and blessing to the seven Churches of Asia Minor (symbolic of the universal Church) in 1:4–8, John makes reference to his own difficult personal situation in 1:9. He proceeds to recount the details—both auditory and visual—of his first experience of Jesus Christ in 1:10–20, the glorious Face of God Almighty and the eternal voice of the invisible Father.

John's Vision: The Face of Jesus and the Face of God

In the first instance, John describes himself as being "in the Spirit" in Revelation 1:10, an important expression that occurs at critical points in the book and serves to underscore the book's solemn, inspired status (cf. 4:2; 17:3, 21:10). In response to the sound of a loud voice "like a trumpet" (1:10), John turns to see who is speaking to him. And from the midst of the seven Churches (symbolized by the "seven golden lampstands" in 1:20), Jesus Christ appears as a glorious, shimmering, fiery presence in the form of an angel (1:13–20). That Christ appears at the center of the circle of seven golden lampstands leads us to turn our immediate focus to the ongoing presence of Jesus in the everyday life of the Church—in the here and now— more than to the mystery of His return at the end of time. Jesus is a living, shining presence who is active and alive in the everyday life of the communities of faith, speaking to them the words of life as they journey toward the "end of the age" (cf. Mt 28:20).

The details of John's visions articulate the ways in which Jesus is the face of God, and that Jesus and the Father are one. His use of language to describe Christ invites comparisons with descriptions of God and angels, but also with that of "great kings" and "Israelite high priests" in the Jewish biblical and extra-biblical sources.[14] He walks in the midst of the lampstands and calls out to the faithful in the midst of their hour of crisis. Are they facing persecution and martyrdom (Rev 2:10, 13)? Are they drawn by the allure of the Roman Empire, abandoning their faith willingly for values and beliefs that are contrary to the Gospel

(2:14–15, 20–24)? Are they in danger of losing their faith through utter indifference and neglect (3:2–4, 15–18)?

In this first portrait of Jesus, John evokes images that are well-known from the writings of the prophetic books (particularly Daniel and Ezekiel), even as they resonate with extra-biblical sources. As John develops his vision of this first Face of Jesus, the imagery recalls descriptions of both the mysterious "son of man" in Daniel 7:13 and the divine "Ancient of Days" from whom he is distinguished (cf. Dan 7:9, 13, 22). Scholars note that beyond the scriptural reference to Daniel 7:13 is "the transference to the heavenly Son of Man of imagery linked in Daniel [7:9] with the Ancient of Days."[15] We could say that in John's Jewish-Christian apocalyptic world of vision, the "dividing lines between God and the Son of Man are . . . blurred."[16]

Jesus is described as holding seven stars in his right hand (1:16). One should expect that the stars would be in the hand of God (Gen 1:16; Ps 8:3; 147:4; Job 9:7; 38:31–32; Is 40:12), especially since they are said explicitly to be symbols of the angels of the seven Churches (1:20). The symbol of the sharp two-edged sword issuing from Jesus' mouth (cf. 2:16; 19:15, 21) conveys, in the first instance, the sense of the power of God's living word. According to the author of the Letter to the Hebrews, God's Word is "sharper than any two-edged sword, piercing to the division of soul and spirit, of joints from marrow, and discerning the thoughts and intentions of the heart" (Heb 4:12). Centuries later, St. Bernard of Clairvaux would comment that the Word of God: "melts, warms, illuminates, and cleanses the soul . . . it is also our food and a sword and medicine and encouragement and rest, also resurrection and our consummation."[17] And it is ultimately this Word of God that Jesus both speaks and is (Jn 1:1; Rev 19:13).

In Revelation 1:13–18, the first Face of Christ seems to emerge from the very fire of God's glory. Here is an apocalyptic, otherworldly Jesus (Mk 9:3) whose fiery radiance dazzles. This is the glorified Christ who has come "to bring fire to the earth" (Lk 12:49). John's visions serve "to set the echoes of memory and association ringing."[18] In the Hebrew Scriptures, God's glorious presence is associated with fire (Ex 3:2; 13:21; 24:17; Neh 9:19; Dt 4:24; 9:3; Heb 12:29). But fire is no less a symbol of God's judgment. The prophet Malachi describes God's coming on the Day of the Lord by invoking the image of a refiner's fire (Mal 3:2). The fire from heaven reveals, refines, purifies and transforms, consumes, directs, indicts, and exacts judgment.

The overall effect of this Face of Christ "is one of terrifying majesty."[19] The imagery expresses in highly symbolic and visual terms—drawn from lines of Old Testament biblical and extra-biblical reflection—what Church synods and councils in later centuries would come to express and affirm in creeds and official teachings, namely, that Jesus Christ is the Son of God and equal to the Father. John's vision leads us to consider "the emerging Christian willingness to call Jesus 'God' in sources of the later first century," and provides an apocalyptic "visionary demonstration of the same christological conviction."[20]

John's Reaction to the Fiery Face of the Angelic Jesus

As we see in Revelation 1:17, the manifestation of God's presence evokes a response. Here as elsewhere in the

Bible, the experience of the divine evokes fear (Ex 3:6; 20:18–19; Mt 17:5–7; Lk 1:13, 30). The prophets typically express a sense of their own fear, unworthiness, insufficiency, or sinfulness (Jer 1:6; Is 6:5; Ezek 1:28; Dan 8:18). Upon witnessing the miraculous catch of fish described in Luke 5, Peter acknowledges his own sinfulness as he falls before Jesus (Lk 5:8). Jesus' response to the Seer, inviting him to have no fear, echoes similar words of consolation and encouragement that are spoken many times throughout the Bible, whether by God, the Risen Christ, or God's divine messengers. John also invites us to confront our own fears (or lack thereof) with regard to the divine, and to strive to discern through a life of prayer and the Spirit its meaning in our own relationship with God.

The Voice of Jesus & the Voice of God

Just as Jesus' appearance is described using terms that in the Hebrew Scriptures are applied to God, so too, Revelation's angelified Jesus speaks as God does (cf. 1:8, 21:6). The expression "I am the first and the last" in 1:17 invites comparisons with Jesus' use of the expression "I Am" in the Fourth Gospel. In Revelation 2:23, Jesus states, "I am he who searches mind and heart," while in 22:16 he says: "I am the root and the offspring of David, the bright morning star." In addition to being the "first and last" (1:17; 2:8; 22:13), Jesus refers to Himself as the "living one" (1:18), just as in Jewish tradition God is referred to as "the living God" (cf. Dt 5:26; Ps 42:2; Jer 23:36; Hos 1:10; Mt 16:16; 2 Cor 3:3; 6:16; 1 Tim 3:15; Heb 12:22; Rev 7:2). Once more, the voice of this first Face of Jesus serves to underscore His true divinity. Jesus, rather than the Father, emerges as the holder of the keys of death and Hades. The power and authority of this living one who died but lives forevermore extend to heaven and earth as well as over the powers of death and the underworld.

Jesus, the fiery, angelified face of God is at the same time the living voice of God who speaks to the heart of a Church that dwells not in the wilderness of a desert (cf. Hos 2:14), but in an urban environment. In Revelation 2 and 3, Jesus will issue a challenging call to witness faithfully to the values of the Gospel amid the spiritual confusion that surrounds the Churches. He speaks directly to the situation of the faithful which He seems to know intimately. The voice of the Risen Christ comforts, consoles, exhorts, threatens, and issues a call to conversion (cf. 2:5, 16, 3:3, and 3:19). He calls the faithful to strive to be a prophetic people and, like John of Patmos, to share both in the mystery of Christ's own suffering and in His own victory over the world (Jn 16:33).

The Angelic Jesus Speaks to the Seven Churches as He Stands in Their Midst

Having just described a powerful vision of an angel-like, yet divine Jesus, John is once again instructed to write down what he sees (1:19; cf. 1:11). What follows in chapters 2 and 3 represents a remarkable address to the Churches of Asia Minor. The author presents a striking series of seven "letters" dictated in the first-person singular by the glorified Christ Himself. That Jesus is understood here as more than a glorified angel will emerge with even greater clarity in the letters section that follows. John's lofty understanding of Jesus Christ is further developed in Revelation

2–3 in the form of the prophetic oracles delivered to the audience:[21]

> It is utterly remarkable, however, that these oracles all represent the words of the glorified Jesus, for in the biblical tradition that the author obviously reveres the only legitimate source of prophetic inspiration is the one God (Dt 13:1–5).[22]

Unlike anything that is found in the letters of Paul or in the Gospels, the angelic Jesus of the first chapter of Revelation will go on to deliver a series of well-structured and detailed messages[23] directly to each of the Churches. These messages have significance for each community individually, as well as for the entire Church. Together, these letters constitute a kind of visitation, or assessment of the Churches by the Risen Christ to see whether or not they have prepared for the time of crisis and upheaval that is fast approaching. At the same time, details of these Spirit-inspired proclamations reflect something of the political, social, economic, geographical, cultural, and religious realities of the Churches of Asia Minor toward the end of the first century. Finally, the content of the vision of Christ in chapter 1, along with the seven letters in chapters 2 and 3, serve in an important preparatory capacity. That is, they provide the clues and interpretive keys that will help to orient John's audience to what follows in the lengthy "visions section" (Rev 4–22).[24] Throughout, the voice of Jesus in chapters 2 and 3 provides encouragement, comfort, and consolation. This living voice and Word of God promises rewards to those who are faithful witnesses to the Gospel, even as He admonishes and calls to conversion. Ultimately, the angelic Jesus who walks amid the seven golden lampstands calls the listeners to a transfigured life in the Spirit. So too, it is important for us to read these letters as though they are addressed to us, and to reflect upon our own attitudes and particular spiritual situations as we discern what the Spirit is saying to us in our postmodern era.

The Risen Jesus Continues to Appear and to Speak to the Churches of Asia Minor

In a manner consistent with the other writings of the New Testament, the Apocalypse reflects the early Christian belief that Jesus not only arose from the dead, appeared to chosen disciples, and continued to walk in their midst (Lk 24), but that the Risen Lord "continued to speak" to the early Church.[25] It has been argued that the voice of Jesus in the Apocalypse is not merely one among the one-hundred-and-forty-one voices found in the book, but rather the definitive voice (cf. 22:20), with the result that, "In a certain sense the Revelation as a whole is the voice of Jesus."[26]

Not content merely to describe the letters that have been revealed to him, the power of the Spirit makes the living Christ present through the act of reading the text aloud in a worship setting. Again, the visions in the book represent much more than simply a blueprint for the future. We see—both in the spectacular vision of the Risen Christ in angelic form, and in its accompanying vocal component—that the mystery of the return of Christ is a rather more complex matter. For John is careful to maintain the correlation between the expectation of the final return of Christ at the end of time (cf. 3:11; 16:15; 22:7, 12, 20), and the community's ongoing experience of their Risen Lord in the everyday life of the Church (2:5, 16, 22; 3:3).[27] Thus, the seven letters call out to the congregations to be prepared for the encounter with the living Word of the Risen Jesus in truth and justice not only at the end of time, but at the center of everyday life where God's word is active and alive in our present experience (cf. 3:20).

Thus, Revelation 1 through 3 calls us to be attentive to the various presences of Jesus Christ in the midst of the contemporary life of the Church and to heed His voice as it speaks to us in so many different ways at the heart of everyday life. The Divine Word that He both is and speaks continues to be present in the Liturgy of the Word, in the Liturgy of the Hours, in the practice of *Lectio Divina*, and through the sacramental life of the Church, above all in the Eucharist where Christ is really and truly present. He speaks to us especially through the voices of the poor and suffering, all those to whom in justice we are called to minister to as we await the close of the age (cf. Mt 25:40). Revelation 1 through 3 serve to remind us that we need to be on guard against the oversimplified view that John is giving us a mere timetable of events associated with Christ's return at the end of time.

In the letters, the Risen Jesus offers an assessment of each congregation, beginning with the expression "I know," and followed by a word of exhortation. Characteristically, the faithful are asked to "repent" (cf. 2:5, 16; 3:3, 19), to "remember" (2:5; 3:3), and to "be watchful" (3:2, 3). Not surprisingly, when taken together, the letters reflect a mix of positive and negative attributes. Only in the case of the Letters to Smyrna and Philadelphia do we find exclusively positive comments (2:9; 3:8). Conversely, in the case of the Church in Laodicea we find exclusively negative attributes (3:16–17).

The situation reflected in the letters section is far from ideal. Taken together, these Churches reflect a mixture of faithfulness and unfaithfulness, of ardor and indifference, of bravery and cowardice, of sinfulness and grace. The weeds and the wheat about which Jesus speaks in the parables (Mt 13:24–30) grow together among the seven Churches of Asia Minor. The angelic Jesus who addresses the congregations in the Spirit speaks to the Churches in a decidedly forthright, unembellished, and unadorned way. And while the voice of the Risen and glorified Jesus calls out clearly and consistently to the path of conversion, the respective diagnoses, threats, and admonitions contained in the letters section do not tell the whole story. That is because we also find a series of remarkable promises to the victors (2:7, 10–11, 17, 26–28; 3:5, 12, and 21), in which Jesus Himself guarantees rewards to a prophetic (22:7), priestly and royal people (1:6; 5:10; 20:6) who remain faithful witnesses to the very end. While addressed to the angel of each specific Church and intended for the faithful of that community, these promises extend to all who conquer in Christ (cf. 21:7; 1 Jn 5:4–5). Taken together, the letters serve to articulate for the Churches a comprehensive vision of *why* it is that the faithful should live the Gospel to the fullest. They convey a very exalted vision of a humanity which has also been angelified in Christ, as John describes what the human person has been created for and is called to become through the life of grace (cf. Lk 20:36, and the term *isangeloi*, "like" or "equal to the angels").

The angelic Jesus, in essence, is saying: give courageous witness to the truth of the Gospel before a disbelieving

world and acquire a share in what I Am. Follow courageously the path of the exodus journey that leads along the
narrow road (Mt 7:13–14) that is "situated between two
lights: the anticipatory light of the Transfiguration and the
definitive Light of the Resurrection" on Easter morning.[28]
At the same time, be prepared to suffer as I have suffered,
for "no servant is greater than his master" (Jn 15:20). Do
not be afraid to be rejected, denied, or persecuted for the
sake of the Gospel. Be faithful witnesses (cf. 2:10, 13; 3:14;
17:14) to the end and you will share in my own glorious
transformation. Far beyond the imagery of the faithful
reflected in the Johannine Jesus' admonitions to Peter—
"feed my sheep" (Jn 21:17)—and more profound than the
transition from servants to friends signaled in John 15:15 is
the Seer's vision of a humanity that is being glorified and
transfigured, indeed sealed with God's own glory shining
forth in the Face of Christ (cf. Ps 4:6; 31:16; 2 Cor 4:6).

Jesus Calls the Faithful to Patient Endurance in the Midst of Suffering

While the promises to the victors are marvelous to contemplate, it is very clear that they can only be won at a
considerable cost. Thus the angelic Jesus of the first three
chapters of Revelation beckons the faithful to become a
prophetic people, who, like the author himself, "hear and
keep" the book's words of prophecy (1:3; 22:7), adhere
to the testimony of Jesus (19:10), and conquer the world
through the mystery of Christ's suffering, death, and Resurrection (2:7, 11, 17, 26; 3:5, 12, and 20). When John
first describes his situation in Revelation 1:9 (cf. 1:1, 4;
22:8), he speaks of being a brother and fellow participant

in "the tribulation and the kingdom and the patient endurance" (1:9) that characterize Christian life in Jesus. Does he understand this suffering to be a mark of Christian life at the close of the age (Mt 10:22; Jn 15:18ff)? Is John referring to the great tribulation that is to precede Christ's final return in glory (cf. 7:14)? Certainly, this heightened sense of living in the final hour (1 Jn 2:18) has been a characteristic of the Christian experience of time since the Ascension. Revelation's symbolic universe portrays a world divided between those who strive to share in the values of God's everlasting Kingdom, and those who refuse to dissociate themselves from taking part in the sins associated with the earthly kingdom, symbolized by the city of Babylon (18:2).

These visions invite the reader "to look behind the veil of ordinary experience . . . and see the true order of life"[29] as the fulfillment of God's promise of salvation draws near. Those who live according to the rule of God and Christ do so in the midst of danger and rejection. Along with Jesus and the prophet of Patmos, theirs is a suffering witness to the faith (2:9). What the Apocalypse calls forth in the faithful is patient endurance. Here is "the spiritual alchemy" which transforms the faithful, suffering, and rejected witnesses into the glorified victors who will dwell forever in the New Jerusalem.[30] God's Kingdom will come "Not by might, nor by power, but by my spirit, says the Lord of hosts" (Zech 4:6).[31] The Book of Revelation teaches that it is in faith and patient endurance alone (Lk 21:19; Heb 12:2; 1 Pet 2:21–24), and never through the use of violence, that one achieves victory over the world (13:10).[32] The victors have conquered "by the blood of the Lamb and by the word of their testimony" (12:11).

In summary, Revelation 1–3 introduces the audience to the first of a series of distinctive Faces of Jesus, leading the listeners to reflect upon the mystery of the ongoing presence of the Christ to the faith communities on earth. Appearing transformed and transfigured, like an angel (although clearly more than an angel, since He is equal to God), Christ *speaks*. He reminds the communities who listen on the Lord's Day to the proclamation of the Apocalypse that they need to strive together to prepare for the new heaven and the new earth that are fast approaching (21:1; see also Is 65:17; 66:22; 2 Pet 3:13). For through the power of the Spirit, the glorious throne of God and the Lamb stands at the center of the community gathered together in worship and praise, both as it is in heaven and as it will be revealed at the center of the New Jerusalem at the end of time (21:22). The vision in Revelation 1:10–20 and the content of the prophetic messages in chapters 2 and 3 serve to prepare the audience for a quantum shift to the heavenly realms, as the Seer proceeds in chapters 4 and following to describe what he has seen and heard through an opened door in heaven (4:1). Throughout, the Book of Revelation speaks to its audience "in mystic fashion about the challenge and the comfort of living in two worlds at the same time"—one that is rapidly fading, and one which even now is in the process of coming into being through the power of the Holy Spirit.[33] In this way it challenges us today to a renewed perception of the presence of God in creation and in our everyday lives. Are we actively seeking God's presence? Where do we look for this presence? Where do we find it? Are we living in two worlds at the same time, or only in one?

Endnotes

[1] See, for instance, David L. Barr, "The Apocalypse as a Symbolic Transformation of the World: a Literary Analysis," *Interpretation* 38 (1984), pp. 39-50.

[2] David L. Barr, *Tales of the End: A Narrative Commentary on the Book of Revelation* (Santa Rosa, CA: Polebridge Press, 1998), 171.

[3] For the expression "theatre of reception," cf. A. J. P. Garrow, *Revelation* (New Testament Readings; London & New York: Routledge, 1997), 3–4.

[4] Cf. comments by R. L. Jeske, "Spirit and Community in the Johannine Apocalypse," *New Testament Studies* 31 (1985): 458 and literature cited, especially Arnold van Gennup, *The Rites of Passage* (Chicago: University Press, 1960), 20–1; and Victor Turner, *The Ritual Process: Structure and Anti-Structure (Foundations of Human Behavior)* (Chicago: Aldine, 1969), 106ff.

[5] David L. Barr, "The Apocalypse of John as Oral Enactment," *Interpretation* 40 (1986): 256.

[6] David A. deSilva, *Seeing Things John's Way: The Rhetoric of the Book of Revelation* (Louisville, KY: Westminster John Knox Press, 2009), 95.

[7] Ibid.; deSilva, *Seeing Things John's Way*, 93–94 and literature cited; cf. Wayne A. Meeks, *The Moral World of the First Christians* (Louisville, KY: Westminster John Knox Press, 1986), 144.

[8] See comments by Richard Bauckham, *The Theology of the Book of Revelation*, 7–8.

[9] Cf. Leonard L. Thompson, *The Book of Revelation: Apocalypse and Empire*, 77.

[10] Ibid., 32.

[11] See comments by Richard Bauckham, *The Theology of the Book of Revelation*, 17, 159–60.

[12] DeSilva, *Seeing Things John's Way*, 98. See also the followers of the Lamb in 11:18; 12:11, 17; 13:7; 14:12–13; and the opposing forces in 9:20; 13:8, 12, and 15.

[13] See Barr, *Tales of the End*, 180. See also Rev 14:7; 19:10; 22:9.

[14] See David E. Aune, *Revelation 1–5*, World Biblical Commentary 5A (Nashville: Thomas Nelson, 1997), 117.

[15] See Christopher Rowland, "The Vision of the Risen Christ in Rev. 1:13ff: The Debt of an Early Christology to an Aspect of Jewish Angelology," *The Journal of Theological Studies* 31(1980): 2.

[16] Peter Schäfer, *The Origins of Jewish Mysticism* (Tübingen: Mohr Siebeck, 2009), 105.

17 Daniel Griggs, ed., *Bernard of Clairvaux Monastic Sermons,* Cistercian Fathers Series, no. 68 (Collegeville, MN: Cistercian Publications, 2016), 136.

18 Caird, *The Revelation of St. John the Divine,* 25.

19 Wilfrid J. Harrington, O.P., *The Apocalypse of St. John: A Commentary* (London: Geoffrey Chapman, 1969), 80.

20 Jonathan Knight, "The Enthroned Christ of Revelation 5:6 and the Development of Christian Theology," in *Studies in the Book of Revelation,* ed. Steve Moyise (Edinburgh: T. & T. Clark, 2001), 44.

21 Aune, *Revelation 1–5,* 126 and literature cited.

22 Larry W. Hurtado, *Lord Jesus Christ: Devotion to Jesus in Earliest Christianity* (Grand Rapids, MI: Eerdmans, 2003), 591.

23 On the stereotypical features of the letters, cf. Aune, *Revelation 1–5,* 119–24.

24 Cf. Harry O. Maier, "Staging the Gaze: Early Christian Apocalypses and Narrative Self-Representation" in *Harvard Theological Review* 90 (1997): 136, n. 14 and literature cited.

25 M. Eugene Boring, "The Voice of Jesus in the Apocalypse of John," *Novum Testamentum* 34 (1992): 334.

26 Ibid., 352

27 David E. Aune, *The Cultic Setting of Realized Eschatology in Early Christianity* (Leiden, Netherlands: Brill, 1972), 127.

28 St. John Paul II, *Vita Consecrata,* 25 March 1996, no. 40.

29 See David L. Barr, "Doing Violence: Moral Issues in Reading John's Apocalypse," in *Reading the Book of Revelation: A Resource For Students,* Resources for Biblical Study 44 (Atlanta: Society of Biblical Literature, 2003), 106.

30 R. H. Charles, *Revelation of St. John* vol. 1. (Edinburgh: T. & T. Clark, 1920), 21.

31 See Richard Bauckham, *The Theology of the Book of Revelation,* 110–15.

32 David L. Barr, "Doing Violence," 99.

33 Håkan Ulfgard, "Reading the Book of Revelation Today," in *Is The World Ending?* Concilium 4, ed. Seán Freyne and Nicholas Lash (Maryknoll: Orbis Books, 1998), 38.

CHAPTER 3

The Messianic Lion / Lamb of God

Prior to shifting our focus to the apocalyptic Lion/ Lamb in Revelation 5, John invites us to contemplate the mystery of God, "the King of the ages, immortal, invisible" (cf. 1 Tim 1:17), as the book's perspective makes a quantum shift heavenward, beginning in chapter 4. Having here "no lasting city" (Heb 13:14), the faith communities journey forward along the narrow path between two worlds, in the dawning light of that new city which is to come. Unlike the modern poet who is "caught between two worlds, one dead, the other powerless to be born,"[1] the visionary language of the Apocalypse inspires a priestly and prophetic people to stand together in faith and hope at the "threshold of a new world"[2] as they strive to become even now a new creation in Christ. This journey forward in the Spirit through struggles and trials invites hope and confidence in the God who brings order out of chaos and a new creation from the ashes of the old. As the narrative unfolds, the listeners are invited to consider their loftiest goals and their identity as "pilgrims of the absolute," a people called to continue "seeking the face of God" on life's journey.[3]

God's Heavenly Council

As we see, John's visions reveal a God who does not reign in isolation, but is surrounded by His heavenly host, or heavenly council (cf. Jer 23:18; Ps 82:1). Referred to simply as "one seated on the throne" (4:2), the text provides few details concerning the God enthroned at the very center of Revelation's world of vision. Here is the "negative way" (*via negativa*) of the mystics whose focus is the indescribability of the God who transcends the categories (and limitations) of human thought and expression. We are led to reflect upon the mystery of a God who is known through the shimmering effects of His glorious presence (cf. 21:11) and through the voices of the angels who praise and adore Him. For, "if we are to know God at all, we must know Him as the unfathomable mystery, a mystery to be explored only by the humility of worship."[4]

John's visions—like those of the prophet Ezekiel—serve an important role in sustaining the religious and spiritual identity of a people in crisis, on their journey of faith in the midst of a hostile environment. In Revelation, God's glory moves with His people neither as a pillar of fire nor as a column of smoke (Ex 13:21–22), but as the Risen Christ, who in angel form stands in the midst of the seven golden lampstands illuminating the path of His people on their journey toward the New Jerusalem. These visions serve not only as an "antidote to Christian assimilation into a culture with an alien ethos," but offer the audience divine "assurance about the ultimate outcome of all things."[5] They help to anchor in ultimate reality the religious identity of a people in crisis, through inspired visions of that everlasting throne in heaven which stands forever "beyond the reach" of every earthly power.[6]

Again, John's visions serve to "move the world in which he and his congregations move, relate, and think—or at least, to displace the centers of the public cosmos in favor of the Christian cosmos."[7] Against the violent, arrogant, and self-serving exercise of power in the world, John shows us the world as it ought to be, as God and the Lamb stand together at the very center of life. God is in control. His Kingdom will come. Revelation takes the reader beyond the conventional polemics of Christ vs. Caesar and beyond the bitter internal disputes reflected in the sharp, even violent language of the book (cf. 2:16, 23). Ultimately, the audience is led to reflect upon the mystery of God's approaching holiness, before which only that which has been purified will be able to withstand the brightness of Christ's return in glory. And so what remains for us is to try to discover, recover, or re-discover—and keep before our minds daily—a renewed vision of God and Christ at the center of all things, including human relationships.

The Topography of John's Heaven: Expanding Concentric Circles of Praise

The image of the rainbow around God's heavenly throne leads us to reflect upon the first of a number of concentric circles which radiate outward from the very center of Revelation's world of vision. The circular shape (or topography) of John's heavenly world becomes more apparent as the descriptions expand outward from the rainbow described in 4:3 to include details—at times elaborate— of the various ranks of angelic beings that surround the throne. The four Living Creatures around the throne offer perpetual praise and worship to God (4:6–8). The twenty-four Elders with their twenty-four thrones (4:4) encircle the four Living Creatures and offer responses to their songs of praise (4:10–11). The radius of the circles of heavenly beings will expand further to include a great host of angels, numbering "myriads of myriads and thousands of thousands" (5:11). Eventually these visions will encompass the other dimensions of Revelation's three-storied universe as "every creature in heaven and on earth and under the earth and in the sea, and all therein" add their praises to the growing choruses (5:13). Finally, the "great multitude which no man could number" (7:9) of the martyred righteous who have "washed their robes and made them white in the blood of the Lamb" (7:14) add their voices to the chorus, as the Church in heaven and the Church on earth unite their voices in the praises of God and the Lamb. The circles expand still farther to encompass the faithful to whom the book is addressed, as we too are invited to enter John's inspired world of vision and to join our voices to the songs of the angels.

The Lion/Lamb is Worshipped and Adored Along with Almighty God

As the circles of praise continue their outward expansion, John's focus shifts from the God enthroned in heaven to the apocalyptic Lion/Lamb who now emerges alongside the Lord God Almighty as the principal actor and Lord of history throughout the remainder of the book (Rev 4–22). Again, we should note first of all that the image of the Lamb is introduced only gradually. From images of the Almighty Creator God in chapter 4, the visions will shift their focus to the mystery of God's redemption, as a remarkable portrait of Christ is elaborated in chapter 5, the second panel of the book's throne-room "triptych"(cf. 4:1–6:17). A third panel will complete it, as chapter 6 proceeds to explore the mystery of God's arriving judgment initiated by the Lamb who opens the mysterious scroll that is sealed with the Seven Seals (6:1–8:1), thereby initiating the events that will culminate in the arrival of the New Jerusalem in chapter 21. Notwithstanding the very lofty vantage point afforded by the heavenly throne room visions, the figure of the slaughtered Lamb keeps before the audience the stark reality of the Cross of Jesus Christ and the events of Good Friday.

While we are invited to contemplate the Face of the Lamb who stands in heaven as the Lord of history, we ought not to overlook the invitation to take this imagery and appropriate it for our own spiritual lives. For ultimately, John, like St. Paul, invites us to strive for "the higher gifts" (1 Cor 12:31). Here John's God- and Christ-centered universe in some ways invites comparisons with St. Teresa of Avila's *Interior Castle*, which itself reflects a very coherent vision of life in Christ, one that is God-centered. Although their language and imagery are different, the idea is similar. In the *Interior Castle* St. Teresa pictures the soul as a castle composed of numerous suites or mansions in the center of which Christ is enthroned as King. While for John the divine throne stands at the center of heaven, for St. Teresa it is at the center of the soul that one experiences the mystical encounter with God the Father, Son, and Holy Spirit. What they have in common is that they both invite us to the highest levels of contemplation. They invite us to the loftiest understanding not only of God, of heaven, and of the afterlife, but of human nature and the farther reaches of human potential offered by God through the life of grace. For as St. Irenaeus reminds us: "The glory of God is man fully alive, while the life of man is the vision of God."[8]

Revelation 5:1: The Sealed Scroll in the Right Hand of God

In the first instance, John draws our attention not to Christ, but rather to the mysterious scroll written on the inside and on the back (cf. Ezra 2:10). Is the scroll (*biblion*) to be understood in this context as a "book roll?"[9] It appears to be "in the right hand" of the one seated upon the throne.[10] A compelling symbol of divine might, honor, and authority, the right hand "is always the hand of God's deliverance and blessing."[11] That the mysterious scroll has been sealed with seven seals (cf. Is 29:11; Dan 8:26; 12:4, 9) serves to underscore in superlative fashion the profound nature of the divine secrets that it contains. Once again, the symbolism is rich with allusions and evokes a variety of images.

Is this a "'book of destiny' consisting of God's pre-determined plan for human beings and the world?"[12] Is the scroll to be identified with the "Book of Life"?[13] The nature and extent of what the scroll will reveal certainly exceeds the Book of Life's purpose of listing the names of the redeemed and of recording their deeds (20:12). Or, again, is the scroll to be understood as a symbol of Sacred Scripture, more specifically of the Old Testament, which remains sealed until re-read and re-interpreted in light of the Christ-event?[14] Moreover, why is it that the scroll remains sealed? According to the drama described in Revelation 5:2–4, no one has been found worthy to open the scroll and to reveal its mysterious contents. Nowhere in "heaven and earth or the underworld" has anyone been found worthy to take the scroll and open its seven seals— no angel, prophet, priest, king, or hero from the past—only the book's central actor and ultimate revelation of God: the Lamb who was slain "for the life of the world" (cf. Jn 6:51).[15] The scroll is a symbol of Christ's *sovereignty*, as the angelic praises that break forth in reaction to the transfer of the mysterious scroll from God to the Lamb eloquently attest (cf. 5:9 and 5:12).

As the Lamb breaks open the seals, horses and their riders suddenly appear and begin to inflict devastation upon the world (6:1–8). Violent earthquakes erupt (6:12) and stars fall from the sky (6:13) as the cosmos is shaken to its core. Throughout the visions of approaching judgment, it is not so much a question of information being provided to the listeners or of indictments being read aloud before the heavenly court. Rather, with the opening of each successive seal the divine judgments appear to be activated or set in motion by the Lion/Lamb of God (cf. 6:1–8:1).[16] At the same time, it should be noted that the descriptions of plagues and images of destruction that have so fascinated readers throughout the centuries are in each case prepared for by scenes of heavenly praise and worship, which serve "as the context and setting" for the presentation of the dramatic visions of judgment.[17]

Patterned Repetition: Are John's Visions Parallel Accounts of the Same Events?

Finally, are the visions of the various series of plagues (again, respectively, the seven seals in 6:1–17; 8:1, trumpets in 8:2–11:19, and bowls in 15:5–16:21) to be understood as unfolding chronologically (as in a series) or are they to be understood as parallel accounts of the same events? The question of "recapitulation" or "patterned repetition" in the Apocalypse has puzzled commentators ever since the late third century when St. Victorinus of Pettau identified and commented upon this remarkable phenomenon in the earliest extant full-length commentary on the Book. According to Victorinus: ". . . what was said under the trumpets, though potently proclaimed, was said in lesser measure (*minus*), and . . . the same was said under the bowls more liberally (*propensius*), so that there was no progression in the sense of historical narrative sequence (*ordo*) where the Holy Spirit was just speaking again of the same time of the end."[18]

This is a complex and difficult question, but something more than strictly parallel accounts of the events described is needed to advance the plot from the opening of the seals beginning in 6:1 to the fulfillment of God's judgment (signaled by the arrival of the bowls visions in Revelation 15:1f, and along with it the dire consequences depicted in 15:1–22:6). The bowls visions are clearly described as "the *last*" series of plagues (Rev 15:1), underscoring, again, the need to understand these visions as something more than strictly parallel accounts.[19] At the same time, the remarkable phenomenon of patterned repetition—or "recapitulation," as identified by Victorinus—serves as a

caution to the reader against simply reducing the eschatological visions to a linear series of predictions. At the
very least, this important feature of the text attests eloquently to the literary genius of these visions and of John's
remarkable Spirit-inspired command of the "medium of
apocalypse."[20]

Revelation 5:5: The Lion of the Tribe of Judah, the Root of David

The image of the crucified and risen Christ that emerges
is quite different from what John himself appears to have
expected. For the vision combines two different images
resulting in a powerful yet paradoxical symbol of a Christ
who is both Lion and Lamb (cf. 5:5–6). Details of the portrait of Christ developed in chapter 5 evoke a "militaristic"
image of the new Messiah, a new David who achieves
victory over the enemies of Israel, while the images of the
Lamb that was slain serve to express John's "Jewish Christian reinterpretation" of contemporary Jewish messianic
hope and expectation.[21] Beyond a sacrificial lamb that is
led to the slaughter (cf. Ex 29:39f; Is 53:7), this apocalyptic
and all-powerful Lamb with seven horns and seven eyes
is a magnificent symbol of Christ victorious and represents "the most impressive rebirth of images he anywhere
achieves."[22] While the portrayal of Jesus' death in these
terms was already familiar in Christian tradition, in the
words of one scholar, "by placing the image of the sacrificial victim alongside those of the military conqueror, John
forges a new symbol of *conquest* by sacrificial death."[23] At
the same time, we should note the distinctively Christian
nuances of John's re-interpretation of Jewish messianic

expectation. The image of the Davidic warrior who represents the hopes of an oppressed people is here reconfigured
as God's king and anointed one who has achieved victory
not through the exercise of force, but by His self-emptying
upon the Cross (cf. Phil 2:5–8). In the Apocalypse, God
brings about His everlasting Kingdom (the New Jerusalem)
through the self-sacrifice of His messianic Lamb, despite
the concerted efforts of those powers—both visible and
invisible—which would oppose God's plan of salvation.

Revelation 5:6: The Slain Lamb of God of the Apocalypse

While the use of animal symbolism in the Jewish Scriptures and extra-biblical literature is not unknown,[24] John's
particular Christian adaptation of it is both striking and
original. The biblical image of the lamb evokes a number
of associations, including Isaiah's Suffering Servant who
was oppressed and afflicted like a lamb that is led to the
slaughter (cf. Is 53:7), the image of the paschal lamb
rooted in Exodus typology (Ex 29:39f; 1 Cor 5:7), and
John the Baptist's acclamation of Jesus as the "Lamb of
God who takes away the sins of the world" (Jn 1:29). At
the same time, a careful study of the text reveals something rather more complex and paradoxical. John employs
the term *"arnion"* or "little lamb," but this same word can
also be translated as "ram."[25] Thus, John's use of language
serves to underscore the contradictory tensions inherent in
this symbol of a Christ who is *simultaneously* the Lion and
Lamb of God. In this fusion of imagery, "the Lion shows
what Jesus did and the Lamb shows how he did it."[26] The
Lion has conquered through His suffering self-sacrifice,

"The *one* true sacrifice with universal relevance."[27] At the same time, "the violence through which Jesus is said to conquer evil is the violence done to him."[28] The Book of Revelation's Lamb/Ram is ultimately the self-sacrificing "messianic conqueror," as the commentators observe.[29] These visions allude "to the irony in the Christian proclamation that the one on the cross reigns as king" (see 1 Cor 1:23–24).[30] The reader is confronted with the astonishing image of an apocalyptic, all-powerful, yet slaughtered Lamb (cf. 5:6, 9, 12; 13:8).

As one scholar observes: "However touching the image of a lamb in the arms of God may be, that is not the Lamb of the Apocalypse!"[31] This is made clear in the reference to the number of the Lamb's seven horns, a symbolic fullness that points to Christ's all-powerful might. It is also evident in later passages, such as Revelation 6:15–16. Again, John develops an understanding of Jesus that is far more complex than that conveyed in the image of a meek little lamb. Here is a Lion/Lamb who "gathers an army but never leads a charge" and whose "wrath is never portrayed."[32] This is the apocalyptic Lamb/Ram whose "conquest is not through violence inflicted; rather it is through violence suffered."[33]

The Seven Eyes of the Lamb & the Seven Spirits

In Revelation 5:6, the seven eyes of the Lamb are identified with the "seven spirits" (mentioned earlier, in 1:4, 3:1, and 4:5; cf. Is 11:2–3).[34] The seven spirits may be seen as the author's way of speaking of the fullness of the Holy Spirit in relation to God and Christ, as well as to the mystery of the Church's prophetic witness to the world.

Both images, it may be argued, pertain to the book's symbolism concerning the Holy Spirit.[35] It is the Spirit who calls the seven Churches on earth to discern and to heed the significance of Christ's prophetic messages (2:7, 11, 17, 29; 3:6, 13, 22). It is in the Spirit that the door to heaven is opened within the context of angelic worship (1:10; 4:1; cf. 19:11), permitting the community of faith a share in the prophet's visions of heaven (4:2), of impending judgment (17:3), and of the cosmic renewal that God is in the process of bringing about amid the sufferings and sorrows of the age (21:10). Ultimately, it is through the power of the Holy Spirit (cf. Zech 4:6: "Not by might, nor by power, but by my spirit, says the Lord of hosts") that God will bring about His final victory over the visible and invisible forces that conspire to oppose His divine plan.[36]

The seven eyes of the Lamb (cf. the "eyes of YHWH," Zech 4:10) symbolize "the fullness of God's power sent forth into all the earth."[37] Moreover, it is the Holy Spirit who permits the community on earth, in turn, to begin "to see with the eyes of God and Christ,"[38] and so to partake in a renewed and unified vision that allows them to experience—within the worship assemblies on earth—what Andreas of Caesarea calls "one Church of angels and human beings." Divine grace will definitively reunite the voices of the saints—those among the seven Churches and those in heaven—only after the present age has passed and the storms of time have ceased.[39] Within the Apocalypse, the earthly and the divine intersect and so the Church possesses "both an earthly and heavenly aspect, historical, and super-historical," simultaneously, living in authentic union with the heavenly ranks.[40] And when the beleaguered, persecuted Churches on earth gather together in worship and join their voices to those of the heavenly hosts, it becomes possible for them to experience even now the joy of the Church victorious. It is in the power of the Spirit that the faithful are called to begin to see both the open heaven and the passing world around them with the eyes of God and the Lamb, as they witness prophetically to the eternal Gospel (14:6) against the values of the empire (2:10, 13; 3:10). John encourages the faithful to begin now to prepare for their own passage to the heavenly homeland through the purification of their spiritual vision (3:18).

The Transfer of the Scroll & the Proclamation of the Worthiness of the Lamb

The praises of the heavenly beings described in Revelation 5:9 and 5:12 speak of the "worthiness" of the Lamb "to receive power and wealth and wisdom and might and honor and glory and blessing," elements that are properly accorded to God alone (cf. 4:11; 7:10). The worthiness of Christ is further underscored by the Seer's statement that the sealed scroll is *taken* by the Lamb, not given to Him (cf. 5:7–8). No action of God is described, nor is one implied. In the hymn of creation that follows (in 5:9–14), the Living Creatures, the twenty-four Elders, the myriads of angels (5:11), and "every creature in heaven and on earth and under the earth and in the sea, and all therein" (5:13) unite in song to proclaim the worthiness of the Lamb to receive adoration and praise alongside the Lord and God who is seated upon the throne. All of creation is united in the worship of God and the Lamb (Phil 2:10). These visions reflect a lofty understanding of the relation between Christ and the God of Revelation, namely, that "the throne of

Both is one and the same" and "the worship offered to Each is also one and the same."[41]

While the divinity of Christ is never in question in the inaugural vision described in Revelation 1:12–20, it is through the figure of the apocalyptic Lion/Lamb at the center of the heavenly court in chapter 5 that the Risen Christ is shown to be enthroned in heaven, not only above all angelic powers (Heb 2:5–9) but also over all earthly powers. So it is that the figure of this Lamb becomes "the means of bridging the gap between heaven and earth which injustice and disobedience have brought about."[42] Paradise lost through the sin of Adam is here proclaimed as paradise regained through the sacrifice of Christ the Slain Lamb, who is the true bridge between the earthly and the heavenly worlds. As the Lamb begins to open the seals of the mysterious Scroll—thus inaugurating the first series of dramatic judgment oracles in Revelation 6:1— His role as Lord of history will be further clarified. The Lamb proves to be the Lord of history as He sets in motion the events that will bring about the arrival of the New Jerusalem in Revelation 21 and 22.

The New Song of the Living Creatures and the Elders

In the description of the praises of the Living Creatures and the Elders in 5:9a, we encounter for the first time the expression "a new song" (14:3), which also occurs in the Old Testament (cf. Is 42:10; Ps 33:3; 40:3; 96:1; 98:1; 144:9; 149:1). The new song in Revelation 5:9–14 with the other scenes of heavenly worship in the Apocalypse play an important role, as they invite the audience to begin to experience amid the sorrows of this passing life that "newness" of life and grace which God and the apocalyptic Lamb—the new Adam—are bringing about even now, in the midst of suffering, chaos, and disorder. The Lamb has forever opened the door to the heavenly sanctuary through His suffering sacrifice, and the faithful thereby already have access to heaven through the power of the Spirit in worship. Before the opening of the seven seals of the mysterious scroll (beginning in 6:1ff.), John invites the reader to celebrate together with the angels—indeed with all of creation—the victory of the Slain Lamb who opens heaven to His faithful. The new song appropriately celebrates the new situation that has come about in virtue of the Lamb's suffering sacrifice (cf. Heb 8:1–2; 10:19f). Do we have an appreciation of the newness of life to which we are called in Christ (Rom 6:4)? Do we experience something of the newness of God's grace at work in our own lives of prayer and worship?

"Worthy Is the Lamb to Take the Scroll and to Open Its Seals"

The heavenly proclamation of the worthiness of the Lamb functions as a response to the question posed by the angel in Revelation 5:2, "Who is worthy to open the scroll and break its seals?" The worthiness lacking in any other creature (5:3)—either to open the book or to gaze at its contents—is now attributed to the Slain Lamb, underscoring Christ's unique role. The worthiness of the Lamb—the "inner ethical presupposition of the ability . . . to open the Book" (cf. Mt 8:8; Mk 1:7; Jn 1:27)—accentuates yet again the understanding that Jesus is equal to God and worthy to receive worship alongside the one who is seated upon the throne.[43] The angelic proclamation of the Lamb's worthiness to take the scroll and to open its seals reflects early Christian devotional attitudes toward Christ the Lord, as it asserts the divine authority of the Lion/Lamb to inaugurate the process of judgment and transformation that will bring about a new heaven and a new earth.

The Lamb's Sacrifice and Its Effects

The new song of the angels extols the sacrificial and expiatory dimension of Christ's unique sacrifice and its relevance for universal redemption. By His blood the slaughtered Lamb (cf. 5:6, 9, 12; and 13:8) has ransomed for God people "from every nation, from all tribes and peoples and languages" (cf. 7:9, as well as: 11:9; 13:7; 14:6). Elsewhere in the New Testament, the association of the forgiveness of sins with the blood of Christ is a very early notion. It is found in the words of institution of the Eucharist in Matthew 26:28 and comes to be associated with baptism at an early stage of Christian reflection. But in the Book of Revelation, the suffering sacrifice of Christ, the blood of the Lamb, and their salvific effects extend beyond the obliteration of sin. In Revelation 7:14 the saints victorious are depicted as having "washed their robes and made them white in the blood of the Lamb." In addition to clear baptismal associations, the paradoxical image of the white garment purified by the blood of the Lamb speaks to the promise of the transfigured existence of the faithful, realized specifically through the mystery of Christian suffering. The transformation is won at great cost (3:4, 5, 18). In Revelation 12:11, those who have achieved victory in the cosmic struggle against the invisible forces of evil are said to have done so "by the blood of the Lamb and by the word of their testimony." It is through their testimony that the faithful are called to imitate the Lamb and share in His "conquest by sacrificial death."[44] By their faithful witness the victors will win a share in the Lamb's own "postmortem vivification and vindication."[45]

Throughout the entire book "it is the power of Christ-like witness that 'conquers.'"[46] Indeed, Revelation 12:11 alludes to the active role to which Christians are called as they witness prophetically to the values of the Gospel and openly denounce the idolatries of the age before the hostile powers of the empire in imitation of Christ the true and faithful witness (1:2; 3:14). Thus, beyond conveying the Lamb's own worthiness to receive the scroll and along with it the worship otherwise accorded to God, John sets the figure of the slain Lamb before the audience as the model for Christian life in this world. Beyond passive resistance, the faithful are called to a bold and active witness inspired by the example of Christ Himself (cf. 5:5–6). Indeed, "passivity in the face of spiritual crisis is part of the problem, not the answer."[47]

He Has Made Them a Kingdom and Priests for God

The Lamb is not only celebrated for having ransomed people from every tribe and language and people and nation, but also for having radically altered their status, making them a kingdom and priests for God (cf. 1:6; 20:6). Indebted to the rich lines of reflection in Exodus 19:6, John articulates the belief that Christ has conferred upon the faithful a share in His own royal and priestly dignity.

Indeed, Revelation 1:6, 5:10, and 20:6 all "refer back to the cardinal text for Israel's self-understanding in Exodus 19:6 (cf. Is 61:6),"[48] as they speak to the Christian understanding of that new Exodus brought about by the messianic Lion/Lamb. A royal and priestly people of the Apocalypse is called not only to share in the sacrifice of the Lamb, but to fellowship with the angels (cf. 19:10; 22:9). As John shows us, the victors will not merely see God, but will bear His Name on their foreheads (14:1, 22:4) and ultimately will reign with God and the Lamb in a renewed creation (3:21; 22:5).

Moreover, the Book of Revelation's Lamb extends on a universal scale the promises of Jewish salvation history to include all people. Both the Lion of the tribe of Judah (Rev 5:5) and the 144,000 sealed from the tribes of Israel in Revelation 7:4–8 have a place in previous Jewish tradition. But here, they have been reconfigured, once more, in the key of Christ (to borrow a musical analogy). So it is that Revelation 7:9 "as a reinterpretation of 7:4–8 indicates not so much the replacement of the national people of God as the abolition of its national limits."[49] Indeed, the apocalyptic Lamb has not come to abolish but to fulfill (Mt 5:17; Rom 1:16), as we see in chapter 21:12, where the names of the twelve tribes of the Israelites are written on the gates of the New Jerusalem, which Christ has opened to all nations (21:24–26). The Seer's understanding of the Church (or ecclesiology)—too often neglected in the scholarship— reflects here the early Church's understanding of itself as "the spiritual Israel."[50]

Ultimately, the righteous come to share in the royal and priestly dignity conferred by the Lamb even in this present life, even though the reign of the faithful with Christ promised here does remain a potentiality not fully realized until Revelation 20:4.[51] Christian life in this world is marked by this dynamic tension between the already and the not yet, as evident in Jesus' own teachings concerning the Kingdom (Mt 4:17; Lk 17:20–21). This same tension is at work in the Apocalypse as the beleaguered faithful share—though not yet fully—in the royal and priestly dignity of a redeemed people during the time in between Christ's Ascension and His return in glory at the end of time. Certainly the question of how to understand the nature of this reign of the faithful (cf. 1:6; 3:21; 5:10)—which seems to be realized fully only in the vision described in 20:4—does remain. At the same time, the notion that the Church in this world may already be spoken of in terms of the Kingdom of heaven certainly was not lost among the early commentators. According to St. Augustine:

> Consequently, the Church, even in this world, here and now, is the kingdom of Christ and the kingdom of heaven. Here and now Christ's saints reign with Him, although not in the way they are destined to reign hereafter; but the "weeds" do not reign with Him, even now, though they grow along with the "wheat" in the Church. . . . We conclude, therefore, that even now, in time, the Church reigns with Christ both in her living and departed members.[52]

For an audience beset by the conflicting allegiances and colliding values of eternal kingdom and fleeting world empire, the challenge is precisely that of sharing willingly in the heroic witness and patient endurance (1:9; 2:2, 19; 3:10) which are the marks of the Kingdom and priesthood of the Lamb. Throughout, the faithful are called to reject the idolatrous worship of the empire and to render fitting praise to God and the Lamb alone. Again, beyond the pastoral image of flocks of sheep fed by faithful shepherds (Jn 21:15–17), and the titles of servants, or even friends of Christ (Jn 15:15), the language and symbolism of Revelation 5 speak to us of a humanity that is in the process of being *sealed with the glory of Christ's own face*, as St. Ambrose reminds us.[53]

The Praises of the Myriads of Angels and of All Creation

As the cosmic hymn of the universe continues to unfold (5:9–14), the circles of praise expand still further to include the voices of the "myriads of myriads and thousands of thousands" of angels (5:11). The angels' elaborate response to the praises rendered by the Four Living Creatures and the Twenty-Four Elders in Revelation 5:12 contains no less than seven words of praise (cf. 7:10). Echoing the highest ranks of heavenly beings, the angels repeat in a loud voice (cf. 7:10; 11:15; 12:10; 19:1) the shouts of "worthy," as they expand the lexicon of praise for the Slain Lamb who is worthy to receive "power and wealth and wisdom and might and honor and glory and blessing!" This use of a remarkable seven-word formula of praise (here and in 7:12) occurs nowhere else in the Bible. The formula invites comparisons with Second Temple Jewish liturgical prayer, but likely finds its closest analogue in the seven words of wonder rendered by the angels to God (which are referred to but never actually revealed) among the "Songs of the Sabbath Sacrifice" from the Qumran texts.[54] Throughout

John's hymns Christ is worshipped in terms that are "equal to God, with language reserved for God."[55] The entire passage is "highly suggestive of the devotional attitude of the Asiatic Church in the time of Domitian towards the Person of Christ."[56] Again, when the gathered faithful join their voices to the victory song of the heavenly choirs, it becomes possible to experience even now the joy of the Church victorious. In this manner, John's hymns—like the Psalms—are not only world moving but "world-making."[57]

The glorified Christ's ascent to God's throne has opened the door to the heavenly sanctuary (cf. 4:1; 11:19; 15:5), permitting the audience to stand with the angels in the praises of God and Christ. Again, God's grace will reunite definitively their voices after the storms of time have ceased. The compelling descriptions of worship in chapters 4 and 5 serve not merely to strengthen and console, but effectively to draw the earthly community into the "virtual experience of presence in the heavenly temple."[58] It is to this newness of the spiritual life in Christ that John draws our attention, the newness of the cosmic praise of the angels and of all creation, as well as to the profound transformation that this newness has the power to effect in the lives of the seven Churches.

How can we help our people today recover this kind of vision of Christ at the center of things in a society dominated by the roar of anti-God forces in a postmodern world with its fragmented sense of truth and meaning? In our own time, more and more people seem to be living out their lives in a so-called post-Christian state of liberation from many outmoded notions, including that of the God revealed by Jesus Christ. One author observes that "many . . . even nominal Christians, are favoring more worldly, less demanding gurus than Jesus. Promises of peace, energy, and enlightenment have, for some, more appeal than life everlasting and the forgiveness of sins."[59] And yet, there is no reason to despair amid all the problems facing the world, for we must never doubt what the Spirit can accomplish in and through us if we are faithful to our own call to find God and Christ at the center of all things. According to St. Teresa of Calcutta:

> If we really center our lives on Jesus, if we really understand the Eucharist and nourish our souls with the Bread of Life and the word of God, we would not only be able to recognize the likeness of God in ourselves and others but we would also be able to restore it to those who seem to have lost it.[60]

The Enthronement of the Reader

The lofty theological significance of the visions in Revelation 4 through 5 should not obscure the fact that this revelation is given for the sake of the faithful who struggle to preserve their religious identity within a world dominated by the values of the Roman Empire. John's depiction of Christ the Lion/Lamb of God serves to address the needs of those early Christian communities by shedding light on the meaning of life in Christ during the time between the Resurrection and the end of time (1 Cor 10:11). Drawing the listeners' focus *heavenward* to the glorified Lamb as they journey forward in time in the presence of the angelic Jesus, the book's visions serve to address the question of human suffering, while extolling its redemptive value. The Book of Revelation does not teach us "how to avoid suffering, but how to suffer," namely, by joining our sufferings to those of Christ Himself.[61] For those who share in the sufferings and patient endurance of the Lamb, what is predicated of Christ by nature also comes to be predicated of His faithful witnesses by participation.

God's renewal of heaven and earth also involves a process that includes the transformation of the reader. Indeed, all of these remarkable transformations have their humble beginnings in the present life. Already now—in and through their *adoration* of God and Christ in the Spirit— the members of a priestly and royal community begin to stand together with the angels in a renewed creation. The faithful of the seven Churches are, beginning even now, priests forever with the saints and angels in heaven within the sacred time and space of the gathered worship assembly. Will we join our voices to those of the angels and saints in this cosmic hymn of creation?

Endnotes

1 Cf. James Hollis, *Tracking the Gods: The Place of Myth in Modern Life* (Toronto: Inner City, 1995), 24; Matthew Arnold, "Stanzas from the Grande Chartreuse," in *Poetry and Criticism of Matthew Arnold*, ed. A. Dwight Culler (New York: Houghton Mifflin, 1961), 187.

2 J. M. Ford, "The Priestly People of God in the Apocalypse," *Listening* 28: 256; and R. L. Jeske, "Spirit and Community in the Johannine Apocalypse," *New Testament Studies* 31 (1985): 452–466.

3 St. John Paul II, *Agenda for the Third Millennium* (London: Harper Collins, 1996), 18; and Ps 4:6; 27:8; 31:16; 42:2; 80:3, 7; and Song 2:14.

4 Caird, *Revelation*, 63.

5 Charles H. Talbert, *The Apocalypse: A Reading of the Revelation of John* (Louisville, KY: Westminster John Knox, 1994), 111–113. Christopher Rowland, *Revelation* (London: Epworth Press, 1993), 72–73: "In the old order worship maintains the identity of those who refuse to see things as the world sees them."

6 See Samson H. Levey, ed., *The Targum of Ezekiel*, Aramaic Bible 13 (Wilmington, DA: Michael Glazier, 1987), 3. Phillip B. Munoa, III, "Jesus, the *Merkavah*, and Martyrdom in Early Christian Tradition," *Journal of Biblical Literature* 121 (2002): 315 and literature cited.

7 DeSilva, *Seeing Things God's Way*, 103.

8 St. Irenaeus, *Against Heresies*, 4.20.7.

9 Cf. R. H. Charles, *Revelation of St. John* vol. 1, 136–37 and Ezra 2:9; 3:1; Ezra 6:2; Ps 40:7 (LXX 39:7).

10 Or is the scroll "[U]pon the palm of the right hand"? Cf. Henry Barclay Swete, *The Apocalypse of St. John*, 3rd ed. (London: MacMillan, 1911), 75. See also R. H. Charles, *Revelation of St. John*, vol. 1, 136: "The book-roll lies on the open palm of the right hand, not in the hand." Aune, *Revelation 1–5*, 339, points out that the early commentators Tyconius (fourth century) and Beatus (eighth century) render *supra dexteram* "on the right hand." Or is the scroll "at the right *side* of" the one seated on the throne?

11 David L. Barr, *Tales of the End*, 80. See also Ps 20:6; 48:10; Is 41:10; Mt 26:64; Lk 22:69; and 1 Pet 3:22.

12 See comments in Aune, *Revelation 1–5*, 344–45.

13 Ibid., 345. See also Rev 3:5; 13:8; 17:8; 20:12, 15; and 21:27.

14 Ibid. "The view that the sealed scroll of Revelation 5 is all or part of the Old Testament is very old and if found as early as Hippolytus (*Comm. in Dan.* 34.3), Origen (*Comm. in Joh.* 5:4; *Hom. in Exod.* 12.4; *Hom. in Ezek.* 14.2; *Philokalia* 2.1; 5.5), and Victorinus (*Comm. ad Apoc.* 5.1)." See also Lk 4:21; 24:25–27; and 2 Cor 3:15–16.

[15] Ibid., 348.

[16] G. B. Caird, *Revelation*, 71–72.

[17] Leonard L. Thompson, "Cult and Eschatology in the Apocalypse of John," *Journal of Religion* 49 (1969): 342.

[18] See Charles Homer Giblin, "Recapitulation and the Literary Coherence of John's Apocalypse," *CBQ* 56 (1994) 81–95, esp. 81–82.

[19] DeSilva, *Seeing Things John's Way,* 290; See also James L. Resseguie, *Revelation Unsealed: A Narrative-Critical Approach to John's Apocalypse* (Leiden, Netherlands: Brill, 1998), 160ff.

[20] DeSilva, *Seeing Things John's Way,* 195.

[21] Richard Bauckham, *The Climax of Prophecy: Studies on the Book of Revelation* (London: T. & T. Clark, 1993), 214–215. See also Caird, *Revelation,* 75.

[22] Caird, *Revelation,* 73. See as well, Austin Farrer, *A Rebirth of Images* (1949; repr., Boston: Beacon Press, 1963). See orig. (Westminster: Dacre Press, 1949), 17–18.

[23] Bauckham, *The Climax of Prophecy,* 215.

[24] See Aune, *Revelation 1–5,* 369–70.

[25] Most scholars deem this translation unlikely with regard to Christ in the Book of Revelation. See Matthias Reinhard Hoffmann, *The Destroyer and the Lamb,* (WUNT, II, 203; Tübingen: Mohr Siebeck, 2005), 89, n. 261. J. Jeremias, art., *"amnos, arēn, arnion,"* TDNT, vol. I, pp. 340–341.

[26] David L. Barr, "The Lamb Who Looks Like a Dragon?," in *The Reality of Apocalypse: Rhetoric and Politics in the Book of Revelation,* Society of Biblical Literature Symposium Series 39 (Atlanta: Society of Biblical Literature, 2006), 209.

[27] Martin Hengel, *Studies in Early Christology* (Edinburgh: T. & T. Clark Publishers, 1995), 229, n. 5.

[28] Barr, "The Lamb Who Looks Like a Dragon?," 209.

[29] Bauckham, *The Climax of Prophecy,* 184.

[30] Leonard L. Thompson, *The Book of Revelation: Apocalypse and Empire* (Oxford: Oxford University Press, 1997), 48. See also comments by David E. Aune, *Revelation 1–5,* 352.

[31] Loren L. Johns, *The Lamb Christology of the Apocalypse of John: An Investigation into Its Origins and Rhetorical Force* in WUNT 167 (Tubingen, Germany: J. C. B. Mohr [Paul Siebeck], 2003) 148–49. See also Rev 6:16; 14:10; 17:14; as well as 2:16 and 2:23.

[32] Barr, "The Lamb Who Looks Like a Dragon?," 208.

[33] Ibid., 209.

[34] Cf. Isaiah 11:2–3 and comments by Oecumenius, as quoted in William C. Weinrich, ed., *Ancient Christian Commentary on Scripture: New Tes-*

tament XII: Revelation (Downers Grove, IL: InterVarsity Press, 2005), 77: "Isaiah has interpreted for us the 'seven eyes, which are the seven spirits of God sent into all the earth,' saying, 'And there will rest upon him the spirit of wisdom and understanding, the spirit of counsel and strength, the spirit of knowledge and piety. The spirit of the fear of God will delight him.'"

35 Bauckham, *The Theology of the Book of Revelation,* 113–114.

36 Cf. Ibid., 111.

37 Ibid., 109.

38 I am grateful to Professor Ugo Vanni for his insightful comments in this regard.

39 Jean Daniélou, *The Angels and Their Mission* (Allen, Texas: Christian Classics, 1957), 114.

40 Petros Vasiliadis, "'Εἰκών' and 'Ἐκκλησία' in the Apocalypse," *Greek Orthodox Theological Review* 38 (1993): 114. See also Aimo T. Nikolainen, "Der Kirchenbegriff in der Offenbarung Johannes," *New Testament Studies* 9 (1962–63): 353, 359.

41 Charles, *Revelation of St. John* vol. 1, 151.

42 Rowland, *Revelation,* 75.

43 Charles *Revelation of St. John* vol. 1, 139.

44 Bauckham, *Climax of Prophecy,* 215.

45 DeSilva, *Seeing Things John's Way,* 102.

46 Ibid., 224.

47 Loren T. Johns, "Identity and Resistance: The Varieties of Competing Models in Early Judaism," in *Qumran Studies: New Approaches, New Questions,* ed. Michael Thomas Davis and Brent A. Strawn (Grand Rapids, MI: Eerdmans, 2007), 268.

48 Håkan Ulfgard, *Feast and Future: Revelation 7:9–17 and the Feast of Tabernacles,* Coniectanea Biblica New Testament 22 (Stockholm: Almqvist & Wiksell, 1989), 46.

49 Bauckham, *Climax of Prophecy,* 225.

50 Charles, *Revelation of St. John* vol. 1, 199.

51 R. H. Charles, *The Revelation,* vol. I, 16: ". . . in the spiritual kingdom of Christ . . . all the faithful are already kings and priests to God (i. 6)."

52 St. Augustine, *De Civitate Dei,* XX.7–17, in *The City of God, Books XVII–XXII,* ed. Gerald G. Walsh, et. al. Fathers of the Church 24 (1981): 276; and XX.9, 278.

53 St. Ambrose, "From the Explanation of the Psalms," Ps 43, 89–90: Corpus Scriptorum Ecclesiasticorum Latinorum 64 (324/326); *Enarrationes in* xii. *Psalmos Davidicos.*

54 See Carol A. Newsom, *Songs of the Sabbath Sacrifice: A Critical Edition* (Atlanta: Scholars Press, 1985), 177.

55 David R. Carnegie, "Worthy is the Lamb: The Hymns of Revelation," in *Christ the Lord: Studies in Christology Presented to Donald Guthrie,* ed. H. H. Rowdon (Downers Grove, IL: InterVarsity, 1982), 256.

56 Swete, *Apocalypse,* 84.

57 Cf. Walter Brueggemann, *Israel's Praise: Doxology Against Idolatry and Ideology* (Philadelphia: Fortress Press, 1987), 7ff.

58 Carol A. Newsom, "Merkabah Exegesis in the Qumran Sabbath Shiroth," *Journal of Jewish Studies* 38 (1987): 14.

59 Sharon Doyle Driedger, *Maclean's Magazine,* December 15, 1996, "Is Jesus Really God?" 41.

60 As quoted in Fr. Lawrence J. Gesy, *The Hem of His Garment: True Stories of Healing* (Huntington, IN: Our Sunday Visitor Publishing, 1996), 81–82.

61 DeSilva, *Seeing Things John's Way,* 102; and Clifford Geertz, *The Interpretation of Cultures* (New York: Basic Books, 1973), 104.

CHAPTER FOUR

Jesus Christ the Divine Warrior

From visions of a fiery, angelic Christ walking in the midst of and speaking directly to the Churches on earth, to images through an open door in heaven of the Lion/Lamb who is adored and glorified by the angels alongside the Creator God, John now shifts our attention *forward* to the mystery of Christ's return at the end of time (the Parousia). With the dramatic appearance of the messianic Divine Warrior returning in glory, John introduces "one of the most powerful and impressive portrayals" in the book.[1] Here is the Word of God (19:13), the "King of kings and Lord of lords" (19:16), who rides out from heaven upon a white horse accompanied by the armies of heaven (19:14). While the messianic Rider represents the key figure in the Seer's portrait of Christ the Divine Warrior, two other images are relevant to the discussion: the "Messianic Child" in 12:4–5, and the angelic "one like a Son of Man" who is seated upon a white cloud in 14:14ff.

The Divine Warrior and Revelation 19:11–21

John's Divine Warrior who judges the world in justice and truth (15:3; 16:7; 19:2) crystallizes important aspects of the book's reflections concerning divine judgment—aspects which are implicit in the first two Faces of Jesus. This can be seen in details of the description of the Rider and the ominous language used by the angelic Christ in His address to the seven Churches (2:16, 22–23, 27), as well as in direct associations between the Lamb and the arrival of God's judgment (cf. 6:16–17; 14:10; and 17:14). This third Face of Christ leads us to reflect upon the meaning of Christ's victory over death on the Cross and His final return in judgment. At the same time, it offers consolation to Christians in crisis, reassuring them concerning the final outcome of history.

The Divine Warrior and the Return of Christ in the New Testament

While John's Divine Warrior offers a magnificent, awe-inspiring image with which to convey of the mystery of Christ's return at the end of time, the imagery has little in common with what we find elsewhere in the New Testament.[2] Although early Christian reflection speaks of His dramatic appearance upon the clouds (Mt 24:30; Mk 13:26), and of the mighty angels who accompany Him (cf. 2 Thess 1:7–9), neither in Paul's reflections concerning the return of Jesus (cf. 1 Thess 4:13–18; 1 Cor 15:51–57) nor anywhere in the Gospels (cf. Mk 13; Mt 24; Lk 21) do we find a parallel for this striking "Rider on a White Horse," "from whose mouth issues a sharp sword," and who in righteousness "judges and makes war."[3] At the same time, John's language does recall a number of texts from the Old Testament and early Judaism in which God (or His Messiah) is depicted as a warrior. The image of the deity who intervenes in military conflict is not unique to Israel, but is widespread in Ancient Near Eastern texts, where the thunderous voice of the storm god "shakes heaven and earth."[4]

The Complexity of the Imagery

Details used to describe the Divine Warrior pose a number of challenges to the reader and questions arise. First of all, is the Rider in Revelation 6:2 to be identified as a Face of Christ? The identification is difficult to sustain.[5] Moreover, how are we to reconcile the figure of the obedient Lamb who has conquered through His suffering sacrifice, with the language of divine retribution and violence contained in the Seer's description of the Warrior (19:11–16), as well as in the drastic consequences that await Christ's enemies (19:17–21)? The ethical problems posed by this language can neither be ignored nor easily dismissed. Again, the Apocalypse—in a manner consistent with the other writings of the New Testament—teaches that it is through faith and never through violence that one comes to share in Christ's victory over the world (13:10).[6] The basic attitudes of humility and patient endurance exemplified by the Lamb must also be present in those who would be His faithful witnesses (1:9; 5:9–10; 13:10; 14:12). Ultimately, the strong language aims to transform the behavior of the audience and has "repentance as its primary goal."[7]

The Holy War Theme in the Bible

According to Thomas B. Slater, in the Hebrew Bible we find four principle motifs with regard to the notion of God as Divine Warrior: (i) the Lord of hosts "makes war against the enemies of Israel";[8] (ii) God "slays the sea monster and brings about order from chaos";[9] (iii) He "judges and punishes evil";[10] and finally, (iv) God "liberates His people."[11] Here in Revelation 19:11–21, John adapts and re-interprets these Divine Warrior traditions (cf. 12:7–9; and the hymn in 12:10–12).[12] The theme may be divided into two basic forms: (i) traditions in which God battles *alone* (cf. Ex 14:13–14; Is 59:16; 63:3) or with His celestial army (Joel 3:11, Zech 14:5); and (ii) conflicts which envision the collaboration of God's people[13] with Revelation reflecting a "much more complex combination of sometimes contradictory eschatological perspectives."[14] Whether as witnesses to God's mighty deeds, or as active participants in the spiritual warfare depicted, John invites the faithful to *choose sides.*

Spiritual Struggle: God and Christ Do Battle Along with the Faithful

While the holy war represents an important theme in the Book of Revelation, it is to be understood symbolically and spiritually rather than literally. If one were to interpret the text literally, one would misunderstand John's purpose, for ultimately the prophet "is showing how the death of Jesus has the power to destroy evil, using the graphic imagery of holy war."[15] By unveiling for the Churches the hidden truth concerning the drama of the spiritual war that rages in heaven (and on earth), John edifies his readers concerning the nature of the struggle for those who would count themselves among the followers of the Lamb, and so join the white-robed faithful (cf. 7:9) who have achieved victory by means of their witness to the point of death. This spiritual war—waged not by violence but by suffering self-sacrifice—"founds the world, overcomes evil, abolishes chaos, establishes order and justice."[16]

The Holy War Thematic in the Hymns of Revelation

In Revelation 4–22 John shows us that "the God whose voice shook Sinai will once again shake heaven and earth."[17] Among Revelation's songs of the angels, the holy war motif emerges in 11:15–18, which signals the arrival of God's Kingdom. It is present in 12:10–12 where a loud voice proclaims Satan's fall from heaven. It resounds in 15:3–4 in the voices of those who have conquered the beast and sing the Song of Moses and the Lamb. The hymn in 16:5–7 sings the praises of God's justice, while the magnificent, concluding Hallelujah hymn (which figures in the *Hallelujah* chorus of Handel's *Messiah*) celebrates the fall of Babylon (19:1–4) and the arrival of the marriage supper of the Lamb (19:5–8). Together, the songs of the angels celebrate the past, present, and future mighty deeds of God. They proclaim His power and glory, praise the salvation brought about by God and the Lamb, while welcoming the arrival of the Kingdom of ancient promise symbolized in the New Jerusalem.

The Importance of Prayer and the Worship of God and Christ Alone

Once again, John's visions and the theology of the book reflect the principle that "people resemble what they revere, either for ruin or for restoration."[18] Thus, the Seer calls his audience to worship God (and God alone; cf. 14:7; 19:10; 22:3, 9). While the faithful are not described as exercising an active role in the defeat of the enemies portrayed in the book, the prayers of the saints find their own place within the drama of the spiritual struggle portrayed (8:3f). The incense of the prayers of the saints is gathered together and applied, as it were, by God and the angels directly onto the course of time and history, exercising thereby its own distinctive impact within the process of transformation that will culminate in the arrival of the New Jerusalem. Indeed, "behind the veil of God's wrath, the prayers of the saints determine everything."[19]

Revelation 19:11: The Open Heaven and the Appearance of the Rider

The visions section began in Revelation 4:1 with the magnificent image of an open door in heaven (again, "a major vision-marker"[20]) that signals the beginning of a divine revelation (cf. Ezek 1:1; Mk 1:10 and parallels; Acts 10:11; Rev 11:19; 15:5). The recurrence of this image here in 19:11 expands the reader's perspective still further. John's visions of the heavenly world invite the audience not merely to question and reconsider their place within the existing social and political order, but serve as a corrective to the splendor of Roman imperial cult ceremonial, as they offer instead an exalted "counterexperience of awe that will expose the other as counterfeit."[21]

John's Reversal of the Roman Empire's Symbols of Military Victory

So it is that details used in the description of the Divine Warrior incorporate images which serve to contrast Christ with the illustrious warrior hero of Roman imperial might.[22] The Divine Warrior rides forth from the open heaven. He is the Word of God (cf. 19:13; Wis 18:15–16) who is crowned with "many diadems" (19:12). The divine power and otherworldly splendor of this King of kings and Lord of lords far surpasses the grandeur and majesty of the Roman generals and emperors. The armies that accompany Christ emerge from heaven. The war that He wages is a spiritual one whose field of battle is cosmic in scope and proportion. The enemies that He vanquishes are Death and Hades (Rev 20:14), along with the powers of evil that oppose God's will (20:10). The decisive victory of God's Divine Warrior was won upon the Cross on Mount Calvary on Good Friday. At the same time, in John's Rider from heaven we see a striking reversal of the figure of Jesus riding a young donkey in the Gospel accounts of His triumphal entry into Jerusalem. For in the Book of Revelation, Christ returns "not as the convicted criminal but as God's eschatological judge."[23] The irony of this reversal of images is one that would not have escaped the faithful of the early Christian communities, who were awaiting with faith and hope the triumphant return of their Risen Lord and Messiah (22:20).

The Symbolism and the Spiritual Struggle of the Soul

At the same time, the cosmic, "from above" perspective of the Apocalypse should not obscure the fact that the battle waged and won by the Divine Warrior and Word of God represents a spiritual victory whose consequences are equally decisive at the level of the human soul. Notwithstanding the cosmic scope of John's visions, the symbolism is to be appropriated at a personal and spiritual level. The unfolding story speaks eloquently to that struggle within the human heart which leads to paradise regained, uncovers the treasure hidden in the field (Mt 13:44), acquires the pearl of great price (Mt 13:45–46), and transforms the soul into that "well-ordered city" in which God and Christ are enthroned at its very center.[24] Do we aspire to such lofty spiritual ideals in our own life of prayer?

Revelation 19:12–13 and the Description of the Divine Warrior

The Divine Warrior's "eyes . . . like a flame of fire" recall the eyes of the angelic Jesus in Revelation 1:14 (cf. 2:18) and both texts are indebted to Daniel 10:6. The Warrior's "many diadems" evoke once again Roman triumphal imagery. Elsewhere, God's enemies—both Satan, who has "seven diadems on his heads" (12:3) and the "beast from the sea" with ten diadems on its horns (13:1)—share this symbolism in common with the Warrior. Thus, reference to the many diadems worn by the Rider—a "literary counterpoint" to those worn by His enemies in 12:3 and 13:1—underscores Christ's superiority over His adversaries, both visible and invisible (cf. 17:12).[25]

The reference to a "secret name" (in addition to those revealed; cf. 19:11, 13, 16) evokes Old Testament images of the mysterious being encountered by Jacob in Genesis 32:29 as well as the angelic being who appears to Manoah in Judges 13:11–18. At the same time, the expression serves to underscore the Divine Warrior's heavenly origins. The name is inscribed upon the Rider himself (cf. 3:12; 14:1; 22:4; as well as 13:1) rather than upon the diadems.[26] This unknown name speaks to the fact that Christ's "nature, his relationship to the Father, and even his relationship to humanity, transcend all human understanding,"[27] for "when they have joined all the glorious names that adoring wonder can ascribe to him, he still confronts them with an ultimate mystery."[28] David Aune draws attention to Rev 2:17, which promises to the one who conquers a white stone "with a new name inscribed that no one but the recipient knows," as well as 3:12 where the Christ inscribes the names of God, the name of the New Jerusalem, and His own "new name" upon the victor.[29] Just as the Seer has not ceased to underscore Christ's equality with God, neither does he neglect to provide the audience with indications concerning his hopes for their ultimate transformation in Christ (Rev 22:4).

Revelation 19:13 and the Divine Warrior's Vestment

Details of John's description recall a number of Old Testament texts, among the oldest being Isaiah 63:1–6 and the prophet's violent description of God's victory over Edom. At the same time, the question of how to interpret the presence of the blood on the garment of Revelation's Divine Warrior arises. Is it the blood of the Rider Himself? Is it that of His followers? Is it that of God's enemies? Given the complexity of the Seer's symbolism, is it to be interpreted as that of all three at the same time? Does John include this graphic detail because the war has *already been waged and won*? It is, after all, the Lamb's *own* blood that has been shed upon the Cross, achieving thereby decisive victory over the powers of sin and death (5:9, 12).[30] While the violent language in Isaiah 63 (itself a nuanced re-interpretation of Israel's holy war tradition; cf. Ex 15), affords an important context for interpreting John's Divine Warrior, the original language and symbolism of the holy war are, again, reversed and reinterpreted in the key of Christ. John has reversed the image of Isaiah's "avenger splattered with the blood of his enemies," for it is ultimately the Lamb who has been pierced (1:7).[31]

At the same time as there are points of comparison with the Hebrew Scriptures, the imagery evokes once again—and in striking fashion—the red and purple robes of Roman imperial splendor.[32] Although here the majesty of the robe's color derives not from the lavishness of the red or purple cloth from which it was woven, but from the blood sacrifice of the slaughtered Lion/Lamb—an irony that was not lost upon the writers of the Gospels (cf. Mk 15:17; Jn 19:2, 5). For the final victory of Christ and His followers is achieved not in imitation of the military might of the Roman emperors and their generals, but through the complete reversal of power inherent in the Lamb's self-sacrifice upon the Cross, and the patient endurance of His witnesses (even "until death," 2:10).

Could the blood be that of the martyred righteous who cry out to God that He "judge and avenge" their blood "on the inhabitants of the earth" in Revelation 6:10 (cf. 7:14; 12:11; 16:6; 17:6; 18:24; and 19:2)? Is it the blood of the Lamb intermingled with that of the faithful witnesses?[33] Finally, is this the blood of the Rider's *enemies*? Admittedly, the fact that the robes of the Warrior are described as "dipped in blood" *prior* to the battle in no way precludes the interpretation that the text is alluding to the blood of the Rider's opponents, particularly given the account of the destruction of Babylon in chapters 17 and

18.[34] However, the Divine Warrior's sword is God's Word, while the "winning weapon" of Christ's followers in this holy war is their faithful witness.[35] Thus, John describes for us a messianic warrior "who has conquered not by killing His enemies, but by allowing himself to be killed, and who invites his followers to do the same."[36] Or as Primasius comments, the robe sprinkled with blood is symbolic of "the tokens of his passion, whether this be in the Head himself or in his body, which is the church."[37]

The Divine Warrior Is the Word of God

The reference to Jesus as "the Word of God" in 19:13 invites, in the first instance, comparisons of the Gospel with Letters of John and the wisdom texts to which they are indebted (including Prov 8, Sir 24, and Wis 7–8). However, the expression appears to allude more specifically to Wisdom 18:15–16,[38] and the appearance of God's Word as Divine Warrior: "The personification of God's will suddenly made lethally present in the disobedient world."[39] The Rider's appearance is not only dramatic, but "fulfills all our expectations: appearing out of heaven on a white horse, with exalted names, an honorable reputation, in command of heavenly armies, bearing the accouterments of war."[40] The profound reversal of images represented by this Divine Warrior—who "leaped from heaven, from the royal throne, into the midst of the land that was doomed" (Wis 18:15)—vindicates the hopes of the faithful (1:9; 3:10; 6:9; 12:11; 20:4), whose crucified Lord re-appears at the close of the age not as the slaughtered victim of Roman justice, but as God's Messiah and judge of the cosmos. Ultimately, this messianic figure "is like divine speech made manifest in human form, faithfully representing God's message to humankind: The Word of God is faithful and true to God."[41] Finally, the angelic overtones of John's portrait recall not only the image of God's Word leaping forth from heaven in Wisdom 18:15–16, but also the figure of the angel of Exodus 23:20–23 that bears the name of God.

Revelation 19:14: The Rider and the Armies of Heaven

The image of Christ returning at the end of time accompanied by the heavenly host resonates with early Christian reflection concerning the return of the Son of Man in judgment (cf. Mt 16:27; Mk 8:38; Lk 9:26; 1 Thess 3:13). That the unarmed "armies of heaven" (whether angels, or the saints, or both) should be described here as wearing fine linen (cf. 15:6) suggests they are more appropriately clad for a wedding banquet (cf. 19:7, 9, 17) than for the decisive battle with God's enemies—a battle in which they do not appear to be actively engaged (19:21). This is consistent with the view that Revelation's symbolism is better suited to explore the theological meaning of the return of the victorious Christ at the end of time than to depict a violent battle against the forces of evil (a struggle engaged elsewhere by Michael and the angels, 12:7–9);[42] for "Christ does whatever fighting is required, and that by his word."[43]

Revelation 19:15: The Rider's Sword

The striking image of the sword emerging from the mouth of the Rider recalls a detail of the angelic Jesus in 1:16 (cf. 2:12, 16). While the Face of Christ has been transformed once again, the final result is the same: "the nations have been judged, found wanting and punished" (cf. 1:7; 2:26–28; 3:10).[44] John's reconfiguration of the image of the weapon in the hand of the personified Word of God in Wisdom 18:16 as emerging from *the mouth* of his messianic Divine Warrior, creates a striking metaphor that may well be original.[45] The symbolic association of the sword with God's divine Word is found elsewhere in early Christian reflection (cf. Eph 6:17; Heb 4:12). The enemy is overcome by the power of the Word of God which the Divine Warrior both *is* and *speaks*. Again, no battle is described (cf. 2 Thess 2:8), for "it is, throughout, John's position that the only battle, the decisive battle, fought by the Lamb was on the cross."[46] Once again, the Warrior of Revelation 19 is not "the slaughtered Lamb turned slaughterer, but it is the witness turned judge."[47] His appearance signals nothing less than the arrival of the definitive transformation of heaven and earth, for the arrival of God's Word "does not precipitate the end of the world but a re-creation of it."[48] As Jürgen Moltmann reminds us:

> The biblical apocalypses are not pessimistic scenarios for the destruction of the world which seek to disseminate anxiety and terror and to paralyse people; they hold fast to the hope of God's faithfulness to his creation in the terrors of this age. "When all this begins to take place, then lift up your heads, for your redemption is near," promises Luke (21.18). Prophetic hope is hope in action, apocalyptic hope is hope in danger, a hope which is capable of suffering, patient and persistent: whatever may come, in the end there is God.[49]

John's visions of a new heaven and earth invite us to look beyond our fears, beyond the terrors of the age, to live always in the *light of Christ's return*, and so to prepare to meet Him at the end of time through our encounters with Him *in the present*: in our life of faith and in our service of the poor, the sick, the dying, the abandoned, the marginalized, where we encounter Christ broken every day in our midst. C. S. Lewis reminds us that "the Present is the point at which time touches eternity," and that it is only in the present—neither in the past nor the future—that "freedom and actuality" are offered to us.[50]

Revelation 14:14: The Rider & One Like a Son of Man Seated upon a Cloud

Reference to the Rider's sword evokes Revelation 14:14, where the Seer describes one like a Son of Man (cf. 1:13; Dan 7:13) who is seated upon a white cloud (cf. 1:7), with a golden crown on his head and holding a sharp sickle in his hand (14:14, cf. 14:17). As in the case of the first Rider in Revelation 6:2, the imagery is open to more than one interpretation. If the figure is to be understood as a depiction of Christ, why are no additional details provided that would favor a clearer identification, as is the case with Christ's portrait in 19:11–16?[51] The ambiguous reference to "another angel" in 14:15 seems to imply that the figure described in 14:14 is an angel, and invites further clarification, as do both the subsequent *command* from the other angel in verse 15 to the one seated on the cloud to use the sickle and reap, as well as the angel's providing the reasons for doing so ("for the hour to reap has come"). If the figure of the one like a Son of Man in 14:14 is to be understood as an image of Christ, then it should be considered together with the symbolism of the Divine Warrior in 19:11–21 and the broader portrayal of the return of Christ as judge that will reach its apex in Revelation 19:17–21 and 20:7–10. Even if the figure in Revelation 14:14 is, admittedly, a "somewhat blurred and abstract vision" of Christ, it is difficult to imagine that the verse would not have evoked the Judge who is "standing at the doors" (Jas 5:9) in the minds of the original audience.[52]

Revelation 19:15: The Divine Warrior's Rule

The rod of iron (cf. Rev 2:27, 12:5) is a clear allusion to Psalm 2:9 (see also Is 11:4) and serves here to assure the messianic understanding of the figure of the Divine Warrior.[53] Despite the power of the emperor in the present age, the hour of deliverance from the evil world-empire approaches when Christ will rule. At the same time, the transference of the imagery in Psalm 2:9 to the faithful in Revelation 2:26–27 ("I will give authority over the nations; to rule them with an iron rod") reflects John's remarkable hopes for the victors, who will acquire a share in Christ's own messianic power and glory.

Revelation 12:5: The Divine Warrior and the Messianic Child

Reference to the Divine Warrior as ruling the nations with a rod of iron recalls Revelation 12:5 and the figure of the messianic child (cf. 12:2, 4, 13) born of the Woman Adorned with the Sun (12:1–6, 13–17), adding yet another dimension to the Seer's portraiture of Christ the messianic judge. The imagery is certainly complex. Is the Woman a symbol of *Israel* bringing forth her Messiah? Is this an image of *Mary* the Mother of Jesus (cf. LXX Is 7:14)? Is the Woman a symbol of the *Church* engaged in the perennial struggle to bring forth Christ into the world in the face of great spiritual opposition? Or is she to be understood as the *New Jerusalem*, the Bride of the Lamb referred to later in the book (19:7–8; 21:9–10)?[54] Does the nature of the book's symbolism permit us to adopt all of the aforementioned possibilities simultaneously?

The figure of the unnamed messianic male child born of the Woman (cf. Is 66:7) who is destined to rule with a rod of iron and who is spirited up to heaven, "to God and his Throne" (12:5), certainly sheds light upon the figure of the Rider in Revelation 19. As such, this messianic child must be considered within the larger context of the book's storyline. The child returns at the conclusion of the story as God's Divine Warrior riding "upon a white charger with the symbols of revenge, victory, and judgement."[55] The audience is led to reflect upon the complex juxtaposition of images (at times antithetical) at work in the book's subtle and intricate portrayal of Jesus Christ.

Revelation 19:15: The Wrath of God

The Seer's description of the arrival of God's judgment (cf. Is 63:2–6; Joel 3:13) re-elaborates details introduced within the context of Revelation 14:18–20. John's circumspection with regard to God in Revelation 4 gives way here to the use of anthropomorphic language, as the fury of His wrath becomes the focus of reflection (cf. 11:18; 14:10,

19; 16:19; of God and the Lamb in 6:16–17). But it is ultimately the power of God's Word *to judge* that is being depicted here. The sharp sword emerging from the Rider's mouth (2:16; Is 11:3f), the Messiah's rule with a rod of iron (2:27; 12:5; Ps 2:9), along with the image of the Word that treads the wine press of the fury of God's wrath (14:10, 19; Is 63:1–6) have all been characterized as "representations of the word of Christ by which he executes with indisputable authority the judgment of God."[56] As God's Word, the Divine Warrior is "the communicator" of that judgment.[57]

Revelation 19:16: The King of Kings and Lord of Lords

The title "King of kings and Lord of lords"—associated primarily with God (cf. LXX Dan 4:37; 1 Tim 6:15)—is transferred here to the messianic Divine Warrior (and to the Lamb in 17:14), reaffirming Christ's "universal supremacy."[58] It also vindicates the audience's faith, while strengthening their hope in the new creation that is to come. Whether as Lamb of God in 17:14 or as Divine Warrior in 19:16, the King of kings and Lord of lords "wins the victory for those who cannot win it for themselves."[59] The question of how to interpret the placement of the name "on his robe and on his thigh" is debated and is perhaps best understood as "written or embroidered on the garment covering his thigh."[60] Again, here is a Lord whose origins are divine and whose splendor far exceeds that of the gods of the Roman pantheon.

The Number of Jesus: 888

Scholars have pointed out that when the title King of kings and Lord of lords is reverted into Aramaic (omitting the word "and"), its numerical value totals 777, "the victorious counterpart and antidote to 666,"[61] the number of the beast (Rev 13:18). Others point to a text from the *Sibylline Oracles* (I, 324–31) that dates from the second half of the second century, in which the numerical value of the Greek letters of the name of Jesus (*Iēsous*) is the peerless "888."[62] While theories concerning the number 777—calculated in Aramaic and omitting one of the words—may exceed the evidence, the text from the *Sibylline Oracles* attests eloquently to early Christian interest both in calculating the number of Jesus and in affirming the superiority of the name that is above every other name (Phil 2:9; cf. Heb 1:4; Rev 22:4).[63]

Revelation 19:17–21 and the Battle That Is Not Described

The marriage feast of the Lamb—into which the faithful gain entry (19:7, 9; 21:2)—finds its antithesis in the "nightmare feast" of the "great supper" of God's wrath, described in 19:17–21 (cf. Ezra 39:17–20).[64] The dreadful (and at times grotesque) language here should be approached less for its literal meaning than for its effect upon the faithful who are reminded of the crisis signaled by the grim reality of God's final judgment (1:7; cf. 11:15–18; 16:14) and of "the paramount importance of living now . . . so as to be found a loyal servant of God."[65]

The anticipated climactic battle between the forces of good and evil (cf. 19:19) is not described, for again, the death and Resurrection of the Lamb have already achieved God's ultimate victory over the powers of sin and death (5:9). So it is that the dramatic description of the beast, the kings of the earth and their armies—gathered to make war against the Divine Warrior and His army in 19:19—is followed immediately in verse 20 by the capture of the beast along with the false prophet and by the account of their relegation to the lake of fire (to be joined in 20:10 by Satan, who is bound in 20:2 but granted a temporary reprieve in 20:7). The devastating outcome of the encounter between the remaining opponents and the Divine Warrior/Word of God is described in 19:21. Is the absence of detail concerning the battle between Christ and His opponents to be interpreted as a statement by the Seer that the sovereign Christ "is too exalted to contend personally with the devil" who in any event, "is no worthy combatant"?[66] Clearly, the enemy is no match whatsoever for the Divine Warrior and is unable to do anything without divine leave—and even then only for a limited time.[67] Overall, the book's much anticipated account of the definitive battle between the forces of good and evil proves to be less of a "battle and triumph," than a juridical reflection upon the declaration of a "verdict and execution" of a sentence.[68] Indeed, Revelation 19:17–21 and its description of the great supper of God may be interpreted as "a parody of the messianic banquet, a symbol of eschatological joy,"[69] and a macabre antithesis of the early Christian celebration of the Eucharist.[70] Yet again, the scene serves to underscore the stark, black and white, either/or choices that the Seer of Patmos places before his audience.

To sum up: in 19:11–16 Christ appears as the messianic judge and Divine Warrior who emerges from heaven at the end of time in order to manifest God's just judgment. As is the case with regard to the other two Faces of Jesus, John continues to describe Him using terms which in the Hebrew Scriptures are otherwise associated only with God. While Christ judges the unjust, ultimately, God's righteous judgment is not reserved exclusively for the enemies of the Divine Warrior, but extends both to God's people and to the nations, to the just and the unjust, to the good and to the evildoer (cf. Ps 9:8; 72:2; Tob 3:2; Eccles 3:17).[71] Those who have proven to be good and faithful witnesses to Christ will be vindicated, and will come to share in His own victory, while God's opponents—whether visible or invisible—will be destroyed. Again, as we see in 19:17–21, no fighting is described and the much anticipated battle "takes place offstage."[72]

Along with this third Face of Christ belong the figures of the messianic Child who is born of the Woman Adorned with the Sun and is caught up to heaven in 12:5, as well as the angelic one like a Son of Man described in 14:14–16. Thus, beyond the stark either/or language and symbolism of the book, John's audience is left to contemplate the splendor, the glory, and the complexity of the Faces of a Christ who is contemporaneously a "Lion," a "conqueror," and a "messianic ruler," but also a "Lamb," a "child," and an angelic "one like a Son of Man."[73]

How is it that Christ should be depicted in such different ways? According to St. Irenaeus, God is not seen through human effort. Rather, God is seen "when He pleases . . . by whom He wills, and when He wills, and as He wills."[74] St. Maximus the Confessor (580–662) elaborates these ideas further:

The Lord does not always appear in glory to those who stand before Him. To beginners He appears in the form of a servant (Phil 2:7); to those able to follow Him as He climbs the high mountain of His transfiguration He appears in the form of God (cf. Mt 17:1–9), the form in which He existed before the world came to be (cf. Jn 17:5). It is therefore possible for the same Lord not to appear in the same way to all who stand before Him, but to appear to some in one way and to others in another way, according to the measure of each person's faith.[75]

The seven Churches—then as now—constitute what Augustine refers to as a mixed entity, a *corpus permixtum,* an admixture of saints and sinners, of saintliness and sinfulness, of faithful witness and unfaithful or lukewarm adherence to the Gospel, of those who strive to live as a people who have been made a kingdom and priests, and of those who remain too deeply immersed in the values of world.[76] For according to Augustine, not only are there many sheep within and many wolves without, but "many sheep there are without" and "many wolves there are within."[77] Moreover, these inclinations are also at work in a human heart that is divided. St. Gregory the Great compares the Church's progress to the early morning sky, in which the dawning light is "intermingled with darkness" (cf. Song 6:10; Rom 13:12).[78]

Finally, for the faithful during the time leading up to Christ's return, this third Face of Christ offers reassurance concerning their own salvation, while describing powerful visions of the overthrow of evil and, with it, the end of a political, social, and economic system that has persistently rejected Christ and His Gospel, while persecuting His followers. Once again, the imagery speaks eloquently to the mystery of the everlasting reign of Christ along with His saints, who have proven victorious in the epic spiritual battle described (Rev 22:5; Mt 19:28; Lk 22:30).

Endnotes

1 George R. Beasley-Murray, *The Book of Revelation,* New Century Bible, based on the Revised Standard Version (London: Oliphants,1974), 277.

2 David E. Aune, *Revelation 17–22* vol. 52C, World Biblical Commentary, 1046.

3 Cf. Rev 19:15; cf. 1:16, 2:12, 19:11; and Aune, *Revelation 17–22,* 1053.

4 Moshe Weinfeld, "Divine Intervention in War in Israel and Ancient Near East," in *History, Historiography and Interpretation: Studies in Biblical and Cuneiform Literature,* ed. Hayim Tadmore and Moshe Weinfeld (Leiden, Netherlands: Brill, 1986), 121.

5 See the discussion in David E. Aune, *Revelation 6–16,* 393–94. Allen Kerkeslager, "Apollo, Greco-Roman Prophecy, and the Rider on the White Horse in Rev 6:2," *Journal of Biblical Literature* 112 (1993): 116–121, argues that the symbolism associated with the First Seal portends the arrival of false messiahs and false prophecy.

6 D. L. Barr, "Doing Violence," 99. R. B. Hays, *The Moral Vision of the New Testament* (San Francisco: Harper San Francisco, 1996), 175: a book ". . . that places the Lamb that was slaughtered at the center of its praise and worship can hardly be used to validate violence and coercion."

7 Brian K. Blount, *Revelation: A Commentary* (Louisville, KY: Westminster John Knox Press, 2009), 358.

8 Thomas B. Slater, *Christ and Community: A Socio-Historical Study of the Christology of Revelation* (Sheffield, England: Sheffield Academic Press, 1999), 210. Cf. 1 Sam 15:2; Is 1:24; Jer 46:10; Mal 1:4–5.

9 Ibid. Cf. Ps 74:13–14; Is 27:1; Job 41.

10 Ibid. Cf. Josh 24:20; Is 3:11–15; 31:2–3; Zeph 1:1–13; Hag 1:5–11.

11 Ibid. Cf. Ex 14:1–15; Is 35:3–4; 40:3–5.

12 Ibid., 211.

13 Richard Bauckham, "The Apocalypse as a Christian War Scroll," *Neotestamentica* 22 (1988): 17.

14 See Aune, *Revelation 17–22,* 956.

15 Barr, *Tales of the End,* 138.

16 Ibid., 104.

17 Richard Bauckham, "The Eschatological Earthquake in the Apocalypse," *Novum Testamentum* 19: 232. Heb 12:25–29.

18 Gregory K. Beale, *We Become What We Worship: A Biblical Theology of Idolatry* (Downers Grove, IL: IVP Academic, 2008), 284.

[19] Hans Urs von Balthasar, *Theo-Drama: Theological Dramatic Theory, IV: The Action, I* (San Francisco: Ignatius, 1994), "Under the Sign of the Apocalypse," 54, n. 3.

[20] Leonard L. Thompson, *Abdignon New Testament Commentaries: Revelation* (Nashville: Abingdon, 1998), 175.

[21] DeSilva, *Seeing Things John's Way,* 195.

[22] Aune, *Revelation 17–22,* 1051.

[23] Slater, *Christ and Community,* 218.

[24] Cf. "Origen on Prayer," trans. William A. Curtis, Chapter XV, "Thy Kingdom Come," *Christian Classics Ethereal Library* (2015): 47.

[25] Aune, *Revelation 17–22,* 1054.

[26] See Aune, *Revelation 17–22,* 1055.

[27] Beasley-Murray, *The Book of Revelation,* 280.

[28] Caird, *The Revelation of St. John the Divine,* 242.

[29] Aune, *Revelation 17–22,* 1055.

[30] Barr, *Tales of the End,* 137–38.

[31] Harrington, "Worthy is the Lamb," 66.

[32] See Aune, *Revelation 17–22,* 1057.

[33] Ian Boxall, *The Revelation of St. John,* Black's New Testament Commentary, Book 19 (Grand Rapids, MI: Baker Academic), 274.

[34] Beasley-Murray, *The Book of Revelation,* 280; Charles, *Revelation of St. John* vol. 2, 133.

[35] Blount, *Revelation: A Commentary,* 354.

[36] Boxall, *The Revelation of St. John,* 274.

[37] Primasius, "Commentary on the Apocalypse," 19.13, as quoted in: *Revelation,* ed. William C. Weinrich, 311.

[38] Roger Le Deaut, *La Nuit Pascale* (Rome: Pontifical Biblica Institute, 1963), 334, on John's indebtedness to wisdom tradition.

[39] John P. M. Sweet, *Revelation,* TPI New Testament Commentaries (London: SCM Press, 1979), 283. Slater, *Christ and Community,* 218.

[40] Barr, *Tales of the End,* 137.

[41] Slater, *Christ and Community,* 218.

[42] Charles H. Giblin, *The Book of Revelation: The Open Book of Prophecy,* Good News Studies 34 (Collegeville, Minnesota: Liturgical Press, 1991), 181.

[43] Ben Witherington, III, *Revelation,* New Cambridge Bible Commentary (Cambridge, UK: Cambridge University Press, 2003), 243.

[44] Slater, *Christ and Community,* 226, n. 49.

[45] See Aune, *Revelation 17–22,* 1060.

[46] Harrington, "Worthy is the Lamb," 67.

[47] Bauckham, *The Theology of the Book of Revelation*, 105.

[48] Blount, *Revelation: A Commentary*, 349.

[49] Jürgen Moltmann, "In the End – God," *Is The World Ending? Concilium* 1998, ed. Seán Freyne and Nicholas Lash (London: SCM & Maryknoll: Orbis Books, 1998), 123.

[50] C. S. Lewis, *The Screwtape Letters, with Screwtape Proposes a Toast* (New York: Harper Collins, 2001), 75.

[51] Peter R. Carrell, *Jesus and the Angels: Angelology and the Christology of the Apocalypse of John*, Society for New Testament Studies Monograph Series, Book 95 (New York: Cambridge University Press, 1997) 188–89.

[52] Matthias Reinhard Hoffmann, *The Destroyer and the Lamb*, WUNT, II, 203 (Tübingen, Germany: Mohr Siebeck, 2005), 251.

[53] Aune, *Revelation 17–22*, 1061.

[54] Wilfrid J. Harrington, O.P., *Revelation*, Sacra Pagina 16 (Collegeville, MN: Liturgical Press, 1993), 128ff.

[55] Ragnar Leivestad, *Christ the Conqueror: Ideas of Conflict and Victory in the New Testament* (London: SPCK, 1954), 233.

[56] Beasley-Murray, *The Book of Revelation*, 281.

[57] Giblin, *The Book of Revelation: The Open Book of Prophecy*, 181.

[58] Ibid., 182. See as well: Thomas B. Slater, *Christ and Community*, 219. Aune, *Revelation 17–22*, pp. 953–55. For the expression "King of kings" cf. 2 Macc 13:4; 3 Macc 5:35, 1 Enoch 9:4; while "Lord of lords" occurs in Deut 10:17; Ps 136:3.

[59] Slater, *Christ and Community*, 219–20.

[60] Giblin, *Revelation*, 182. Charles, *The Revelation of St. John*, vol. II, 137. Cf. the discussion in Aune, *Revelation 17–22*, 1062.

[61] Witherington, *Revelation*, 244; Giblin, *Revelation*, 182; Patrick W. Skehan, "King of kings, Lord of lords (Apoc. 19:16)," *Catholic Biblical Quarterly* 10 (1948): 398.

[62] Jean-Pierre Prévost, *How to Read the Apocalypse* (Ottawa: Novalis, 1991), 40. J. M. Ford, *Revelation*, Anchor Bible (New York: Doubleday, 1975), 226.

[63] Aune, *Revelation 17–22*, 1063.

[64] Beasley-Murray, *The Book of Revelation*, 282.

[65] DeSilva, *Seeing Things John's Way*, 110.

[66] Rev 12:13; 13:7ff; 20:1–3; Job 1:12; 2:6. Leivestad, *Christ the Conqueror*, 234.

[67] Leivestad, *Christ the Conqueror*, 234.

[68] Ibid., 234.

[69] Aune, *Revelation 17–22*, 1063–64.

[70] Barr, *Tales of the End*, 138.

71 Aune, *Revelation 17–22*, 1053.

72 Blount, *Revelation: A Commentary*, 354: "Even there, it is unclear whether John intends combat of a traditional sort. After all, the primary weapon is a sword not of steel but of God's word."

73 See again comments by Barr, *Tales of the End*, 111.

74 St. Irenaeus, *Adversus Haereses* 4.20.5 in: *Ante-Nicene Fathers, Vol. I: The Apostolic Fathers with Justin Martyr and Irenaeus*, ed. Alexander Roberts and James Donaldson, trans. Philip Schaff (repr. 1885; Grand Rapids, MI: Christian Classics Ethereal Library, 2010), 817.

75 St. Maximus the Confessor, "Second Century on Theology," *Philokalia*, vol. II, (London: Faber & Faber, 1981), 140.

76 *The City of God* 18.49. Cf. *The City of God by St. Augustine*, trans. Marcus Dods (New York: The Modern Library/Random House, 1950), 660.

77 Cf. "Tractates on the Gospel of John," 45:12, in *The Fathers of the Church: St. Augustine, Tractates on the Gospel of John, 28–54*, vol. 88, ed. John W. Rettig (Washington, DC: Catholic University of America, 1993), 198.

78 Cf. St. Gregory the Great, "Moral Reflections on Job," XXIX, 3–4; in *Morals on The Book of Job by S. Gregory the Great*, in 3 vols., James Bliss and Charles Marriott (Oxford: John Henry Parker, 1844–1850), 303–304.

CHAPTER FIVE

A Fourth Face: A Reflection

The "Apocalypse of Jesus Christ" (1:1) is only partially understood without some appreciation of the sacred author's hopes for the reader as these emerge in the text and in the choices that are set before the audience. And yet, the history of the discussion of this last book of the Bible demonstrates clearly that very little attention has been directed to the figure of the human person in the Apocalypse,[1] and particularly to the Seer's lofty understanding of the "farthest reaches of human nature" in Christ. God's promise to make all things new (Rev 21:5) holds particular significance for those called to be faithful witnesses and victors in the spiritual battle depicted. In this regard, the Seer articulates his own compelling version of what it means to become a new creation in Christ, indeed to be clothed with Christ (Gal 3:27), the prototype of a redeemed and renewed humanity (Col 1:18; Rev 1:5), as the narrative sets before the audience images of Christ and of the new self, created in God's image, "in true righteousness and holiness" (Eph 4:24). Thus, the electric, visionary, Jewish-Christian apocalyptic colors of the book's story world not only bring to life a portrait of Jesus Christ, the Son of God that is unique in the New Testament, but this

multi-faceted Jesus also comes to function as the mirror
through which to reflect back to the seven Churches the
prophet's highest hopes for them in their time of crisis,
in the form of a fourth Face. As the reader gazes into the
kaleidoscopic swirl of oscillating visions in the Apocalypse,
the churning images—these shifting crystals of visionary
glass and sand—will fuse to reveal some inspiring images
of the human person transformed in Christ. In addition
to the three Faces of Christ in the Book of Revelation,
a Face of a different kind emerges for the reader's consideration: namely, Jesus' own Face as it has come to be
reflected, refracted, deformed, and misshapen in the face
of a fallen and sinful humanity once created in God's own
image and likeness (Gen 1:26–27). Again, it is precisely
here, as we shift our focus from the Faces of Jesus to this
remarkable fourth Face, that I would like to slow the pace
of our reflections and to enter into greater detail concerning the spiritual transformations signaled in the text, so
as to better appreciate their meaning and significance not
only for John's original audience, but for us today.

St. John and Apocalyptic Spirituality

This line of reflection leads us, in the first instance, to
consider the text from the perspective of the spiritual and
psychological depths out of which the story emerges. That
the book has a great deal to say concerning spirituality and
the inner life has long been recognized. Indeed, "the battle
between good and evil takes place not only in the arena of
history but also in human hearts."[2] The vast supernatural
canvas upon which the story of the Apocalypse is painted
should therefore also be considered from the perspective

of the author's own inner life, and the spiritual and "psychological explosion" out of which these visions emerge.[3] Again, beyond the powerful visions of a new heaven and a new earth, the book narrates a compelling account of one early Jewish-Christian prophet's own experience of "paradise now."[4] The apocalyptic drama that transpires in the story's symbolic universe, with its clash of images, finds its analogue in the struggles at work within the *human heart*. Or in the words of the fourth-century Syrian monk, known as Pseudo-Macarius:

> The heart itself is but a small vessel, yet there are also dragons and there are lions; there are poisonous beasts and all the treasures of evil. And there are rough and uneven roads; there are precipices. But there is also God, also the angels, the life and the kingdom, the light and the Apostles, the treasures of grace—there are all things.[5]

According to Judeo-Christian tradition, the human person has been created in the image and likeness of God. The soul is "capable of God" (or *capax Dei* in the words of St. Augustine), with image aspiring to reflect archetype (2 Cor 3:18; Eph 4:24; Col 3:1, 10) in such a way as to participate more and more deeply in the life of the Spirit.[6] So it is that a magnificent vision of the human person emerges in the Bible and extra-biblical literature, in the writings of Origen, St. Gregory Nazianzen, St. Gregory of Nyssa, and in later reflection, including St. Thomas Aquinas, and the late fourteenth-century Renaissance Neoplatonists such as Marsilio Ficino (1433–1499) and his student Giovanni Pico Della Mirandola (1463–1494). The human soul is spoken of within these lines of reflection as a "microcosm," a world in miniature (*parvus mundus*).[7] Here, the fullness of being (*magis esse*) consists in striving to discover, to aspire toward, and to recover one's own deepest identity as contained within the infinite mystery of God. This ideal stands in stark contrast to the diminished state of "privation of the being" (*minus esse*) of those who have defected from, ignore, or are simply no longer able to perceive their own higher calling and destiny.[8] In this way, the Seer's portrait of the human person offers a powerful critique of contemporary society's de-divinized, secularist humanism. Where the "Light of revelation is obscured,"[9] humanity is deformed by a loss of "ontological density."[10]

Beyond apocalyptic literature's perspective that looks with dread (and fascination) to approaching judgment along the forward-looking, horizontal axis and the upward-looking, vertical axis which draws the human imagination up into inspired visions through an opened door into heaven, an interior, mystical dimension of this literature also speaks to us of the soul's longing for paradise regained. Whether to live in the shadow of Christ's return (Rev 6:15–17) or in its light (Lk 21:28) is a choice that is left to each individual. But for the exiled Jewish-Christian prophet John, both are transcended in the experience of the open heaven as we are led to contemplate the relationship between the cosmic and the personal,[11] of "the great world . . . within the small" and "the inner theater of the Christian soul" to whom such visions have been granted by the Spirit for the life of the community of faith.[12] And while the visionary is taken up "in the Spirit" (Rev 4:2), this journey is not without its own dangers, as reflected in a number of texts which underscore the need for some sort of spiritual preparation.[13]

The fourth Face and a consideration of the experience of apocalypse as a spiritual and psychological expression of the human soul's desire for God take us beyond the study of Christ (Christology) to the meaning of salvation (or soteriology), and ultimately, to a consideration of John's portrait of the victorious, transfigured faithful who have conquered the world through the power of the Cross. For the present, it should suffice to say that the mythic, macrocosmic perspective at work in Revelation's electric world of vision finds its analogue in the personal, interior struggle of the individual to live in accord with the Holy Spirit. Although the narrative of the Book of Revelation is cast in cosmic terms and epic proportions, it ultimately gives voice to the drama at work at the level of the human heart, and the mystery of the spiritual struggle in which the soul (Rom 7:14ff)—created as it is in God's own image and likeness—strives to bear the divine image.

The Book of Revelation: Text and Icon

Once again, the text is more than a *window* into John's world in late Mediterranean antiquity, even if points of contact between the text and the world of the author's time are not lacking, as the commentators have long observed. The text is also more than "a mirror" before which the postmodern reader is able to construct (or de-construct, as the case may be) its meaning in conversation with the clues provided within the narrative.[14] It may be argued that the text of the Book of Revelation is also a door to the sacred which offers us something more than the written record of the visions of an early Jewish-Christian prophet recorded nearly two thousand years ago.

Beyond ancient artifact, the text is a "literary vehicle."[15] These mystical texts may be seen as "verbal maps" and "verbal icons"[16] designed to draw their audience into the heavenly world they portray. According to this view, John's aim is "not just to tell but to reveal."[17] Again, it is through the text—as door and gateway—that the Seer's revelatory experience is "re-presented or re-actualized"[18] in the reading aloud of the text of the Book of Revelation by the gathered community on the Lord's Day (1:3, 1:10). It is precisely in this act of reading aloud and of responding to the text that the audience is offered the opportunity not only to overhear but to enter into the Seer's world of vision mediated by the text in the power of the Spirit. For as St. Clement of Rome observes, it is ultimately through Jesus Christ "that we look straight at the heavens above. Through Him we see mirrored God's faultless and transcendent countenance. Through Him the eyes of our heart were opened."[19] Indeed, "By Him are the eyes of our hearts opened . . . (to behold) His wonderful light."[20] In the context of comments concerning Revelation 5:6, the eyes of Christ are a way of speaking of the Holy Spirit, which allows the community of the faithful who contemplate the Faces of Christ to see *with His own eyes*, to see through His eyes and to see ourselves both as He sees us in the present moment and as He hopes to see us in the future.[21]

The Book of Revelation: Text as Icon

So it is that the reading of the text—as icon and door— opens our mind, created after God, to its "inward likeness to the archetype," in the words of St. Stephen the Younger.[22] In what ways might this approach to the text of the Book of Revelation as icon assist the contemporary reader to begin to sound the depths of the Seer's symbolic universe along with its *spiritual* meaning? First of all, the relationship between icon and Sacred Scripture has been the subject of a long and rich tradition of theological reflection associated with the Christian East, where Holy Scripture and Holy image are understood to be "mutually revelatory."[23] The icon may be understood to be "theology in color,"[24] or "'theology in images,' parallel to theology in words."[25] Icons have been called "markers on our path to the new creation" that both "reveal a transfigured universe" and allow us "to participate in it."[26] Ultimately, the icon as door "opens up to us an immense vision which embraces both the past and the future of the universe."[27]

The significance of Eastern Christianity's lines of reflection concerning Scripture and Icon for acquiring a better understanding of the Book of Revelation is enhanced further when one appreciates something of the distinctiveness of the Seer's *use of language*. In fact, to an extent "greater than other apocalyptic texts," the language of the book "is visionary language that deals in pictures rather than propositions."[28] John's language "stands on the border between word and picture,"[29] impacting the reader in a manner that goes beyond words to express, as they point beyond themselves to ultimate reality, that is, "to God's transcendent world and the ultimate goal of the creation."[30] And these images are themselves profoundly shaped and rooted in biblical tradition. From the tree of life (Gen 3:22, 24; Rev 2:7; 22:2, 14, 19), to the use of motifs in the Book of Exodus, to images of the temple, through to the arrival of the New Jerusalem, the Seer's world is steeped in biblical thought and imagery. At the same time, the book reinterprets and reconfigures the words, motifs, and symbols of the Jewish Scriptures, transposing them in the key of Christ. In this process the Seer offers an unveiling (the literal meaning of apocalypse) of the transcendent world described beyond the opened door to heaven (4:1). For, in the final analysis, the Book of Revelation is concerned not only with what is to take place in the future, but with ultimate realities and "what is" (literally "the things that are," 1:19).[31] In a manner reminiscent of the Prophet Ezekiel, the story aims to engage not only the intellect but also to inspire the religious imagination of the reader in such a way that the audience is invited to step into the new world that John describes, a world which, once again, is profoundly biblical. In this way, the text of the Apocalypse is an icon and door that opens up the path toward the New Jerusalem. It calls the audience to prepare with a sense of urgency for the arrival of a new heaven and a new earth, and so to be transformed and transfigured in the process. Ultimately, the Sacred text functions not only as an icon, but as "a door which leads to divine life."[32]

Text, Icon, and Perspective: Rublev's Trinity

Most readers will be familiar with a well-known Russian icon, commonly referred to as Rublev's Trinity. Painted by St. Andrew Rublev (c.1360–70 to 1427–30) in the fifteenth century, it presently adorns the walls of Moscow's Tretiakov Gallery. This "unexcelled jewel of iconography" is inspired by Genesis 18 and the mysterious encounter between Abraham, Sarah, and the three mysterious visitors, a story that later came to be read and interpreted in the light of Christian theological reflection on the Blessed Trinity.[33] Long before St. Andrew Rublev painted his Trinity, iconographic tradition had been inspired by the story of the three mysterious visitors who enjoy the hospitality of Abraham and Sarah by the oak at Mamre, with the earliest extant evidence being found in the catacombs of the Via Latina in Rome (dating to the fourth century).[34] The icon of the Trinity depicts three angelic figures seated around a small table at the center of which is a chalice. While most would identify the angelic figures proceeding from left to right as the Father, Son, and Holy Spirit, others argue that "authentic iconographic tradition does not represent in human form either the Father or the Holy Spirit because they did not become incarnate, did not assume human form, and therefore remain indescribable."[35]

With regard to the icon itself, one author observes: The "dominant impression is brightness. The yellows, greens, and lilacs are very light and transparent."[36] Others speak of "an intense spiritual beauty . . . which the most beautiful theological texts could never convey."[37] The basic form of the composition is a circle, which is a central image in John's visions of the open heaven. Owing to the icon's particular use of perspective, the lines of the outer circle formed by the three figures appear to converge toward a point outside of the icon, such that the person standing before it becomes the fourth person at the table, the fourth person in the circle.[38] To the one who stands before the icon, a space is opened at the table inviting the viewer to "join them around the table" and so enter into the conversation with the three persons of the Blessed Trinity.[39] Rublev's Trinity "opens to welcome the viewer, whom the icon leads into sacred space, to communion at the table of God."[40] Or as Henri Nouwen expresses the idea, the icon invites the person who stands before it to enter into the circle of the love of the Trinity, "a circle that could not be broken by the powers of the world."[41] Experts on iconography observe that the use of this type of inverse perspective is typical of iconographic tradition.

The Book of Revelation's Inverse Perspective

In a manner not unlike these icons, the lines of meaning of the text of the Book of Revelation—as both icon and door—may be seen to converge outside of the text in such a way that they draw the audience into the Seer's world of inspired vision, values, and Jewish-Christian apocalyptic logic. As with the icon of the Trinity, the Book of Revelation invites the faithful of the seven Churches to *complete the circle* and become a part of the text's world of meaning, along with the reversal in perspective of the story's symbolic universe. The text's inverse perspective—like that of the Gospels—reaches out to encompass the reader, inverting entirely the values of the world in favor of the values of the Kingdom of God taught by Jesus in the Gospels. As one author suggests:

> By using inverse perspective, iconography has embraced the entire concept of those Gospel teachings like the Sermon on the Mount, which completely reverse our secular, earthly values. And this also reminds us that it is God who takes the initiative to come forth and encounter humanity.[42]

Both icon and Scriptural text serve to contextualize the life of the Christian within this same inverse perspective and its "logic of reversal," a divine logic that is at work throughout the Bible.[43] Indeed, from the story of the Fall in the Book of Genesis, through the story of the Exodus, in the writings of the prophets, to paradise regained in the mysteries of Christ's death, Resurrection, and glorification we see this inverse perspective at work. In Luke's Magnificat, Mary proclaims the greatness of a God who "has brought down the powerful from their thrones, and lifted up the lowly; [who] has filled the hungry with good things, and sent the rich away empty" (Lk 1:52–53). In the God and Christ-centered world of the New Testament, the Word of God became Flesh (Jn 1:14), and the first will be last and the last first (Mt 20:16). So it is that this reversal of perspective is not merely aesthetic, but calls for a complete reversal of the ego, "the reversal of the intellect."[44] Or as Jesus says, "Unless a grain of wheat falls into the earth and dies, it remains just a single grain; but if it dies, it bears much fruit" (Jn 12:24).

The logic of reversal at work in the Seer's story world reflects a comprehensive vision of human transformation in Christ, according to which those who follow the Lamb on the royal road of the Cross shall acquire a share in His glory. The Book of Revelation—as icon—invites its audience to strive to attain to the likeness to Jesus Christ, the Icon of God (cf. 1 Cor 15:49; 2 Cor 4:4). For, again, "Icons are like the markers on our path to the new creation, so that, according to St. Paul, in contemplating "'the glory of the Lord, [we] are being changed into His likeness' (2 Cor 3:18)."[45] In this way, just as the person standing before Rublev's icon becomes a fourth person in the circle, the

person standing before the text of the Apocalypse—as icon
and door to the sacred—is called to live the faith in such
a way as to become a living reflection of Jesus, indeed, a
fourth Face of Christ.

A Fourth Person in the Circle

Having looked intently upon and contemplated the Faces
of Christ in the Book of Revelation (cf. Ps 27:8; 4:6; 31:16;
80:3), St. John of the Cross describes what happens when
God looks back at us through the eyes of Christ:

> Scattering a thousand graces, he passed through
>   these groves in haste,
> And, looking upon them as he went, Left them,
>   by his glance
> alone, clothed with beauty.[46]

The Gospels record the miracles of Our Lord and show
us how it is that when Jesus passes by, what was broken
is made whole, the sick are healed, the dead rise again,
the powers of darkness scatter in haste. When Jesus passes
by, the faded images of a fallen creation which has been
estranged from the Face of God are restored and made
beautiful once more. In and through His words, His works,
His miracles, a beauty shines forth that is not of this world.

We have been contemplating the Faces of Jesus from
the perspective of our own efforts of looking at Him in the
apocalyptic icons depicted in the Book of Revelation. What
St. John of the Cross leads us to meditate upon is the mystery
of the transformation that comes about when Christ looks
back at us, leaving us gloriously transformed by His glance

alone. St. John Chrysostom expresses the view that those who have pleased God "will be invested with such glory as these eyes cannot even look upon," for while the face of Moses shone with glory, "the face of Christ shone far more brilliantly than this."[47] Indeed, biblical and extra-biblical literature hold up for us examples of people who have been so transformed by their encounter with the living God's transforming grace, that—in a manner reminiscent of the image of Jesus transfigured on Mount Tabor—they shine, if only momentarily, with the divine fire of God's Spirit.[48]

When we contemplate the mystery of the transformation of the human person in Christ through the Book of Revelation, as with all attempts to speak of mystery, words are inadequate. Various expressions are used within complementary lines of theological reflection that help us to begin to sound the depths of the mystery of human transformation, whether we speak of divinization, theosis, apotheosis, metamorphosis, "transformation soteriology,"[49] Christ mysticism, or in terms of adoption (*huiothesia*).[50] Others speak in terms of "a *continuum* between angels and transformed human beings"[51] within biblical and extra-biblical reflection. At the same time, the question does remain as to whether or not these texts—which, characteristically, have "oscillated between metaphor and mysticism"—are to be understood literally (cf. Dan 12:3).[52] Moreover, the interpreter is left to ponder whether these transformations by grace are to be thought of as exclusively within the realm of future possibility, or whether and to what extent they are to be understood as being realized (at least in part) in the here and now (or what scholars refer to as "realized eschatology", as we anticipate the end of the story while we are still in the present).

Clothed in the Beauty of the Lord: Biblical Images of Human Transformation

There are streams of biblical and extra-biblical reflection that speak of individuals who are transformed by God's grace and acquire some manner of exalted status in the heavenly spheres.[53] The figure of Enoch in Genesis 5:24 is said to have "walked with God," while later tradition describes his glorious transformation into the angelic being Metatron (cf. 2 Enoch 22:8–10; 3 Enoch). Elijah, "a prophet like fire" (Sir 48:1), ascends into heaven in a whirlwind, in "a chariot of fire" with "horses of fire" (2 Kings 2:11; Sir 48:9). The face of Moses, transformed by the glory of God, shines with an otherworldly light (Ex 34:29f, 35; cf. 4 Ezra 7:97; 1 Enoch 38:4; Judg 5:31).[54] A second-century text relates images of a transformed (if not deified) Moses who ascends to heaven and is seated upon God's throne,[55] while the writings of Qumran (4Q374, 4Q377) and Philo of Alexandria proceed along analogous lines of reflection.[56] According to the prophet Daniel, "Those who are wise shall shine like the brightness of the firmament; and those who turn many to righteousness, like the stars for ever and ever" (12:3).

Jesus teaches that the righteous "will shine like the sun" in the heavenly Kingdom (Mt 13:43), and that those who follow Him faithfully and share in His sufferings "will also sit on twelve thrones, judging the twelve tribes of Israel" (cf. Mt 19:28; Lk 22:29–30). A number of passages in the New Testament speak of the miracles performed by Jesus' followers. Peter, for example, walks on water (Mt 14:28–31). The disciples exercise a ministry not only of preaching, but of healing and deliverance (cf. Mk 6:13,

20; Lk 9:6). Indeed, "many signs and wonders were done among the people by the hands of the apostles" (Acts 5:12; cf. 1:8; 2:43; 4:16). The Johannine Jesus makes the remarkable statement that "he who believes in me will also do the works that I do; and greater works than these will he do, because I go to the Father" (cf. Jn 14:12). St. Luke records Jesus' command to the seventy to heal, as well as their ability to perform exorcisms (10:1, 17). The Acts of the Apostles recounts the miracles of Peter (cf. Acts 3:6–7; 5:15–16; 9:34, 36–42), as well as the extraordinary miracles that God worked through Paul (Acts 19:11). Stephen, who was filled with power and grace is said to have done "great wonders and signs among the people" (Acts 6:8; cf. 6:15). Moreover, at the time of his martyrdom, Stephen, "filled with the Holy Spirit," is able to see the heavens open and "Jesus standing at the right hand of God" (cf. Acts 7:55–56). In his Letters, Paul—who alludes to his own experience of the third heaven (cf. 2 Cor 12:1f)—expresses through various images the mystery of being transformed into (cf. 2 Cor 3:18) and conformed to the image of Christ (Rom 8:29), and exhorting his audience to have the mind of Christ (Phil 2:5; 1 Cor 2:16).[57] The writings of Paul reflect an exegetical tradition that speaks of Christ as the image of God and the believer as the "image of the image" (cf. Gen 1:27; 2:7; 1 Cor 15:44b–49; 2 Cor 3:7–4:4; Rom 8:29–30; Col 1:15; Phil 2:6; Heb 1:3), inviting comparisons with the writings of Philo.[58] John's approach is more narrative in nature, and as we shall see, although his symbolic language and stark rhetoric contrast strongly enough with Paul's language of human transformation in Christ (cf. 2 Cor 3:18), in the Apocalypse we are transformed in accord with the object of our worship and, ultimately, become what we worship (14:9–11; 16:2; 19:10; 22:3, 9; cf. Gal 6:7–8).[59] As we saw earlier, just as Daniel transferred to the Son of Man details from descriptions of the Ancient of Days, John transfers to Christ what in the Hebrew Scriptures is predicated of God alone. So too, a study of the content of these promises—to which we now turn—will suggest that the dividing lines between Christ and the victors have been analogously "blurred,"[60] allowing John to achieve, again, through the shifting sands of his kaleidoscopic word-pictures, a portrait of the faithful Christian who is called to become an image of the Image, or fourth Face of Christ.

John's Portrait of a Transformation in Christ

Again, in a style and manner that is appreciably different both from the narratives in the Gospels and Acts, and from the lines of discursive reflection concerning the mystery of "participatory union"[61] with Christ in the Letters of Paul (cf. Gal 3:26–27; 2 Cor 5:17), the Book of Revelation articulates a most compelling portrait of the transformation of the human person in Christ. And it is precisely in the book's noteworthy capacity to draw its audience into the world of vision it portrays that we should begin to look for the lines of meaning as they extend forth from the text (as verbal icon) toward an audience that is "poised on the boundary between earth and heaven."[62] The text (again, as literary vehicle and/or verbal map) is designed to draw the audience into the "symbolic transformation of the world" effected by the reading aloud of the text in a worship setting on the Lord's Day (1:10) as they learn to walk with the angels in this present life, to stand side by side with the heavenly ranks,[63] and to join their voices to the expanding circles of praise.[64] Again, "one Church of angels and human beings" unites in adoration of God and the Lamb as the vision of the open door into heaven serves to shift and expand the audience's perspective from the historical to the supra-historical, from the human into the transcendent beyond. At the same time, we should note that the Seer's motives are not primarily mystical or eso-teric (cf. Col 2:18), but rather, exhortative as he prepares the audience spiritually to enter courageously into the con-flict of the messianic holy war described in chapters 4–22 (a dramatic struggle of epic proportions that will unfold upon a cosmic stage, demanding of the seven Churches nothing less than faithful witness even unto death, cf. 2:10).

Ultimately, it is in the concluding visions in chapters 19–22 that the sparkling details of a renewed and trans-formed creation come to be elaborated most compellingly in the visions of the New Jerusalem, which endures as a powerful symbol not only of God's divine presence and everlasting dwelling place, but of God's holy people trans-formed at the end of time. Again, far beyond the sheep entrusted to Peter (Jn 21:16–17), or the servants and friends of Christ (Jn 12:26; 15:15), Revelation's visionary language develops a remarkable portrait of the victor as an angelified image of Christ.

They will see God's face and bear His Name upon their foreheads (14:1; 22:4; cf. Ex 28:36–38) and will reign forever with God and the Lamb (3:21; 22:5). Again, the text of the Apocalypse is an icon, and this icon is a door that opens onto the heavenly world. And it is here, as the inverse perspective of the narrative reaches outward to encompass the audience with visions of everlasting blessings and rewards, that we find a host of echoes and resonances with the promises made to the victors in Revelation 2–3.[65] Here, through the oracular address of the living Christ (who speaks in the first-person singular, "I Jesus"), John effectively places the reader between the specific challenges and hardships (both internal and external) faced by the Churches on earth, and the consolation offered both in the promises of Christ and in the details of visions of the ultimate fulfillment of these eschatological transformations by the God of hope who makes all things new (Rom 15:13; Rev 21:5).

As discussed earlier, the authoritative voice of the angelified Jesus of Revelation 1 addresses the Churches, issuing challenges, threats, and words of consolation appropriate to the life circumstances of each community as He accompanies the faithful upon their dangerous journey toward God's new creation. Again, these congregations represent an admixture of courageous witnesses and lukewarm adherents to the Gospel, of those living in a manner that befits a royal and priestly people, and of those who are deeply immersed in the values of the Roman Empire.

Throughout, the voice of Christ emphasizes the reality of judgment and the need to repent (2:5, 16; 3:3, 19; cf. 2:21–22; 9:20–21; 16:9, 11). He reminds the Churches of the importance of love (2:4–5, 19) in the face of a range of conflicts encompassing both external threats (2:10; 3:10; 7:14; 11:7; 13:7) and internal divisions (2:6, 9, 15; 3:9). Along with exhortations to hold fast (2:13, 25; 3:11; cf. 14:12) and to offer courageous witness to the Gospel against the powers of evil and the idolatries of empire (even "until death," 2:10; cf. 12:11),[66] the victors are promised a remarkable series of rewards that—when taken together—

articulate an inspired vision of human transformation in Christ and of the everlasting fellowship with God and the Lamb that this entails.

The Promises to the Victors

Addressed to the respective angels of the seven Churches of Asia Minor, the promises to the victors (cf. 2:7, 10–11, 17, 26–28; 3:5, 12, 20–21) are found within the so-called "letters section" in Revelation 2–3.[67] And as noted previously, these prophetic messages reflect a clearly discernable structure and are written with the aim of providing consolation and strength for the "spiritual lives of the churches."[68] While the promises to the victors are the subject of ample study in the commentaries, they have been too infrequently examined together as a group.

Discussions may be entertained as to whether a single overarching concept might provide a network of meaning for approaching these promises. Certainly, the strong echoes and resonances between them and details of the visions of the definitive arrival of God's glory in Revelation 19–22 have led some to speak in terms of a relationship between "promise and fulfillment."[69] Others suggest that they be approached in light of the story of salvation history, leading from paradise, to paradise lost and exodus, and culminating with paradise regained and co-regency with Christ (cf. Rev 22:5).[70] However we choose to study them together as a group, these promises prove to be an essential aspect of John's portrait of the divine life and glory to which God has called the faithful in Christ, in this life and in the next. At the same time, John's rhetorical strategy (with its stark either/or logic) demands that these promises of ultimate transformation in Christ and everlasting reward always be considered in light of the book's threats of everlasting punishment (cf. 21:8; 22:15; Mt 13:49–50; 25:41–46). For if we "nullify the reality of apostasy in these texts then we also cheapen the value of those who overcome."[71]

John's Use of the Verb "To Conquer"

With regard to the language itself, the verb "to be victorious over" or "to conquer" (*nikaō*) occurs some seventeen times in fifteen verses. John appears to use the term "without any attempt at definition."[72] While the language evokes military associations as well as athletic connotations (cf. 4 Ezra 7:127–28; 4 Macc 6:10, 17:15),[73] it is the narrative's dramatic depiction of the spiritual warfare or cosmic conflict between the forces of good and evil (cf. Rev 12:7–9) that provides the broader context for approaching the text. The victor (or conqueror) is the one who does the works of Christ faithfully until the end (cf. 2:26), such that their witness is analogous to that of Christ himself (cf. 3:21). Like the messianic, Davidic Lion/Lamb who has conquered in 5:5 (cf. 3:21; 17:14; and Jn 16:33), the faithful are exhorted to share in Christ's victory, conquering by the "blood of the Lamb" and by their own testimony (12:11; cf. 2:11, 17, 26; 3:5, 12, 21; 12:11; 15:2; 21:7), and never by the use of force. Again, the messianic Lion/Lamb has conquered "not through violence inflicted" but "through violence suffered."[74] Victory is said to be over "the beast and its image and the number of its name" (Rev 15:2). Conversely, among the eschatological opponents described, the "beast from the sea" (or Antichrist), for instance, is permitted to "make war on the saints and to conquer them" (Rev 13:7; cf. 6:2, 11:7). The victor then, is called to resist the forces of evil—both visible and invisible—which oppose the will of God, by keeping the Word of God with courage and patient endurance (1:9; 2:2, 3, 19; 3:10; 13:10; 14:12) while never denying His name (Rev 3:8). They have offered heroic witness to Christ and have conquered through their acquired share in the sufferings of His Cross (cf. 7:14; 22:14).

The promise of reward to those who conquer assumes a conflict—indeed, a conflict of epic proportions—one that calls the audience "to engage this conflict victoriously, by not yielding to the pressures to purchase security at the cost of justice and one's very soul."[75] The victor, then, is the Christian "warrior for Christ"[76] in whom the Lion/ Lamb "wins afresh with the weapons of love the victory of Calvary."[77] For ultimately, "the victory of Christ is the victory of the Father who sent him, and the victory of the conqueror is the victory of Christ" (cf. 5:9f; 7:14; 12:11; 21:2, 3; Lk 22:28–30; and Jn 16:33).[78]

The Language and Symbolism of the Promises

Although the symbolism is rich, powerful, and at times borders on the otherworldly and mystical (cf. 2:17, 28), the language is not without distinct echoes and resonances with the teachings of Jesus in the Gospels.[79] For instance, the expression at the conclusion of each of the letters, "Let anyone who has an ear listen to what the Spirit is saying to the churches" (2:7, 11, 17, 29; 3:6, 13, 22; cf. 13:10), recalls Jesus' own admonition in the Gospels: "He who has ears to hear, let him listen" (cf. Mt 11:15; 13:9, 43; Mk 4:23; Lk 8:8; 14:35). The commentaries point to

John's use of symbols of transformation in Revelation 2–3: the paradisal image of the tree of life (2:7; 22:2), the crowning of the victors (2:10; cf. 3:11; 4:4, 10; 12:1), and a share in the hidden manna (2:17). The victorious witness will be robed in white vestments (3:4–5, 18), will receive a new name (2:17), a share in God's authority over the nations (2:26), the morning star (2:28), and be enthroned with Christ (3:21). All of these images speak in some way to the acquisition of some share in the glorification that attends the messianic Lamb's own victory over the powers of the Cross and death, even as all are predicated upon the necessity of living to the full "lives of dangerous witness" to the Eternal Gospel (14:6) whether or not this witness (*martyria*) should involve death (cf. 2:10; 12:11).[80] Finally, each of these promises "places the final reward in a light which gives it special attractiveness," given the specific circumstances in which the local Church finds itself.[81]

A Fourth Face: The Transformation of the Victors: The Challenges and the Promises

Let us focus, then, upon the content of the Letters to the seven Churches in Revelation 2 and 3, with a view toward arriving at a deeper appreciation of what Jesus asks of His audience—both ancient and postmodern—and what is promised to those who are prepared to share resolutely in His own sufferings. The aim throughout will be to offer a comprehensive perspective more than a detailed study of the text. Again, the textual icon's inverse perspective (no less than the Gospel's logic of reversal) invites us to approach these verses not only as educated observers concerned with analyzing and assessing the text's original meaning, but also with the understanding that it is God who has taken the initiative to come forth and encounter us in Christ through the power of the Holy Spirit (cf. Jn 15:16). The text as icon (and door), then, challenges us to precisely that "reversal of the intellect" (or *metanoia*) and reversal of the ego that the mystery of the Cross itself demands (cf. 2:5, 16; 3:3, 19).[82]

And as we reflect upon both the *challenges* (threats and warnings) issued by the voice of the living Christ and the *content* of the promises to the victors (and the ultimate transformations that they presage in Revelation 19–22), we should look for the lines of the text as icon as they reach out to embrace the faithful who are called to complete the circle and to become a fourth Face of Christ. While the challenges help the audience to appreciate and focus on the loftier purpose (*telos*) to which the angelified Jesus calls them in the midst of the struggles, uncertainties, and terrors of the present age, the promises convey consoling images of the ultimate transformation of the human person in Christ (again, whether we speak of *theosis* or *Christosis*) with the arrival of the fullness of God's everlasting promise at the end of time to make all things new (21:5).

What, then, is John's understanding of the ultimate fulfillment of our reality as persons? What is the completion to which we are called within the context of the life of the Trinity? What does the voice of the risen and glorified Christ call forth in me? On the journey toward completion in the life of grace, what does Christ call me to do? To be? To become? What difficulties or flaws does He call us—whether individually or as members of Christian communities—to identify, to repent of, and to overcome?

John's Spirit-inspired visions invite us to the spiritual discernment of God's offer of grace in Christ in the depths of the present moment as it opens forth into the infinite, and to be ever mindful of the challenges that we face in responding to the divine purposes and calling amid the many and complex demands of this present life. Where is the bright newness of God's promise of transformation in Christ at work in the midst of the darkness, confusion, and sufferings that I may be facing in the present moment? How do these images help us to appreciate more fully—and to strive to follow with greater energy and enthusiasm—the upward, forward, and inward trajectory of God's call to us to be transformed through the mystery of the Cross and the glorification of Christ, the Alpha, Omega (22:13), and Morning Star (22:16)?

To the Angel of the Church at Ephesus

A prosperous center of trade and commerce, Ephesus was among the most important cities in the Roman province of Asia. The city was renowned for its temple to Artemis— in Roman mythology, Diana—the Greek goddess of hunting and fertility (cf. Acts 19:24–35).[83] At the same time, temples dedicated to Roman Emperors Hadrian and Domitian (along with others) attest to the city's status as *"neokoros"* ("temple-keeper"; cf. Acts 19:35), an honorary title accorded to important centers of emperor worship. In addition, magic and sorcery were widely practiced at Ephesus (Acts 19:13–19). As the largest city of Asia Minor, it would become one of the pre-eminent centers of early Christianity, and figures in a significant way in the ministry of St. Paul (Acts 18:19–28; 1 Cor 15:32), as well as in the life of St. John.[84] The city would also come to be associated with an important ecclesiastical council held in the year AD 431.

The letter to the Church at Ephesus (like all of these prophetic oracles) is addressed to the angel of the Church (2:1). As Jesus makes each of His promises to those who prove victorious, the audience is placed in a dynamic tension between a "flashback" to details of John's vision in Revelation 1, and a "flash-forward" to inspiring details of the glorious transformations that will accompany the arrival of a new heaven and new earth.[85] The evocation in Revelation 2:1 of the earlier image of Christ holding the stars in His right hand (cf. 1:16) and walking "among the lampstands" (cf. 1:13, 20), serves to underscore the *divinity* and the definitive *authority* (in heaven and on earth), as well as the ongoing *presence* of an omniscient Christ who speaks directly to the life situation of His audience with knowledge of the details of their interior life and attitudes (cf. 2:2–3, 9, 13, 19; 3:1, 8, 15). As with all of the letters, Jesus is revealed in a specific way to each of these Churches, and He speaks directly to the community in such a manner that "this revelation, the situation of the church, and the promise of victory correspond and imply a certain story," one that anticipates the arrival of a new creation, amid the clashing images of approaching judgment and heavenly worship.[86]

The Challenge to the Church at Ephesus

Prior to issuing His challenge to the Church at Ephesus, Jesus commends the faithful for their works, their toil, and their patient endurance (2:2), as well as for their discernment and zeal in not tolerating false teachers who claimed the authority of apostles (cf. Acts 20:29–30; 1 Tim 4:1–8; 6:2–5). Mention is made in Revelation 2:6 of the Nicolaitans (cf. 2:15). While little is known concerning the details of their beliefs and doctrines, the group is associated with the practices of idolatry, emperor worship, immorality, and sacrifice to pagan deities.[87] The Church at Ephesus has proven to be steadfast in its rejection of false apostles and unwavering in its refusal to compromise with the enticements of a form of pluralism (cf. 2 Jn 1:9) that extolled both idolatry and immorality as expressions of spiritual freedom.[88] At the same time, Jesus admonishes this community for having neglected (or abandoned) the love that they had demonstrated initially (2:4–5; cf. Eph 1:15). Their lack of love (cf. Mt 24:10–12) occasions a call to repentance (*metanoeō*) and is accompanied by the threat that their lampstand will be displaced unless they adhere to Christ's message (Rev 2:5).

This message serves as a warning to the faithful in every age, that while one may be virtuous, keen, discerning, zealous, and orthodox—indeed one may be as virtuous as the angels—without the love of God and neighbor, the Christian is little more than a proverbial "noisy gong" or "clanging cymbal" (1 Cor 13:1). The Lord's admonition underscores the importance of speaking the truth with love (Eph 4:15) while placing that charity into action concretely through the service of others (1 Jn 3:18). Beyond the demands of moral precepts and codes of canon law, it is the call to practice charity in all things—including the love of one's enemies (cf. Mt 5:44)—that serves to identify the Christian as a true and authentic disciple of Christ (Jn 13:35). Indeed, abiding in the love of God is associated with nothing less than the fullness of Christian joy (cf. Jn 15:10–11). Certainly, any Church that possesses the gifts of discernment while seriously neglecting the primacy of Christian charity is no longer capable of reflecting God's love and light to others, and as such is one that is well on its way to losing its identity, for "a church that has forgotten to love is a church that has ceased to be a church."[89] Or in the words of one commentator, "Orthodoxy without orthopraxy is a false religion."[90] It is only by aspiring to bring to others that love of God which "endures forever" (1 Chron 16:34; Ps 106:1; 107:1) that we can be confident that we are doing our own part to build the faith upon solid rock and not sand (Mt 7:24–25). By abiding always in the love of the Father, the Son, and the Holy Spirit, the community endures safely as part of that vine (Jn 15:4) which produces "fruit that will last" (Jn 15:16).

The Promise to the Victors: To Eat of the Tree of Life in Paradise

The challenge to the Church at Ephesus is followed by the promise in Revelation 2:7 that the victor will be given "permission to eat from the tree of life that is in the paradise of God" (cf. Rev 22:2, 14, 19; and Gen 2:9; 3:22, 24). In the first instance, the imagery recalls the story of Adam and Eve in the Garden of Eden and paradise lost, while anticipating the return to the blessedness of paradise regained. The text serves to juxtapose the story of creation in the Book of Genesis (Gen 2–3) with John's account of a new creation in this last book of the Bible (cf. 1 Enoch 24:4–5; 25:4–7; 3 Enoch 23:18; 4 Ezra 8:52; Test. Levi 18:11).[91] The inspiring imagery contained in this promise will find

its fulfillment in chapter 22 and in details of the visions of
the New Jerusalem. In Revelation 22:1 the tree is said to be
beside the "river of the water of life, bright as crystal." The
river itself is said to flow forth from the throne of God and
the Lamb. The tree of life produces twelve kinds of fruit,
and its leaves are "for the healing of the nations" (22:2).
Thus the promise offers to the Ephesians the reassurance
of Christ's love for them despite the serious challenge that
has been identified, while setting before them images of the
brightness of God's promise in Christ that offer hope and
inspiration in the face of the real difficulties that they must
address in the present life of the Church.

    This first promise—like all of these promises to the
victors—points beyond this world to the next as, indeed,
"the entire Apocalypse is an exposition of this concept."[92]
So it is that the richness of the symbolism has inspired
a multiplicity of interpretations. The image of the tree
of life is understood as a metaphor for salvation just as
the content of the promise speaks of a return to the state
of blessedness and fellowship with God that had been
intended from the very beginning of creation but was lost
when Adam sinned and God forbade access to the tree
(cf. Gen 3:24; Ezra 31:2ff). Thus, according to Andrew of
Caesarea, to eat from the tree of life is "to share in the
blessings of the future age."[93] In this regard, the symbol
functions as a symbol of that ultimate reality where God
dwells. According to David Aune:

> The tree of life is not simply a symbol for eternal
> life alone but also represents the *cosmic center of
> reality* where eternal life is present and available,
> and where God dwells. The cosmic tree or tree of

life represents the sacrality of the world in terms of its creation, fertility, and continuation and, therefore, is a tree of immortality.[94]

At the same time, the tree of life can also be understood as a metaphor of the community of the elect (cf. Is 60:21; Ps 1:3; and Prov 3:18; 11:30; 13:12; 15:4).[95]

The tree is ultimately a compelling symbol of Christ and the Church. According to Bede the Venerable, "the tree of life is Christ," and "by the vision of him holy souls are nourished both in the celestial paradise and in the present body of the church."[96] Caesarius of Arles identifies the image with the fruit of the Cross,[97] while according to Tyconius, the tree of life is "the wisdom of God, the Lord Jesus Christ" (cf. Prov 3:18), and to eat of the tree of life is to eat "from the fruit of the cross."[98] Certainly, John's use of the noun *xylon* for "tree" supports the association with the wood of the Cross (Acts 5:30; 10:39; Gal 3:13; 1 Pet 2:24). For it is ultimately the death of Jesus upon the Cross that has destroyed the powers of sin and death (Rom 6:8–10), accomplishing God's plan of redemption, and making it possible for a transformed humanity "to inherit the paradise of God."[99] The symbol leads us to reflect upon the far side of the suffering and death symbolized by the Cross and the fruit that it has borne in the era of the post-Resurrection. Its wood has been transformed through the crucifixion of Christ into the tree of life itself. One may ask: why did God not simply prevent Adam from sinning? According to St. Thomas Aquinas (echoing St. Paul in Romans 5:20), if God permits evil, it is "to draw forth some greater good" (*Summa Theologica* III, q. 1, a. 3, ad 3). John's visions offer one account of human nature raised up to something greater in the New Jerusalem where suffering and death are no more (21:4; cf. 20:14) and the saints enter forever into their "final joy . . . in the presence of God and of Christ."[100] Finally, the image is a most fitting one to set before a Church located in a city that was the site of a primitive tree-shrine dedicated to the goddess Artemis, a shrine over which a succession of later temples "of increasing magnificence" would be built and in which food was sacrificed to idols (cf. 1 Cor 8:1ff).[101]

The Fruit of the Tree of Life in Paradise: Postmodernity's Lost Metanarrative

Today, the archeological ruins of Ephesus attest to the faded glory of a city that had been among the wonders of the ancient world, and serves as an impressive reminder to the faithful in a postmodern era that the glories of this passing world are destined to fade (Is 40:6–8; Heb 13:14). The challenge and the promise of Christ underscore the importance of striving to seek first God's heavenly Kingdom (Mt 6:33) in all things, as we endeavor—through our witness to the values of the Gospel and our own patient endurance—to build up that New City (Rev 21:2) which is even now in the process of taking shape in our midst.

As the text *qua* icon reaches out to find its completion in the reader in a postmodern world, the narrative of God's creation transformed into a new creation invites but also challenges us to consider the meaning of John's message for us today. As we journey from paradise lost to paradise regained, the living voice of Jesus invites us to an authentic spiritual discernment that is able to perceive what is of God (1 Jn 4:1), but not without speaking the truth of the

Gospel with love and charity. At the same time, the text as door to the sacred encourages us to strive toward Christ's promise to eat of the fruit of the tree of life as we allow our hearts to be transformed into that garden in which God is present through the power of the Holy Spirit. In his treatise on prayer, Origen exhorts his audience to resist every sinful inclination "that the Lord may walk in us as in a spiritual garden," so that—even now—we may "live amid the blessings of regeneration and resurrection."[102]

As we continue to live out our lives in the final hour (1 Jn 2:18), we are invited through a spiritual life deeply lived to begin by eating of the fruit of the tree which is Christ in the present life of the Church—in His Word and the Eucharist—and so to experience the healing power of the leaves of this tree. Above all, the text issues a challenge to the faithful who live in the midst of a narcissistic culture shaped by gnostic tendencies to make the very counter-cultural choice of embracing the mystery of the Cross in our own lives. Here is the reversal of the ego that the text as icon calls forth in us. At the same time, we are called to discern where it is that repentance is most needed both within ourselves and within our communities of faith. To refuse to do so, again, is to run the risk of no longer being a Church and a lampstand capable of bearing the light of Christ before the world (2:5). To carry the wood of the Cross upon the exodus flight through this passing world of illusions, through a life of courageous witness to the Gospel, and to do so in a manner that reflects God's love and light to others is to journey resolutely upon the narrow road that leads to the reward of the fruit of the tree of life, which is everlasting fellowship with God and the Lamb.

To the Angel of the Church at Smyrna

Renowned for its great wealth and beautiful architecture, Smyrna was also an important center for science and medicine (with a temple appropriately dedicated to Asclepius, the Greek god of medicine).[103] The first city in Asia Minor to establish a temple in honor of the goddess Roma (*dea Roma*), it was—like Ephesus—recognized as an important center for emperor worship. Smyrna would rise to prominence within early Christianity, with tradition chronicling visits by both St. Paul and St. John.[104] According to Eusebius, St. Ignatius of Antioch wrote pastoral letters to four Churches from Smyrna, and later, while in Troas, composed letters to the Christians of Smyrna and Philadelphia (as well as to St. Polycarp, Bishop of Smyrna), all while on his way to Rome to face execution.[105]

The allusion to details of John's vision of Jesus in Revelation 1:17–18—"The first and the last and the living one, who was dead and came to life,"—serves to emphasize Christ's divinity and lordship. Again, we see that John's apocalyptic one like a Son of Man is not only described in terms that are used for God in the Hebrew Scriptures, but that Jesus speaks as God does (cf. 1:8; 21:5) with the expression "the first and the last" (cf. 2:8; 22:13) echoing God's own self-referential speech in Isaiah 44:6 (see also Is 41:4; 48:12). Our Lord's self-designation as the one who "was dead and came to life" would have held special significance for the inhabitants of a city that was destroyed by the Lydian army in the sixth century BC and rebuilt only after several centuries.[106]

The Challenges Facing the Church at Smyrna

Worthy of note is that Jesus' address is comprised solely of words of encouragement, with the grave challenges facing the community being the result of external factors (cf. 2:8–11). Along with the letter to the Church of Philadelphia, Smyrna is the only community of the seven accorded praises without warnings or rebukes. The community is praised for its perseverance in living deeply the mystery of the Cross through a life of tribulation (cf. Job 7:1) and in its exemplary witness to the Gospel through a life of poverty that has made it rich (cf. Lk 6:20; 2 Cor 8:9; Jas 2:5). This poverty—which contrasts sharply with the economic and material richness of the Church at Laodicea in Revelation 3:17—is most likely the direct result of a resolute unwillingness to compromise the faith with the values of the Roman empire, given that it was "almost impossible to have a share in a city's public life without also having a part in some aspect of the imperial cult."[107] Pressures in this regard would have included economic sanctions, the risk of expulsion from trade guilds, the loss of property, and even imprisonment (Heb 10:32–36).[108] Through this message Christ "speaks to every church that is poor in spirit yet possesses all things," (cf. 2 Cor 6:10)[109] reminding us thereby that a community's spiritual wealth is assured only where the treasure hidden in the field abides within their hearts, as Andrew of Caesarea reminds us (cf. Mt 13:44).[110]

In addition to their affliction and material poverty, the faithful suffer the slander of their opponents (2:9; cf. 3:9; Acts 13:45). Questions arise concerning the identity of the group to whom the author is referring, and a number of possibilities are discussed in the scholarly literature. Is John referring to Gentiles (or Gentiles claiming to be Jewish) who are speaking out against the Christians? Are they Jews from outside of the Jesus movement, or perhaps Jewish-Christians, whom John is accusing of slander (cf. Lk 3:8; Jn 8:44; Jn 8:44; Mt 23; Rom 2:28–29)? What is likely is that the text permits us to overhear the bitter rivalry that existed between two minority groups, with John's characterization of the slanderers as saying that they are Jews although they are not serving as an indication that he is claiming this title "for himself and his community."[111]

The Crown of Life

Following His words of encouragement to the faithful not to fear what they are about to suffer, and exhorting them to remain faithful even in the face of martyrdom, Jesus states that He will give them "the crown of life" (cf. 2:10; 3:11; Jas 1:12)—a most appropriate prize for the beleaguered faithful of a city that was renowned for its athletic games.[112] In the ancient world, crown symbolism encompassed a vast range of connotations: from glory, honor, and status, to "victory or achievement," to expressions of "joy and celebration," to "cultic and religious uses," as well as denoting immortality and lasting peace.[113] In the Book of Revelation, the crown symbolism expresses a number of concepts. In addition to victory, it is a metaphor for "royalty, divine glory, and honor."[114] In Revelation 2:10 John uses the term "crown" (*stephanos*), rather than "crown of gold" (*stephanos chrysos,* as in 4:4 and 14:14; cf. 4:10; 9:7), suggesting here a wreath of leaves (cf. 3:11, 6:2), such as that awarded to those who are victorious in an athletic contest or who have achieved military victory.[115] Although the crown of life is mentioned only here and in the Letter to James (cf. Jas 1:12), Paul speaks of the "crown of righteousness" (2 Tim 4:8), of an "imperishable wreath" (1 Cor 9:25), and of a crown in which we "boast" or "glory" (cf. 1 Thess 2:19–20). In the early Christian literature, St. Polycarp is said to have been "crowned with the wreath of immortality and has borne away an incontestable prize" (*Martyrdom of Polycarp*, 17:1).[116] In addition to athletic and military associations, the crown symbol is used in descriptions of celestial beings that are crowned with light (cf. 2 Enoch 14:2, 3; Bar 6:1). They wear diadems that have been set upon them by the Holy Spirit. The "unfading" crown of glory is found in both Jewish and Christian sources (cf. 1 Pet 5:4; LXX Jer 13:18; 1QS 4.7).[117] So too, those who are faithful will be crowned with glory (cf. 1 Pet 5:4; Heb 2:5–10). Like the promise made to the Church at Ephesus in 2:7 to "eat from the tree of life," the crown of life promised here in verse 10 speaks to that state of eternal blessedness which will be the reward of the righteous in the world to come. According to Henry Barclay Swete: "The crown consists of life, so that the promise is practically equivalent to that of [verse] 7, though it is presented under another aspect."[118]

The Promise to the Victors: Protection from the "Second Death"

The consoling image of Christ's gift of the crown of life is reinforced by the promise to the victor that they will not suffer the "second death" (2:11). The expression is found only here in the New Testament, although it does occur among the writings of Qumran (cf. 1QH 3:28–36; 17:13–14; 1QpHab), as well as the Aramaic paraphrases of the Old Testament, or Targumic literature, which speak of "a second death by which (death) the wicked die in the world to come."[119] The expression serves to contrast the death "which all must suffer and the fate of those who are doomed never to escape its power, whether because they do not qualify for the resurrection, or because they suffer judgment in the world to come" (cf. Mt 10:28; Lk 12:4–5).[120] The promise would have held particular significance for a city referred to by the ancient Athenian statesman Aristides as the "phoenix," in virtue of the fact that, again, it had died and come back to life, after having been destroyed and rebuilt several centuries later.[121]

The promise finds its fulfillment both in Revelation 20:6, where those who share in the first resurrection at the beginning of the thousand-year reign are described as "blessed and holy," and in 20:14, where the second death is practically equated with the lake of fire at the final judgment. John's use of the expression in Revelation 21:8 serves to underscore once again the starkness of his either/or rhetoric, as the second death is said to await those who stand with the powers of evil on the dark side of the book's partitioned humanity. Again, the text calls for a choice between the eternal reward awaiting those over whom the second death has no power (who will be priests who reign with God and Christ, in 20:6), and the eternal punishment destined for those whose place is in the lake of fire and sulfur (cf. 21:8).

The Crown of Life and Protection from Second Death in a "Post-Death" Era

As the voice of Jesus, the "first and last who was dead and came to life" (2:8; cf. 1:18), and this text as icon, reach out to us today, John's message inspires a postmodern audience to assess the quality of their Christian witness. Does it reflect the Gospel's logic of reversal in such a way as to point others to the Kingdom of God? Does it have eschatological sign value? That is, does the quality of our witness serve to point others to the truth and the power of the inbreaking Kingdom in the present time? Is it resolute in the face of opposition and persistent in its refusal to compromise with the values of a secularist culture? The words addressed to the community at Smyrna serve to remind us in this post-Christian era that those who live the faith in a manner that is uncompromising are destined to incur the opposition of the world. It may lead to derision, marginalization, social and economic sanctions, persecution, and even martyrdom (cf. 12:11; Heb 12:4). And yet, no external threat—including the threat of death itself—should lead the faithful to sacrifice the transforming power of the Cross upon the altars of social and economic compromise and political expediency.

At the same time, John's use of the crown imagery leads us to contemplate not only the glory that awaits the righteous in the age to come, but the mystery of the God who glorifies us in our struggles *in this present life.* Here is a profound Christ-mysticism that speaks to us of a God who is not only present to us in the trials of life, but who works within us through the power of the Spirit to transform us in our strivings, like Jacob who struggled with beings both human and divine and was blessed by God (Gen 32:24–31). And it is precisely this association that St. Cyprian develops in his words of exhortation to the martyrs and confessors of the faithful in Africa during the third century. The Christ-mysticism of the martyrs is one that is deeply incarnational in its rootedness in the mystery of the Cross (cf. Gal 2:20). But far beyond any imitation of Christ, for those who live deeply the reversal of the ego at the heart of the spirituality of the Cross, it is Christ Himself who struggles within us to achieve victory, and who not only crowns, but *is Himself crowned in our struggles*. St. Cyprian writes:

> If the battle shall call you out, if the day of your contest shall come, engage bravely, fight with constancy, as knowing that you are fighting under the eyes of a present Lord, that you are attaining by the confession of His name to His own glory; who is not such a one as that He only looks on His servants, but He Himself also wrestles in us, Himself is engaged—Himself also in the struggles of our conflict not only crowns, but is crowned.[122]

Once again, the faithful who respond to the call to share in the mystery of the Cross through a life of Christian witness—whether or not this witness results in a martyr's death—come to be transformed and transfigured in such a way as to become living reflections of the divine Face that is contemplated (cf. Ps 4:6; cf. 31:16; 80:3) beginning in the present life. Perhaps it is fitting that the crown of life is not mentioned among the visions of future glory to be revealed in Revelation 19–22. The text can be interpreted

more readily as John's way of underscoring the transforming power of the Cross at work amidst the sufferings of the
present time (cf. Rom 8:18; 1 Pet 5:1).

Spiritual Warfare: The Phoenix
Rises from the Ashes

As the lines of the text reach out to us today, the tribulation of the Church at Smyrna serves to remind us that our
life on earth involves a struggle, indeed a kind of spiritual
warfare (Job 7:1; cf. the Latin: "Militia est vita hominis
super terram," translated as "the life of the human person
on earth is a warfare, i.e., is the state of being a soldier").
According to St. Francis de Sales, life is a struggle "against
the constant danger of moral and spiritual lapse and collapse, against the lingering effects of past misdeeds, and
against the solicitations of the flesh, the allurements of the
world, and the snares of the devil."[123] Our Lord's exhortations to have no fear (cf. Gen 46:3; Mt 1:20; 28:5–10;
Lk 1:30), along with the promise that the victors will not
be harmed by the second death, underscore once more
God's power over the forces of darkness (including death
itself in 20:14). Like a phoenix rising up from its ashes, the
faithful of the Church of Smyrna—who are rich in their
poverty as they endure severe trials—bear within themselves the mystery of the suffering and death of Jesus so
that His life—indeed, His glory—may be made manifest
within them (cf. 2 Cor 4:10). The image of the phoenix
came to be adopted as a symbol of the Resurrection (cf. 1
Clement 24:3–5; 25:1–4) and of Christ Himself in early
Christian literature as the faithful were reassured that they
would "flourish like the phoenix" (cf. Tertullian; Ps 91:13

LXX).[124] In the centuries that followed, the image of this bird which dies and returns to life would come to be seen as a symbol of the angelic life of the ascetics who—like the apocalyptic visionaries of earlier centuries—came to experience within themselves a foretaste of the heavenly life in this world of shadows.[125]

Beyond the images of future glory that adorn the cosmic canvas of John's story world, Our Lord's words invite us to reflect upon the quiet beginnings of our victory over the second death in the present age, particularly in the conversion of heart to which we are called as a co-requisite of public witness to the Gospel. With the victory of the Lamb over the powers of sin and death, the pathway to the angelified or Christified existence envisioned for the victors in the concluding chapters of the book opens up before us in the spiritual struggles of the present moment. Or in the words of one early commentator: "The first resurrection is found in conversion of the heart," in the movement of the soul "from iniquity to justice, from infidelity to faith, from evil acts to a holy way of life."[126]

To the Angel of the Church at Pergamon

The city of Pergamon was "the leading religious center of Asia."[127] Its most celebrated citizen was the Greek physician and philosopher Galen (ca. AD 129–199), who served in the court of Marcus Aurelius in Rome.[128] Famous for its book production, it was the home of "one of the great libraries of the ancient world."[129] It was an important center for the worship of the gods (Zeus, Athena, Dionysus, and others), as well as for emperor worship, with temples dedicated to Augustus and Trajan. The prominence (if not primacy) of the imperial cult in Pergamon and the serious dangers that it posed to the local Christian community are further underscored by the harsh reality that Christians "faced the actual threat of Roman execution" here,[130] a fact that is often cited among the reasons for John's use of the expression the "throne of Satan" (2:13).

The allusion in Revelation 2:12 to John's earlier vision of the one who has the sharp two-edged sword issuing from His mouth in 1:16 serves, again, to underscore the power of the living Word of God that Jesus both is and speaks (2:16; 19:13; Heb 4:12; Is 49:2; cf. 11:4; and Wis 18:15–16), as is further accentuated in the powerful images of the arrival of the Divine Warrior in Revelation 19:11–20 as the book approaches its crescendo (cf. 19:15, 21). A compelling symbol of Roman military might and its exercise of the power over life and death, the *ius gladii* (or "right of the sword") is juxtaposed in these verses with the "sword-bearing" Word of God, serving once again, to displace the power co-ordinates of Rome while issuing a warning to the faithful to beware of the invisible forces of evil that are unmasked in direct references to Satan's throne and dwelling place in 2:13.

The Challenge to the Church at Pergamon

In the first instance, words of encouragement are addressed to the community for having held fast to Christ's name and for not denying their faith even during the days of Antipas, who was martyred for his courageous witness (2:13). Jesus proceeds to issue a strong challenge to the Church in 2:14 concerning those involved in idolatrous worship and immoral behavior, and then goes on in 2:15 to reiterate His earlier admonition in concerning those who adhere to the teachings of the Nicolaitans (cf. 2:6). In contrast with the community at Ephesus which had placed too great an emphasis upon doctrinal integrity, the Church at Pergamon has de-emphasized it, leading to a precarious "over-identification with the world."[131]

The voice of Jesus proceeds to threaten that unless they repent, He will "make war against them" with the sword of His mouth (Rev 2:16). This particular reference to the coming of Jesus on account of those who compromise the faith in 2:16 (cf. 3:11; 22:7, 12, 20) does not seem to refer to the return of Christ at the end of time. Rather, it suggests an *anticipated* return in imminent judgment (cf. 2:22), serving to emphasize once again the complexity of John's understanding of the mystery of the presence of the exalted Jesus to the communities being addressed.[132]

The Promise to the Victors

Having both admonished the Church at Pergamon to repent and threatened in Revelation 2:16 to make war against them with the sword of His mouth unless they comply, the promise to the victors follows in 2:17. Where the promises within the letters to Ephesus and Smyrna are readily associated with the story of creation, with the narrative of paradise lost and regained, as well as with the promise of everlasting life, the language here is admittedly, somewhat more mystical and rarefied as Jesus promises to the victors "hidden manna" and a "white stone" upon which a "new name" is written (which no one knows except the one receiving it).

The image of manna (from the Hebrew, "What is it?") recalls the miraculous bread that fell from heaven during the time of the Exodus (cf. Ex 16:15; Neh 9:15; Ps 105:40; Heb 9:4), and which later reflection would refer to as "the bread of the age to come."[133] That the text refers to this manna as "hidden" certainly renders the verse more difficult to interpret, and a number of possible explanations are discussed among the commentators. Is it reserved exclusively for those who attain the blessed life of the "age to come"?[134] Is the manna hidden in the sense that it was "placed in a jar that was set before the Lord" (cf. Ex 16:32–36; 2 Macc 2:4ff.; Heb 9:4), to be given "to the righteous by the Messiah" at some time in the future?[135] Or are we to understand that the "heavenly manna referred to in the Old Testament will be restored in heaven through eternal life?"[136] Certainly, the hidden manna, like the tree of life, offers yet one more compelling symbol of the blessedness of life everlasting that awaits the victor, "the fullness of the spiritual gifts of the future age," in the words of Oecumenius.[137] At the same time, given the immediate context, associations between this bread from heaven and "food of angels" (cf. Ps 78:25; 2 Esdr 1:19; Wis 16:20) which God once provided for His people on their journey through the desert—and the bread which the Word Incarnate *became* for the "life of the world" (cf. Jn 6:30–35, 48–51)—offer a stark contrast with the food sacrificed to idols alluded to in Revelation 2:14–15.

More elusive (and, admittedly, rich and allusive) is the image of the white stone upon which the new name is written. The Greek noun *psēphos* referred to in the text is usually translated "stone," although "pebble," "gem," as well as magical "amulet" are among the possibilities enumerated in the commentaries.[138] One interpretation likens the image to the ancient practice of using a stone as a ticket of admission to public festivals (or a token of membership in a guild or association). If understood as the victor's "ticket of admission" to the heavenly banquet and messianic feast (cf. 19:9), this coheres well with the foregoing image of the hidden manna.[139] Perhaps the image is an allusion to the ancient practice of using a stone when casting a vote (cf. Acts 26:10), with a white one indicating an affirmative vote and a black stone a negative one. Certainly the imagery achieves an emphatic qualitative contrast between the ultra-durable writing surface of a stone upon which the new name is inscribed, and the "impermanence of parchment, so famed at Pergamum."[140]

Among other interpretations is the view that John is referring to a gem (perhaps beryl), which figures among the precious jewels mentioned in the description of the New Jerusalem in 21:20. The symbolism coheres with both Old Testament descriptions of the jeweled breastplate of the high priest (cf. Ex 28:17–20), and the names of the tribes inscribed upon them, as well as with "the Rabbinic tradition that jewels fell from heaven with the manna" in the wilderness.[141] That the stone is white can be interpreted as a symbol of the glorified state of the conqueror. Elsewhere in the book, the color white is used in the description of the vestments of the twenty-four Elders in Revelation 4:4 who worship before the throne of God (which is described as white in 20:11), of the blessed who have washed their robes white in the blood of the Lamb (7:13–14), as well as of the victors (3:4–5, 18), as we shall have the occasion to discuss further. It also occurs in the descriptions of Christ in 1:14, 19:11 (cf. 14:14). The whiteness of the stone symbolizes victory and is "bright with glory," according to Oecumenius.[142]

Is the name written upon the stone that of God or of Christ (3:12; 14:1)? Is the name that of the victor (Is 62:2; cf. Is 65:15)? For Victorinus the new name "is that of Christian,"[143] while the Venerable Bede suggests that the new name has been written upon the stone so "That we might be called, and in fact be, sons of God."[144] According to John Ruysbroeck: "All spirits receive a name when they return to God—each a special name in accordance with the nobility of its service and the depth of its love . . . which will remain with us for eternity."[145] Finally, while these are consoling symbols of the future blessedness that awaits the victor, neither the hidden manna nor the white stone with a new name written upon it is referred to explicitly in the concluding visions of eschatological fulfillment in Revelation 19–22.

"Kainos" Meets "Telos" on the Journey toward "All Things New"

As the lines of meaning extend outward to embrace the reader, John calls us to listen to the voice of the Spirit as we look for the newness (*kainos*) of God's grace at work in the present—the "point at which time touches eternity," in the words of C. S. Lewis—all as we strive to offer faithful witness to the loftier goals, ends, and purposes (*telos*) of the Gospel.[146] In the letter to the Church at Pergamon, the promise to the victors offers consoling images to a divided, suffering Church living under the shadow of Satan's throne. Again, John's visionary language sparkles like precious gems, permitting the variety of interpretations found in the commentaries. The language here both veils and unveils a facet of the fourth Face; it "neither reveals nor conceals, but gives a sign," as Heraclitus of Ephesus once wrote concerning the oracle at Delphi (cf. Fragment 93).

Along the journey from the blessedness of Eden to the sin of Adam and paradise lost, through the trials, temptations, failures, and miraculous wonders of God's grace in the wilderness, to paradise restored through the sacrifice of the Lion/Lamb, John calls us to hearken to what the Spirit is saying to the Churches. The Lord's call to conversion, to turn, to repent (cf. 2:5, 16, 21–22; 3:3, 19; 9:20–21; 16:9, 11) serves as a warning to the faithful in a postmodern era to guard against the temptation either to abandon our faith (cf. Jude 11) by compromising the Gospel (and the integrity of the Church) with the idolatries of the age, or to submit to threats of coercion, whether overt or subtle (2:13). However countercultural, John's rhetoric serves as a sobering reminder that God's Word is not only "our food . . . medicine, security, rest, resurrection and final consummation," but is also the sword of God's revealed truth in an era that is post-God, post-truth, post-Christian, and post-virtue.[147] God's Word of truth is the sword of the Spirit offering solace and protection in the spiritual combat, along with the "whole armor of God": the "belt of truth," the "breastplate of righteousness," and the "helmet of salvation" (Eph 6:12–17). At the same time the Word's piercing insight indicts with its power to judge the thoughts and intentions of the human heart (Heb 4:12).

The Churches of today, no less than in the time of Pergamon, are offered a foretaste of "the life-sustaining power" of God which is "hidden in Christ" (Col 3:3) within the Eucharist[148]—the "bread from heaven" (Jn 6:32–35)— as we prepare the way of the Lord, making straight "in the desert a highway for our God" (Is 40:3). Here, the image of the desert, or wilderness (no less than the city or temple), leads us to reflect upon the transformations of the soul and the journey of the human heart in stages (cf. Gen 12:9), through the deserts of the world (and those of our own making), a heart that wanders restlessly until it rests in God (as Augustine reminds us in *Confessions* I.1). According to a spiritual writer from the eleventh century:

> If you wish to see the blessings "that God has pre-
> pared for those who love Him" (1 Cor 2:9), then
> take up your abode in the desert of the renunci-
> ation of your own will and flee the world. What
> world? The world of the lust of the eyes, of your
> fallen self (cf. 1 Jn 2:16), the presumptuousness of
> your own thoughts, the deceit of things visible. If
> you flee from this world, then light will dawn for
> you, you will see the life that is in God . . .[149]

John's promises to the victors serve to remind us that through a life of faith lived to the fullest—both spiritually and with regard to our public witness—this desert will one day "bloom with the flowers of Christ" (cf. Is 35:1–2; St. Jerome, *Letters*, 14), as the way of the Cross gives way to the glory and the majesty of the Lord that are to be revealed in us. In this regard, Primasius suggests that the white stone can be translated "pearl" (as is the case in the "Old Latin," or *Vetus Latina* version), which in the case of the victor may be readily likened to the pearl of great price "that the merchant found and valued as equal to all his possessions which he sold"[150] (cf. Mt 13:45–46). Ultimately, it is Jesus Christ who is the sparkling stone given to the one who overcomes and transcends all things, according to John Ruusbroec.

> By this sparkling stone we mean our Lord Jesus Christ, for according to his divinity he is a beam of eternal light, a ray of God's glory, and a spotless mirror in which all things have their life. Whoever overcomes and transcends all things is given this sparkling stone, through which he receives light, truth, and life.[151]

He goes on to caution however, that this stone is also a pebble (*calculus*) that is "so small that a person scarcely feels it" when one "treads it underfoot" (cf. Heb 10:29), hence the need to repent (2:16) as we endeavor not only to avoid placing stumbling blocks before others through our actions, but to strive for a life of ongoing conversion as we flee from the shadow of Satan's throne and draw ever closer to the Throne of God and the Lamb which will last forever (11:15; 22:5).[152] To "put on" Christ (Rom 13:14) is to become a new creation (2 Cor 5:17) and "new self" (Eph 4:24; Col 3:10), indeed, a fourth Face of Christ, and—like the New Jerusalem—to be adorned spiritually with every precious jewel (Rev 21:19).

Finally, in Christ's promise of a new name, the audience is inspired to have no fear (2:10), to look beyond the sorrows and disorders of the present time to that newness of life promised to those who remain faithful witnesses, and so to achieve, thereby, a share in the glorious transformations elaborated in Revelation 21–22. Again, John speaks of the inspired "new song" of the praises of God and the Lamb (5:9; 14:3; cf. 15:3), a new name (2:17;

3:12; cf. Is 62:2; 65:15), the new Jerusalem (3:12; 21:2; cf. Test. Dan 5:12), a new heaven and new earth (21:1; cf. 2 Pet 3:13; Is 65:17), all of which are reflections of God's promise to make "all things new" (21:5). Elsewhere in the New Testament the sacred authors speak of a "new covenant" (Heb 12:24), a "new commandment" (Jn 13:34; 1 Jn 2:7, 8; 2 Jn 1:5), and a "new teaching" (Mk 1:27). The newness that John describes speaks to the mystery of the radically new and "miraculous" thing that God is bringing about, and is an important term in "eschatological promise."[153] It is, therefore, toward this newness of life in Christ (Rom 6:4) that John invites his audience—both ancient and modern—for wherever Christ is present, *there* is the new creation (2 Cor 5:17).

To the Angel of the Church at Thyatira

An eminent scholar once remarked that the "longest and most difficult" of John's letters is addressed to "the least known, least important and least remarkable" of the seven cities of Asia Minor.[154] Originally a military garrison outpost founded in the third century BC, Thyatira would go on to become a prominent center of commerce by the second and third centuries AD. At the time in which John writes, the city was home to a large number of trade guilds, which included "associations of clothiers, bakers, tanners, potters, linen workers, wool merchants, slave traders, shoemakers, dyers"—especially of purple fabrics (cf. Acts 16:14)—"and copper smiths."[155] In addition to shrines dedicated to Apollo and Artemis, and worship associated with the imperial cult, each guild had its own patron deity. The frequent celebration of feasts in honor of these gods came to assume a central place in both the social and commercial life of the city. Finally, little can be said concerning the origins of the Christian faith community in Thyatira, whose history, according to some sources, can be traced to the late first century, when John wrote the Apocalypse. The Acts of the Apostles makes mention of Lydia—a dealer in "purple cloth" who was from the city of Thyatira—and was living in Philippi when she was baptized by St. Paul after hearing him preach (cf. Acts 16:14–15, 40). The local Church would grow considerably in size and stature during the centuries that followed, with the respective Bishops of Thyatira attending the Councils of Nicea (AD 325) and Ephesus (AD 431).

In His address to the angel in Revelation 2:18 Jesus begins by referring to Himself as "the Son of God, who has eyes like a flame of fire" (cf. 1:14), and whose "feet were like burnished bronze" (cf. 1:15). The phrase "the Son of God" does not occur in John's earlier vision described in Revelation 1, and is used only here in the book (cf. Mk 1:1; Mt 14:33; Lk 1:35; Jn 1:49; Rom 1:4). Taken together, details of the text underscore the divinity of Christ, His all-seeing omniscience (cf. 2:23), power, and abiding stability, as well as the shining radiance of His appearance. All serve to subvert claims made by the Roman emperors to be "sons of god."[156] Moreover, the mention of "burnished bronze" among the details of Christ's appearance, effects a striking polemical counterpart to the image of the bronze statue of the radiant sun god Apollo Tyrimnaeus (the primary local patron deity), that was worshipped in Thyatira, a city noted for its bronze production. In the fiery, apocalyptic figure of the Son of God presented in these verses, the Church at Thyatira "had her true champion, irresistibly arrayed in armour flashing like the refined metal from the furnaces of the city. He was the true patron of their work."[157]

The Challenge to the Church at Thyatira

In the first instance, Jesus addresses words of encouragement to the community in 2:19, extolling their practice of four specific virtues, namely, their "love, faith, service, and patient endurance," adding that their latter works exceed the first. He proceeds in 2:20 to issue a strong warning concerning their tolerance of a certain prophetess named Jezebel. The reference is an allusion to the infamous wife of King Ahab (cf. 1 Kings 18:4, 19; 21:25; 2 Kings 9:22, 9:30–37), who led others to worship foreign gods and was responsible for the deaths of many Old Testament prophets (1 Kings 18:4). In the Church of Thyatira, Jezebel is a prominent member of the community who is accused of beguiling the faithful to practice sexual immorality (cf. 2:20–22, although this may be interpreted as an Old Testament "metaphor for idolatry" rather than a reference to immoral acts, as in Ezek 23:36–47), as well as to eat food sacrificed to idols.[158] Given, again, the prominence of the guild associations in Thyatira, the community would have faced no small pressure to join in the idolatrous practice of paying homage to the gods of the guilds, for to refuse to participate could have serious social and economic consequences. Jezebel and her followers, like those adhering to the teachings of Balaam, or the Nicolaitans in Pergamon (cf. 2:14–15), are accused of misguiding and misdirecting the faithful, while the leadership of the Church is admonished for being too tolerant of what is intolerable, and risking in this way the exchange of the deep things of God (Rom 11:33; 1 Cor 2:10) for "the deep things of Satan" (2:24). Indeed, this heightened emphasis upon the falsity of prophecy and teachings may "indicate that the teachers had been permitted to flourish longer than those in Pergamon" (cf. 2:14; 21–23), thereby permitting these dangerous beliefs and practices to become a greater threat.[159] Evidently, the Church of Thyatira (in sharp contrast with the community in Ephesus) has evidently not lost the love it had at first. But is it a mistaken notion of charity which lies at the root of their tolerance for what is false?[160]

The Promises to the Victors

Jesus promises to those who conquer and persevere in doing His works that they will be given power "over the nations" (2:26; cf. 1 Cor 6:2–3; Rev 20:4; 22:5). John appears to be inspired in these verses by Psalm 2:8–9, as reflected in references to the rod of iron (cf. 12:5; 19:15; Is 11:4) and the shattering of clay pots. Primitive Christian exegesis of Psalm 2 is reflected elsewhere in the New Testament (cf. Mt 3:16–17; Mk 1:10–11; Lk 3:21–22; Jn 1:49; Acts 4:25–26; 13:33; Heb 1:5; 5:5).[161] Christ, as God's anointed one, will do battle along with the heavenly host against all powers both visible (cf. 19:14, 19–20) and invisible that wage war against the Lamb and His faithful (cf. 13:4; 17:14) and oppose God's plan to establish His Kingdom (cf. 12:9; 20:2–3). Those who respond generously to Christ's directive to live "faithful lives of dangerous witness" uncompromisingly and until the end will acquire a share in the everlasting rule of God, with the Lamb transferring to the victors a share in His own authority.[162] For those who have purified their robes in the Blood of the Lamb (7:14) will become an image of the Image, ruling along with Christ in the world to come (cf. 20:4, 6; 22:5; Mt 19:28; Lk 22:29–30).

The Morning Star

In Christ's promise to give to the victor the "morning star" in Revelation 2:28, we encounter one of "the most poetic, most incisive, one of the most specifically Christian images in the entire Apocalypse, and also the clearest."[163] The text recalls Daniel's shining righteous, whose appearance is likened to the radiance of the stars (cf. Dan 12:3; 2 Esdr 7:97; Sir 50:5–7). In virtue of Jesus' statement in 22:16 that He is the morning star, what is being promised here appears to be nothing less than a share in the mystery of Christ's own glorified state (cf. Mt 13:43). At the same time, the text represents a clear allusion to the planet Venus. In the Roman pantheon she was the goddess of love and beauty but also of military "victory and sovereignty, for which reason Roman generals owed their loyalty to Venus" and built temples in her honor.[164] Thus, the promise (and allusion) serve to further reinforce what has already been promised concerning power over the nations (Ps 2:9).

The text can also be seen as an allusion to the prophecy concerning the future king of Israel—the star and scepter—referred to in Numbers 24:17, a text that came to acquire messianic associations, as suggested in Matthew's account of the nativity of Our Lord (cf. Mt 2:2, 10).[165] Thus, to be given the morning star is to be conferred a share in the power and authority over the nations of the messianic "King of kings and Lord of lords" (Rev 19:5), as well as to acquire a share in the morning radiance of His everlasting glory. And while the content of the promise points to a future time, it in no way precludes the "foretastes which are given to the faithful in the growing illumination of the mind and the occasional flashings upon it of the yet distant light of 'the perfect day'" (cf. Prov 4:18; 2 Pet 1:19).[166]

The Victors at Thyatira: Co-Regents with Christ & Witnesses to the New Dawn Rising

As the lines of meaning extend outward to encompass the reader today, the challenges and the promises articulated by the living Jesus lead us to reflect upon the struggles and sufferings of the present time in light of the glory to be revealed to us (Rom 8:18; 1 Pet 5:1). At the same time, they invite a postmodern audience to hold together the tension of these opposing realities and embrace the struggle between the darkness and the light which is at work in every human heart. Through Jesus' calls to repent and accompanying threats of destruction, the book's language speaks to us of the inescapable course of upheaval and change that leads to the arrival of the New Jerusalem. While the new creation must be preceded by the dissolution of the old, God and the Lamb will "reconstruct out of the fragments of the old life" all things new (21:5).[167] Again, owing to the fact that the cosmic finds its analogue in the microcosmic, the foregoing may be said of the individual at a personal, spiritual level as well. The fourth Face of Christ promised to the victor emerges from the remnants of the old sinful self that has cast off its corrupted nature and has put on that new self-created in God's image to give witness to the life of holiness and divine justice (Eph 4:22–24; Col 3:10; 2 Cor 5:17).

At Thyatira, the victor—who is promised a share in both the authority and the radiant glory of Christ— may be likened to a sparkling jewel in the royal crown of Christ the King (Zech 9:16). As John continues to elaborate his Jewish-Christian apocalyptic understanding of transformation in Christ (whether we speak analogously of deification or *Christosis*), once again we see that just as "the dividing lines" between God and Jesus have been blurred, so the descriptive boundaries separating Christ and the victor are analogously "blurred" and imprecise.[168] And just as the light of God may be seen to shine in the Face of Christ (2 Cor 4:6), so the light of Christ shines forth from the face of the victor who is to become a shining star and co-regent with Christ. This message speaks to us in a powerful way of our own call to become light bearers to a darkened world. According to Andrew of Caesarea:

> Both John the Baptist and Elijah the Tishbite were called light bringers. For the one foretold of the first rising of the "sun of righteousness," and the other is known as the forerunner of the second rising" (cf. Mal 4:2).[169]

Beneath the allusive, numinous language, Revelation's lexicon of victorious witness speaks directly to the mystery of the baptismal call and vocation of every Christian to be a "light bearer" (2 Pet 1:19), and does so in a manner that adds apocalyptic breadth and dimension to the language in the Sermon on the Mount, where Our Lord exhorts the faithful to be the "light of the world" and the "salt of the earth" (Mt 5:13–16).

Origen observed long ago that what is promised to the baptized will exceed even the miracles that God worked for His people during their exodus in the wilderness (Ex 15). Indeed, much more than passage through the desert or the river Jordan, the divine Word of God promises the baptized "passage through the heavens themselves."[170] Likewise, John's symbolic universe accords the victorious witness an everlasting place in the sky as a star shining brightly alongside Jesus Christ, the Morning Star. At the same time, caution is necessary, since John's message is just as firmly rooted in the realities of this world as it is otherworldly. The virtues of love, faith, service, and patient endurance exercised by the faithful of the Church at Thyatira—and lauded by the Son of God in this letter—"are not mere general deeds of Christian 'service' but are works of persevering witness to the outside world."[171] So too for Christ's followers, the morning star is already rising in the works of Christian virtue and in their sign value before the world, that is, in their capacity to point to the mystery of the inbreaking of that sparkling New City made neither of bronze nor copper alloy, but of gold and precious jewels. Or as the author of the Book of Proverbs reminds us, "the path of the righteous is like the light of dawn, which shines brighter and brighter until full day" (Prov 4:18).

Tyconius suggests that the appearance of the morning star is a symbol both of Christ and the first resurrection "because his appearance scatters the darkness of error and the worldly shadows of the night are put to flight by the approaching resurrection. For, as this star brings an end to the night, so also does it mark the beginning of the day."[172] It is, however, St. Gregory the Great who helps us to reflect upon the arrival of the long awaited new day within the context of an ongoing process rather than a fixed moment in time, as he situates the Church along a spectrum between the darkness of night and the full light of day, comparing the Church to the daybreak or dawn. He writes:

> For because the dawn, or day-spring, is turned from darkness into light, the whole Church of the Elect is, not improperly, designated by the name of dawn, or day-spring. For whilst it is brought from the night of unbelief to the light of faith, it is laid open to the splendour of heavenly brightness, as the dawn bursts into day after the darkness. . . . For Holy Church, seeking for the rewards of the heavenly life, is called the dawn, because, while it leaves the darkness of sin, it shines with the light of righteousness. . . . For the day-spring, or dawn announces that the night has already passed, but yet does not present to us the full brightness of day: but whilst they dispel the one, and take up the other, they keep the light intermingled with the darkness. . . . But the Church of the Elect will then be fully day, when the shade of sin will be no longer blended with it. . . . For what is the place of dawn but the perfect brightness of the eternal vision?[173]

Gregory's reflections help us to appreciate that the lines of meaning extending outward to the audience from the text trace their source and origin beyond the open door of heaven (Rev 4:1). In the promise to the victors at Thyatira,

the Son of God calls us to begin now to shine brightly
before a darkened world through a life of steadfast witness
to the Gospel as we journey through the light and darkness intermingled across the dawn sky, so to be with Christ
a star and scepter before the nations (Num 24:17). The
metamorphoses of the gods from their Babylonian origins
to their Greek versions to their Roman re-incarnations all
attest to the perennial process at work in the refashion-
ing of the dying gods in order to keep them current with
the ever changing times. The words of Christ serve as a
warning against a spirit of syncretism that would accom-
modate the eternal truths of the faith—whether through
a subtle, incremental re-adaptation or a wholesale refash-
ioning of "the Way, the Truth, and the Life" (Jn 14:6)—to
the image and likeness of the gods (and goddesses) of a
postmodern age.

To the Angel of the Church at Sardis

Founded circa 1200 BC, Sardis was among the most
magnificent cities of Asia. Strategically situated on a
number of important trade routes, it became the capital
of the kingdom of Lydia. One of its early kings, Gyges
(from the seventh century BC), is thought to be "the prototype of Ezekiel's 'Gog'" and as such became a symbol
of "the forces of evil" associated with the end times (cf.
Ezra 38–39; Rev 20:8).[174] The city's fabulous wealth was
based upon its commerce and trade in gold as well as its
woven textiles, particularly the manufacturing and dyeing
of wool. Sardis was also an important center of worship
with many temples dedicated to the gods through the centuries, among them a magnificent temple in honor of the

city's principal goddess Artemis, which was one of the largest Ionic temples "known to have been constructed in the ancient world."[175] Destroyed by an earthquake in AD 17—and later rebuilt—the city went on to suffer a number of decisive military defeats, and by the time John writes his Apocalypse, it had become a city "strangely dominated by its illustrious and proverbial past."[176] Archeological excavations in the twentieth century led to the discovery of an ancient synagogue dating to as early as the fifth century BC, serving to confirm the presence of "a Jewish community far larger, wealthier, and more powerful than had previously been imagined."[177] In fact, the evidence speaks to a remarkable confluence of Jewish and Hellenistic life in Sardis, suggesting an "accommodation to their pagan surroundings" (implied in Revelation 3:4 and in Jesus' allusion to the few who had not sullied their garments).[178]

Christ refers to Himself as the one who "has" (or "possesses") both the seven spirits of God (Rev 1:4; 4:5; 5:6), and the seven stars (recalling Rev 1:16; cf. 2:1). As indicated earlier, the seven spirits of God may be interpreted as "a symbol for the various manifestations of the one Spirit of God as localized in each of the seven churches," while the stars are identified explicitly in 1:20 with the respective angels of the Churches.[179] Again, given that both are under the control of Christ, the text offers yet another example of John's tendency to transfer to Him what in the Hebrew Scriptures is predicated of God alone. Here, the language and symbolism speak once again of a sovereign, all-holy, all-knowing, and all-seeing Christ who addresses, assesses, commends, consoles and indicts the Church at Sardis in a manner that recalls His words to the Church at Ephesus (cf. 2:1).

The Challenges to the Church at Sardis

Rather than using the expected words of encouragement and praise at the beginning of the letter (cf. 2:2, 9, 13, 19; 3:8), Jesus proceeds immediately to rebuke the majority of the faithful concerning the inadequacy of their works (cf. 3:15). Have they acquiesced to external pressures to compromise their faith? Or is the Lord's criticism directed against a dangerous and misguided form of false spirituality rather than a lack of action on the part of the faithful? G. B. Caird speaks of "a church which everyone speaks well of, the perfect model of inoffensive Christianity, unable to distinguish between the peace of well-being and the peace of death."[180] By the time in which the Apocalypse was written toward the end of the first century, it would appear that just as Sardis had been "living off a former but no longer existing fame, so the same attitude had infected the church," the only community of the seven which Jesus declares to be perishing spiritually.[181] So it is that the glorified Christ issues a series of exhortations in rapid succession, urging the community to rouse itself from this deadly form of spiritual lethargy, as He calls forth in them alertness, obedience, and repentance (cf. Rev 3:2–3). At the same time, this compromise is less likely related to the teachings and practices of groups such as the Nicolaitans. Rather, Jesus' words here may allude to an accommodation in the opposite direction, namely, that the majority of Church members had struck a compromise, or *"modus vivendi,"* with the local synagogue in order to secure its protection from Rome with regard to the demands of the imperial cult.[182] Thus, the orthodoxy and lack of charity characteristic of the Church at Ephesus find their counterpart in the lethargic and deficient Christian witness of a Church that is diagnosed as spiritually near death.

Promise to the Victors

In sharp contrast with the majority who have been found deficient with regard to their works, Jesus proceeds to commend the worthiness of the few who have not concealed the light of the Gospel before the world (cf. Mt 5:14; Mk 4:21). The promise to the victors of Sardis is tripartite. Jesus promises that those who conquer will be clothed in white, that their names will not be deleted from the Book of Life, and that He Himself will profess their names before God and the angels. First of all, the symbol of the white garment (or robe) occurs with some frequency in the book and conveys a host of positive associations, ranging from notions of "ritual and moral purity" to descriptions of "heavenly messengers."[183] White is the color of the baptismal robes, the bride's wedding dress, as well as the vestments of the priest. God is vested in white in Daniel 7:9 (as are the deities of ancient Greece and Rome). The dead are dressed in white (cf. Rev 6:11). Jesus' garments become exceedingly white in the Gospel accounts of the Transfiguration (cf. Mk 9:2). In ancient Rome, "citizens wore white robes in celebration of military victories."[184] The hope-filled promise of being found worthy to walk with Christ Himself in triumphal procession (cf. 2 Cor 2:14–16; Col 2:15) would have held particular appeal to the faithful of a Church in a city that has known defeat and has "only the bitter memory of past triumph."[185] The white garment purified by the blood of the Lamb is associated with the transformed and transfigured existence of the blessed who have given faithful witness even unto death (7:14; cf. 22:14), while in the hymns of the Apocalypse it is the vestment of those who take part in the angelic praises of God (cf. 4:4; 7:9; 15:6). It would appear that the Seer regards some members of the community as already worthy (cf. 4:11; 5:2, 4, 9, 12) of the future blessing of walking with Christ vested in white robes (cf. 3:4–5). That is to say, what is promised here is not exclusively a future reward, but is a present, lived reality for a worthy few, even if only at an incipient stage.[186] The imagery will reappear in the descriptions of the "fine linen" that is "bright and pure," which symbolizes the righteousness of the saints in 19:8, as well as the vestments of pure white linen in which the heavenly hosts that follow Christ in 19:14 are arrayed.

Jesus' promise not to erase the name of the victor from the Book of Life in Revelation 3:5 evokes the ancient custom whereby each city maintained a register in which the names of its citizens were written. Thus, John's Book of Life is by analogy "the register of citizens of the heavenly city" described in Revelation 21:27.[187] In the Old Testament, Exodus 32:32 refers to that book written by God which contains the names of those who have been faithful to Him (and so have not worshipped gods made of gold [cf. Ex 32:31]), and to have one's name blotted out from this book is a "metaphor for judgment" (cf. Ps 69:27–28; Is 4:3).[188] John's own use of the term may constitute an allusion to the practice of deleting the names of the Christians from the synagogue-register, thereby placing them in danger of losing their "precarious entitlement to safety" from the demands of the imperial cult and Roman justice.[189]

David Aune discusses the small library of at least three types of heavenly books referred to in the Old Testament and early Jewish and Christian literature: the Book of Life, which functioned as a heavenly record of the righteous (cf. 1 Enoch 108:3; Lk 10:20; Phil 4:3; Rev 3:5; 13:8; 17:8; 21:27); the Book of Deeds, or record of the deeds (both good and bad) performed by an individual (1 Enoch 89:61–64; 90:17; 104:7; 2 Enoch 19:3–5); and the Book of Destiny, or heavenly tablets recording the history of the world and/or the destinies of people before they are born (cf. Ps 56:8; 139:16; 1 Enoch 81:2; 93:1–3; 106:19).[190] Finally, Jesus' promise to confess the name of the victor in the presence of God and the angels finds its decisive and definitive fulfillment in Revelation 20:12, "where the Books of Deeds and the Book of Life are distinguished,"[191] and evokes Our Lord's words in the Gospels (cf. Mt 10:32–22; Lk 12:8–9). Were the majority of the Church members at Sardis "ashamed of the name of Christ" and could this promise represent an allusion to their having succumbed to the demand to engage in a form of worship that denied rather than confessed His holy name before the world?[192]

Walking with Christ, Giving Witness to the Light

The voice of the all-knowing, all-holy, all-seeing Christ calls out to the seven Churches among us today with a vigorous warning against self-delusion and spiritual lethargy. This admonition concerning the ineffectiveness of the works of an ancient Church that was diagnosed as nearing the point of death serves as a timely reminder to us today of the radical demands of the Gospel in every generation. In the first instance, this message underscores the vital importance of our being attentive to the voice of God that resounds throughout the ages as He continues to call out to us through His Word, Jesus Christ, in the power of the Holy Spirit. His warning either to adhere to His demands or to be prepared to reckon with the dramatic consequences of His sudden and unexpected return (cf. 3:3–4; 16:15; Mt 24:42–43; Lk 12:39–40) proves in many ways to be more countercultural today than when first pronounced by Our Lord during His earthly ministry. On the one hand, we are reminded again of the eschatological tenor of the Christian experience of time in this world and of the vigilance and spirit of wakefulness to which we have been called in this final hour (1 Jn 2:18). On the other hand, we must pray for the light of the Holy Spirit to grant us the keenness of discernment to be capable of distinguishing clearly the voice of God (at times, subtle [cf. 1 Kings 19:12]), from among the many others that vie for our attention in the era of virtual reality: from the inner voice of the ego that—no differently now than in the time of Adam and Eve—prefers to respond "My will be done" instead of God's will, to the clamor of external voices—both digital and analogue—that entice the postmodern Churches in the direction of new (and ancient) forms of smooth compromise. In this regard, the Lord's call in Revelation 3:3 to remember all that we have received and heard, to guard it, and to repent, seems in so many ways to be not only counter-cultural, but still very far ahead of its time today in a world that seems ever more pre-Christian than post.

The Christian faith is not a private mysticism, but calls forth a dynamic public witness to the power of God's inbreaking Kingdom. This witness cannot be effective without the vibrant interior, spiritual dimension of the life of grace and holiness of which our exterior works are but an outer expression. In addition to watchfulness and wakefulness, we are called to pray always (Lk 18:1–8; 21:36; cf. 1 Thess 5:17; Eph 6:18) and to fast as a means of progress in the spiritual life (cf. Mt 4:2; 6:16–18). Some are called to the life of celibacy for the sake of the Kingdom (Mt 19:12; cf. Rev 14:4). The life of the Gospel lived to the full demands self-denial as we follow Jesus on the way of the Cross (Mt 10:38; 16:24; Mk 8:34; Lk 9:23; 14:27). Finally, St. Andrew of Caesarea reminds us of the importance of the virtue of perseverance when he writes that: "It is not the beginning of good works that crowns the worker, but rather their completion."[193]

Our failure to remember what we have received and heard from our faith tradition (Dt 6:4; Mk 12:28–34) is attested to most eloquently in our postmodern forgetfulness of the reality of sin and its lethal effects. Church documents have spoken for decades now of the crisis of the sense of sin, or what St. John Paul II refers to as "the obscuring of the moral and religious conscience, the lessening of a sense of sin, the distortion of the concept of repentance and the lack of effort to live an authentically Christian life."[194] In fact, as early as 1946 Pope Pius XII observed that "the sin of the century is the loss of the sense of sin,"[195] while philosopher Etienne Gilson—writing in the 1950s—commented that "the real trouble with our own times is not the multiplication of sinners, it is the disappearance of sin."[196] Our Lord's words to the Church at Sardis remind us of how "the Church that goes along with the times disappears with the times" (in the words of an old adage). Unlike the life situation addressed in this letter, we live in an era marked by the notion that there is no God, no grace, and no longer any sin. We have witnessed the gradual muting of a sense of personal responsibility combined with an unformed human conscience rendered ever less capable of desiring the very type of remembrance (and therefore, repentance) to which Jesus called the Church at Sardis. More than forty years ago, Dr. Karl Menninger, an eminent psychiatrist, lamented the virtual disappearance of the term sin from the language of psychology and psychotherapy, warning that people would eventually find themselves without an adequate lexicon with which to adequately address the perennial realities of guilt and personal responsibility.[197] Indeed, "the new narcissist is haunted not by guilt but by anxiety."[198]

The Lord's promise to the victors reaches out to us today far beyond the ruins of a once magnificent city calling us to begin—now—to walk with Him and with the angels on the road toward the New Jerusalem, making of our faithful witness to the Gospel a light before the nations (Rev 21:24; Lk 2:32; Acts 13:47). Again, elsewhere in the Bible, Enoch is said to "walk with God," as does Noah (cf. Gen 5:22; 6:9). In contrast with those deemed to be deserving of punishment in Revelation 16:6 (cf. Lk 12:48; Rom 1:32; Heb 10:29), those who would be proclaimed worthy to walk with Christ dressed in white (cf. 3:4–5; cf. 19:14) must begin immediately to live a life of witness to the Gospel that is worthy of the transformation promised (Eph 4:1; Phil 1:27; Col 1:10; 1 Thess 2:12; 2 Thess 1:5). And while the imagery of walking with Christ certainly implies the blessedness of standing in "close relationship to Him," it also conveys something that extends beyond the traditional understanding of Christian discipleship.[199] When one examines the remaining occurrences of the adjective "worthy" (*axios*) in the Book of Revelation, it becomes clear that it is God and Christ alone who are worthy to receive the praises of the heavenly court (cf. 4:11; 5:9, 12), indeed, of all creation (cf. 5:13). Those declared worthy to walk in the company of Christ are deemed worthy to attain a place in the life to come, and therefore will be equal to the angels (Lk 20:36; cf. 1 Cor 6:3). So it is that the victor must begin now to shine like the sun through a life of virtuous deeds, serving thus as herald of the Gospel and messenger of Christ to a postmodern world. Or as Andrew of Caesarea reminds us:

> One who wins this victory shall shine as the sun because of the garments of his virtuous deeds, and his name will be indelibly entered into the book of the living. And he will be confessed before my Father and his holy powers, just as it is for the triumphant martyrs. For, as he says in the Gospel, "the righteous will shine as the sun."[200] (cf. Mt 13:43)

In the age of information (and disinformation), in which the post-human analogue of the heavenly register is destined to be the digital cloud that serves as the repository of all data, Jesus exhorts us to have no fear in approaching the Cloud of Unknowing as we seek the graces necessary to be effective witnesses to the Gospel, and so to entertain the hope that our names be preserved for eternity in that heavenly register beyond the clouds (cf. Rev 13:8; 17:8; 20:12, 15; 21:27). Moreover, in order that our names be professed before God and the angels (3:5; Mt 10:32–33; Lk 12:8–9), let us—through the integrity of both our words and deeds—profess the Name "above every other name" in all of those places where it is no longer welcomed in the public square. St. Cyprian—like St. John—encourages us to the highest standard of Christian witness when he invites us to live as though we are "temples of God, that it may be clear that the Lord dwells in us."[201]

To the Angel of the Church at Philadelphia

Founded sometime in the second century BC as a center of Greek culture, Philadelphia, the city of "brotherly love," was the most recently established of the seven cities. Its name commemorated the proverbial love and allegiance of Attalus Philadelphus for his older brother King Eumene II of Persia (although it is uncertain which of the two kings founded the city).[202] Located along a major Roman postal road, the "gateway to the east" was ideally situated not only for trade and commerce but also for its admirable strategic military advantage.[203] The region's fertile soil made it particularly suited for grape-growing, and Dionysus—the god of wine and the grape harvest—was fittingly honored as the city's principal deity.[204] Along with Sardis and a number of other cities, Philadelphia was devastated by the great earthquake of AD 17 and its lingering aftereffects. For a time, the city took the imperial name Neocaesarea in honor of Tiberius (Roman emperor from AD 14–37), whose patronage proved instrumental in restoring the city's fortunes, while under the emperor (Flavius) Vespasian (who ruled from AD 69–79) the city took the additional title "Flavia." Nothing is known for certain concerning the origins of the Church, although Philadelphia may have been evangelized by St. Paul along with the other cities in the region. St. Ignatius of Antioch (c. AD 110) indicates that the Church was organized according to the hierarchical structure of bishop, presbyters, and deacons.[205]

Jesus' description of Himself in 3:7 as the "Holy one, the true one, who has the key of David, who opens and no one will shut, who shuts and no one opens" does not quote directly from Revelation 1:1–20. As David Aune points out, the first two titles—holy and true—"are not used together elsewhere in early Jewish or early Christian literature as titles or attributes of God."[206] While the terms do not occur in Revelation 1, they do appear together in an address to God in 6:10 (cf. Is 43:15; Tit 1:2). In the Old Testament, God is referred to frequently as the "holy one" (cf. Ps 71:22; Prov 9:10; Is 1:4; Ezra 39:7; 2 Macc 14:36), while in the New Testament, Jesus is addressed messianically as the "holy one of God" (cf. Mk 1:24; Lk 4:34; Jn 6:69). Elsewhere in the book, God's ways are praised as just and true (cf. 15:3), as are His divine judgments (16:7; 19:2), while Christ the messianic Rider—whose arrival signals the advent of God's judgment—is called "Faithful and True" (19:11). Together, the titles serve to underscore once again Jesus' divinity (cf. Mk 1:24; Jn 6:69; Acts 3:14; 4:12), while conveying the reassuring message to a Church in crisis that God's Word is trustworthy, true, and destined to be fulfilled (cf. 19:9; 21:5; 22:6).[207] The remainder of Jesus' self-designation recalls Isaiah 22:22, while evoking the image of the keys referred to earlier in Revelation 1:18, with the language here serving to emphasize Jesus' divine and royal sovereignty over the powers of death and the afterlife (cf. 20:13–14). Or in the words of Andrew of Caesarea: "Through the image of the 'key of hades' the authority of life and death is ascribed to Christ"[208] (cf. Mt 27:50–53). Elsewhere John refers to the key that opens the shaft of the abyss, thereby releasing the plague locusts in 9:1–3, while in 20:1–3, the key locks the shaft of the bottomless pit into which Satan is thrown, bound for one thousand years.

Praise and Encouragement for a Suffering Church

Along with the letter to the community at Smyrna, Philadelphia is the only Church accorded praises exclusively, without any suggestion of admonition. The Church is commended for having remained faithful by keeping Christ's word and not denying His name despite its weakened condition, thus inviting comparisons with the letter to Smyrna. In fact, a series of elements common to both the letters to Philadelphia and Smyrna suggest that "they should be read side by side."[209] These include: references to allegations of slander; threats of persecution by Rome; the characterization of their Jewish opponents as "Satanic"; the recurrence of the crown imagery; promises of spiritual security; and mention of their spiritual vigor despite their socially inferior status.[210] Thus, the "holy, true one" conveys a consoling message of encouragement to the faithful of a Church with little power, whose vigorous public witness to the Gospel has effectively led to the weakened condition in which they find themselves (3:8). According to Primasius, the Church is to be commended precisely "because she does not have confidence in her own powers but in the power of Christ the king."[211]

Images of an open door which none can shut in Revelation 3:8 (cf. Jn 10:7, 9; 2 Cor 2:12; 1 Cor 16:9; Acts 14:27), promises that the faithful will be vindicated against their adversaries, the reassurances of Christ's love for them in 3:9, the pledge that they will be kept from the hour of trial in 3:10, and reference to the crown image in 3:11, all serve to remind a beleaguered Church of the divine protection of the one who is holy and true, while encouraging them to "hold fast" to what they have (Rev 3:11). Elsewhere in the book, the providence of God is expressed through "the metaphors of 'sealing' (7:1ff.), 'measuring' (11:1–2), and 'nourishment and protection in the wilderness' (12:6, 14–17)."[212] Finally, the assurance of Christ's imminent return to vindicate and to reward the faithful (Rev 3:11) contrasts sharply with the ominous threats of His imminent return in judgment advanced in the letters to Ephesus (2:5), to Pergamon (2:16), and to Sardis (3:3).[213]

The Promises to the Victors

Jesus promises that the victor will be made "a pillar in the temple of my God" and "will never go out of it" (3:12). In addition, He promises to write upon them the names of God, of the city of God, the New Jerusalem, and His own new name. In the first instance, the image of the pillar is used in a metaphorical sense both in Jewish and early Christian literature (cf. Prov 9:1). Paul's Letter to the Galatians refers to the apostles Peter, James, and John as "acknowledged pillars" (Gal 2:9; cf. 1 Tim 3:15). The commentators discuss a variety of possible sources for John's symbolism here. Does the image allude to the local custom whereby "the provincial priest of the imperial cult" would—at the conclusion of his term of service—raise up within the temple precinct a statue of himself inscribed with his own name, as well as the names of "his father and home and his year of office"?[214] Is the text an allusion to 1 Kings 7:15–22 and the two pillars in the temple of Solomon (cf. 1 Kings 7:21); or perhaps the "king's pillar"

in Solomon's temple, referred to in 2 Kings 11:14 and
23:3? Again, given the fluidity of the book's language, it
is probable that no single source accounts for John's use of
the metaphor.[215] If—in light of John's reference to the key
of David in Revelation 3:7—the imagery is to be understood as an expansion of the oracle in Isaiah 22:15–25,
then the stability of the pillar may be interpreted in light
of (and in contrast with) the figure of Eliakim. Isaiah
prophesied that Eliakim would be fastened "like a peg in a
secure place" (Is 22:23) and become like a throne of honor
to his "ancestral house" (v. 24), although, over the course
of time, this peg would give way causing the destruction of
the load it was supporting (v. 25). Here, in sharp contrast,
the victors of the Church at Philadelphia (a city plagued
by the precarious instability caused by earthquakes and
their accompanying aftershocks and tremors) are promised that they will become "not pegs in a wall, but sturdy
pillars in God's temple, at one with him through Christ for
ever."[216] The supplemental assurance that the victor will
never go out of God's temple serves to underscore and
develop further Christ's hope-filled promise of lasting stability and permanence.

Christ's superlative threefold promise to write upon
the conquering "pillar" of the Church at Philadelphia the
name of God (cf. 2:17; 14:1), the name of the city of God,
the New Jerusalem that comes down out of heaven (cf.
21:2, 10; Ezra 48:35), as well as Christ's own new name
(2:17; 19:12) effectively serves to "mark the conqueror as
the property of God and of Christ and as a citizen of the
heavenly city."[217] In the Old Testament, God tells Abraham
that He is *El Shaddai*, or God Almighty (Gen 17:1). He
reveals His holy name, YHWH, to Moses on Mount Sinai

(Ex 3:14; 6:2), and chooses a place for the name to dwell
(cf. Deut 12:11; 2 Sam 7:13; 1 Kings 3:2). God's name and
His powerful protection are over Israel (cf. Num 6:27). His
name is over the ark of the covenant, over the Temple, and
over the city of Jerusalem, while in the post-exilic period,
the divine name comes to denote the glory of God.[218]
Instructions are given to engrave the inscription "Holy
to the Lord" upon the gold plate adorning the forehead
of Aaron, Israel's high priest (cf. Ex 28:36–38; Rev 22:4).
Thus, the inscriptions of the name of God and of the New
City upon the victorious pillar speak not only of the future
promise of God's salvation, but of the mystery of being
consecrated and set apart by and for God to live a life of
holiness (cf. Lev 11:44; 1 Pet 1:16; Rev 22:11). A third-cen-
tury text ascribed to Rabbi Jonathan (AD 220) states that
"Three are named after the name of God, and these are
the righteous, the Messiah, and Jerusalem" (cf. Is 43:7; Jer
23:6; Ezra 48:35).[219] What is the new name of Christ that is
not revealed? Is it the "Word of God" (cf. Rev 19:12–13)?
Or is it a symbol for the "fuller glories of His Person and
Character which await revelation at His Coming" (cf. Rev
2:17)?[220] John's audience is being told that Jesus' identity is
not yet completely revealed, "but remains hidden until the
revelation of his new name."[221]

The Holy Name of God and the Lamb in the Book of Revelation

We are led to reflect briefly upon the symbolism attached
to the name of God and the Lamb and the sharp antithesis
that John has drawn between the followers of the Lamb
and the worshippers of the beast. The followers of Jesus

are to endure hardship faithfully and patiently "for the sake of [His] name" (2:3, 13). They fear God's holy Name (11:18; 15:4) and never deny it (3:8). They conquer the beast, its image, and the number of its name (15:2). The 144,000 are said to bear the name of God and the Lamb upon their foreheads (14:1), just as the name will be upon the foreheads of His servants in the New Jerusalem (22:4; cf. 3:12). The names of the victors will not be omitted from the Book of Life (3:5) but these, again, will receive their own new name (2:17).

Over against the name of God and the Lamb are the "blasphemous names" of God's enemies (13:1, 17:3; cf. 17:5) who curse God's name (13:6, 17:3). Those who ally themselves with God's enemies bear the mark or name of the beast (13:17; cf. 14:11). They neither repent nor glorify God (16:9). Their names are not written in the Book of Life (13:8; 17:8). While the Book of Revelation does resort to the language of threats, John's understanding of the human person in Christ takes the audience far beyond a *quid pro quo* calculus of moral ultimatum. The book conveys the clear understanding that what Jesus is by nature, the faithful are called to become by participation (cf. Rev 1:6; 5:10).

The "Little Church" and the Heavenly Temple

As the lines of the text as icon extend outward from the text toward the reader, John's imagery leads us to consider once again God's strength at work in human weakness (2 Cor 12:10), but not without contemplating at the same time His glory yet to be revealed to us (Rom 8:18). The victor who has endured patiently before a hostile and unbelieving world will be transformed into a pillar of a temple that transcends all physical dimension, in that New City where the temple is the Lord God Almighty and the Lamb (Rev 21:22). Beyond the cosmology of the book's three-story universe, the imagery here leads us to ponder the spiritual fourth-dimensionality of John's symbolic universe *qua* icon and door to the sacred. While certainly a powerful symbol of future eschatological salvation, in the image of the pillar with its superlative, tri-partite divine inscription, the Book of Revelation appears to be "combining the notions about the pillars of the heavenly temple as animate objects and about chosen, holy, and righteous human beings joining with the angels in the divine liturgy."[222] The faithful who stand with John before the open door of the Spirit in the reading aloud of the book on the Lord's Day are called to enter the circles of the heavenly praises before that throne which will last forever, and so join the company of the Living Creatures, the Elders, and the expanding circles of Angels, whose joy will be to worship God and the Lamb eternally (Rev 22:3–5). If we invite comparisons with the Songs of the Sabbath Sacrifice—which seem "to bear witness to the conception that the heavenly pillars belong to the angelic host" (cf. 4Q403)—it appears that the "pledge of Revelation 3:12 is in essence the same as the promise of an angelic destiny," that is to say, "to be a pillar in the heavenly temple would be the equivalent of being an angel."[223]

Indeed the image of the pillar inscribed by Christ with the divine name invites comparisons with Exodus 23:20–21, where God assigns His angel to guide and protect the people on their dangerous journey, warning them to be attentive to the angel's voice and not to rebel against it, for "my name is upon him" (Ex 23:21 [Septuagint version]). In Revelation 3:12 Christ begins by promising that He will write God's name upon the victorious pillar of witness. First of all, the promise to inscribe the name(s) reinforces Christ's divine authority to do what in the Old Testament is the prerogative of God alone. Moreover, the power of the name of Christ—which is above every other (cf. Phil 2:9)—emerges as a topic worthy of consideration in its own right. Paul performs exorcisms, as do the seventy, while Peter performs a miracle in the name of Jesus (cf. Acts 3:6, 16; 16:18; Lk 10:17,). Secondly, the image of an angelified, or perhaps divinized (or Christified), victor is entirely in keeping with the logic of John's portrait of the human person transformed in Christ. Once again, as we have seen in Revelation 2 and 3, the righteous will walk with Jesus vested in white (3:4–5, 18; 7:9, 13–14), they will be seated upon the throne of God and Christ (3:21; 20:4; 22:5; cf. Lk 22:29–30; Mt 19:28), and they will reign with Him (2:26–27; 20:4). Jesus will give to the victor the Morning Star (cf. 2:28; 22:16), just as He will confer upon them God's divine Name, the name of the New Jerusalem, and His own new Name. As mentioned earlier, the idea that the righteous will become like the angels is found elsewhere in the New Testament and extra-biblical literature (cf. Lk 20:36; and the term *isangeloi*, literally "like" or "equal to the angels").[224] So it is that the victors are called to begin now to embark upon that road which will see them transformed into living pillars and divinized mainstays of that new temple which is already in the process of arriving in our midst.

Text as Icon: What Does It Call Forth in Us?

What does the text as icon call forth in us? According to Pseudo-Macarius, Jesus came into the world in order to cast out the powers of darkness and to reclaim us "as his very own house and temple."[225] So it is that he leads us to consider those things that may be hindering our progress in the life of faith:

> We are not yet "glorified with Christ" because we have not yet "suffered with him" (Rom 8:17). We do not yet "carry the marks of him in our body" (Gal 6:17), since we do not live in the mystery of Christ's cross. . . . We have not yet been made "the temple of God" (1 Cor 3:16) and the dwelling place of the Holy Spirit, for we are still the temple of idols. . . . The day has not yet dawned upon us, nor "the day star risen in our hearts" (2 Pt 1:19).[226]

Syriac Christianity's tradition of spiritual reflection upon the "three Churches" articulated in the *Liber Graduum* or "Book of Steps" (from the late fourth or early fifth century), is relevant to these reflections. It speaks of the celestial Church "on high" (described in John's visions beginning in chapter 4), of the Church on earth with its sacramental economy (in which Christ continues to be present and to speak in Revelation 2–3), and of the "little church" of the heart. Or as Alexander Golitzin observes:

> Through God's economy in Christ, the second is the necessary and mediating term which has been called into being in order to open up the first, the

heavenly temple, to access for the third, the human heart.[227]

We are led thus to consider anew John's message as it addresses us at the microcosmic level, issuing the challenge to strive to live a life of witness as a temple of the Holy Spirit and well-ordered city. Or in the words of Pseudo-Macarius, "consider yourself the temple of God."[228] If one is truly the temple of God (1 Cor 3:16), then the heart is an altar, and the Name of the three-times holy God finds a place both to dwell and to walk, along with Christ and the Holy Spirit (2 Cor 6:16; Lev 26:11–12).[229] Where God is present, there is Christ, and where Christ and the Spirit are present, there are the angels, whether in heaven, in the Church on earth, or in the "little church" of the heart (Mt 18:20). This imagery is consonant with the notion that the pillar of the "little church" and "temple of the heart" will come to be incorporated into the celestial temple. Ultimately, the promise implies that the victors are called even now to share in the dignity of Christ's own High Priesthood (cf. Heb 3:1; 4:14), and so to become priests of God and Christ (Rev 1:6; 5:10; 20:6). St. Leo the Great reminds us that "if we are indeed a temple of God and if the Spirit of God dwells within us, then what every believer has within their soul is greater than what they admire in the sky" (cf. 1 Cor 3:16).[230]

To the Angel of the Church in Laodicea

Founded in the middle of the third century BC by King Antiochus II on the site of an earlier outpost, Laodicea on the Lycus was named after "his first wife Laodice."[231] The

wealthiest city in Phrygia, it was situated on an important
trade route and was renowned for the production of textiles. Its luxurious black wool used in the manufacturing of
clothing as well as rugs became a major export for which the
city was famed. Laodicea also became a strategic banking
center and had become so financially self-sufficient that following the earthquake of AD 60, it was able to subsidize
the reconstruction of the city without the usual assistance
of Rome. An important center of medicine, its doctors were
so famous that the names of two (Zeuxis and Alexander
Philalethes) appear on the coins of the city.[232] Like the other
cities addressed in Revelation 2–3, Laodicea too relied upon
aqueducts for its water supply. In the Letter to the Colossians, Laodicea is referred to no less than five times (cf. Col
2:1; 4:13, 15, 16), underscoring the fact that "The Christian
community at Laodicea was closely connected with that of
Colossae."[233] Colossians 4:16 refers to a letter (now lost),
which was written to the Church in Laodicea.

The Christological statement in 3:14 consists of three
rather theologically rich and inter-related titles. Here,
Jesus identifies Himself as "the Amen, the faithful and
true witness, the beginning of God's creation." In the
first instance, the use of "the Amen" as title of Christ
is unique in the New Testament and underscores Jesus'
divine authority, while attributing to Him yet again what
in the Old Testament is associated with God alone. In
light of Isaiah 65:16, Jesus is telling us that His solemn
word is both valid and binding, and that He Himself is
"guaranteeing the truth of his message, just as God's sure
character stands behind his word."[234] The statement that
He is the witness who is faithful and true further elaborates
the meaning of the foregoing title (cf. 1:5), and at the same

time the expression serves to effect a "sharp contrast" with the unfaithfulness of the Church being addressed.[235] Jesus states that He is the "beginning" (or "source") of God's creation (cf. Col 1:15), which serves to clarify and further develop the foregoing. The theological richness of Jesus' self-designation—the "most explicit allusion in the Apocalypse to the pre-existence of Christ"—invites comparisons with the Letter to the Colossians (Col 1:15ff), a letter that John was likely familiar with.[236] Finally, the self-designation is not without a distinctive "liturgical echo," insofar as it serves to remind the audience that Christ is the eternal "Amen" through whom "the community gains access to God", and that it is He who "incarnates the response of the faithful."[237]

The Challenge to the Church at Laodicea

The Church at Laodicea (3:14–22) is unique among the seven addressed. It is the only one deemed lacking in virtually any praiseworthy attribute, and as such is the subject of rebuke and admonition exclusively. Like the Church of Sardis, it is complacency that appears to be the problem. However, unlike the spiritually moribund Church at Sardis, not even a faithful few have been found worthy of Christ's praise (3:4). And in contrast with the Churches at Philadelphia or Smyrna, which are deemed to be spiritually rich despite the financial straits that are the direct result of their faithful witness, Laodicea's abounding wealth and prosperity have rendered it spiritually "wretched, pitiable, poor, blind and naked." This rapid-fire succession of admonitions constitutes a sharp indictment of the Church's spiritual complacency. In Jesus' threat to spit (literally to "vomit") from His mouth a "lukewarm" Church which is "neither hot nor cold" (3:16), the implication is that He will be "rejecting them as dining partners" (rather than being an allusion to the city's water supply).[238] Chided for their spiritual bankruptcy, they are invited to purchase from Christ that gold purified by the fires of suffering and rejection: fires which are encountered in direct proportion to the vibrancy and authenticity of the Christian's public witness to the Gospel. They are prompted to purchase from Christ white robes to conceal their shameful condition, and that spiritual salve which has the power to restore the clarity of its spiritual vision, allowing them to see with the eyes of the Lamb (Zech 4:10; Rev 5:6). And yet, despite the severity of the language, these admonitions are ultimately to be interpreted as an expression of the "faithful Amen's" love for the Church (3:19), as they convey the hope-filled message that there is still time to repent, provided that they turn without delay to Jesus, who alone is "the source of the remedy for the church's hidden needs of spiritual wealth, vision and holiness."[239]

The Promise to the Victors

The promise to the victors is prefaced with a consoling invitation, as the faithful and true witness informs the Church at Laodicea that He stands at the door and knocks. That this door is closed stands in sharp contrast with the image of the open door in Philadelphia (3:8). Moreover, some question remains as to whether the Church at Laodicea will heed Christ's voice and respond to His directives without delay. Jesus has not set any condition on His presence, as He stands at the door of the heart and continues to knock (while patiently awaiting a reply). If the faithful do respond to His invitation, Jesus will enter and dine with them in an intimate communion of table fellowship (cf. Jn 14:23; 14:2–3). The Eucharistic overtones of the language are evident (cf. Jn 6:56),[240] as are the messianic resonances of this meal (cf. Mt 26:29). Is John perhaps inspired by the Song of Songs 5:2, interpreting it in a messianic light (cf. Is 25:6ff)?[241] In any event, the voice of the just judge who admonishes and calls to repentance gives way here to the voice of the loving friend who cares for the faithful despite their serious shortcomings as He beckons them with a sense of urgency to respond to His voice.

The victor is then promised a place upon Christ's throne just as He Himself conquered and is now seated upon the throne of God the Father (cf. 1:6; 5:10; 20:4, 6; 22:5; Mt 19:28; Lk 22:30; 1 Cor 6:2–3; 2 Tim 2:11–12; and Dan 7:18, 27). With regard to the content of the promise, Beasley-Murray comments that "no higher honour than this can be imagined," for here in "the crown of the seven promises to the conquerors and the seven letters themselves," the love expressed by Jesus in 3:19 finds its analogue in the promise made to that Church which appears to be least deserving of it.[242] The fulfillment of the promise is found in Revelation 20:4 and the vision of the martyred faithful who come back to life and reign with Christ for a thousand years, but also in 22:5 where it is said that they will "reign forever and ever" along with God and the Lamb. Here, the promise itself—to be enthroned alongside Christ as He has been enthroned with the Father—appears to be inspired by Psalm 110:1, "one of the most important OT messianic texts in the early Church" (cf. Mk 16:19; Eph 1:20; Heb 1:3; 8:1; 12:2).[243]

The language serves to develop a remarkable transformational symbol that speaks compellingly both of the victor's share in Christ's triumph over death as well as in His power and glory (cf. 2:26–28). Once again, the Seer's art of persuasion offers the reassurance that the victor—here perhaps most clearly of all, the image of Christ, the Image of God—will come to share in the same post-Resurrection "vivification and vindication that Christ enjoyed," and that "the faithful will indeed go where Christ has gone."[244] Finally, the Seer's complex understanding of time and space is such that the faithful—through the person and the actions of Christ—may be seen to share already in the present time, in dimensions of His own High Priesthood, even if these are only to be brought fully to completion in the victor at some future time.

Completing the Circle: A Fourth Face of Christ at the Table of Divine Communion

As the lines of meaning in this text as icon extend forth to find their completion in the heart of John's postmodern audience, they caution against a lukewarm complacency, while urging the faithful to strive without delay to give witness to the contradictions of the Gospel with an authentic sense of Christian zeal. It is not enough to follow Christ from a safe distance; we are called to something much greater. The voice of Jesus that challenges us to repent exhorts us to remain open to all that His loving voice is calling forth in us. For it is divine love and it alone that is "the presupposition for Revelation's warnings and the calls for repentance (3:19), as well as for its promises of salvation (3:9) and exhortations to love others (2:4, 19)."[245]

The closed door before which Christ stands knocking is ultimately the door to the soul as St. Ambrose elaborates for us so magnificently in his *Exposition on the Psalms*:

> Let your door remain open to welcome the one who is arriving. Open up your soul; expand the inner reaches of your mind that you may see riches of simplicity, the treasures of peace, the sweetness of grace. Open wide your heart, run to meet the Sun of eternal light . . . who shines upon every person. . . . Even though He is able to enter, nevertheless he does not want to force His way in as an intruder, nor does He wish to compel the unwilling. Our soul, therefore, has a gate; it has doors . . . if you want to lift high the doors of your faith, the King of Glory will enter in the triumphal procession of His suffering and death. Righteousness too has gates. It is the soul therefore, which has a gate, and which has doors. It is to this gate that Christ comes and knocks; He knocks at the doors. And so, open to Him: he wants to enter and to find His Bride keeping watch.[246]

According to St. Jerome: "Every day, Christ stands at the door of our hearts. He longs to enter. Let us open wide our hearts to him. Then he will come in and be our host and guest. He will live in us and eat with us."[247] Here, in this crown of both the promises and of the seven letters themselves, the lines of meaning now extend forth to encompass the reader completely. Drawn into the circle of fellowship with the divine, the victor is depicted unequivocally as the fourth person seated—indeed enthroned—alongside

Christ at the table of communion with the Holy Trinity, in a manner more reminiscent than ever of Rublev's sacred icon. Thus, the journey from paradise lost to the fruit of the tree of paradise regained now reaches its completion in these images of the victor as co-regent, who, having borne a share in the sufferings and Cross of Christ, now participates in the eschatological power and priestly glory of Christ Himself (20:6; 22:5).

Together with the content of the previous promises, the imagery serves not only to elaborate further, but to fortify, enhance, and infuse a beatific dimension into John's remarkable oscillating portrait of the ultimate destiny of the human person in Christ—crowned, immortalized, angelified, asterified, glorified, and deified through their sharing in the mystery of the Cross. In response to both the challenges and the promises articulated by God's great "Amen," the text as icon calls out to us to add our own "Amen" without delay to Christ's message, by making of our very lives an antiphonal response to the message of the Living Word that resounds within these Letters. John's approach to *Christosis* or deification is a narrative one, when contrasted with Paul's theological reflections on human transformation in Christ. But this is not to say that John's approach reflects a less advanced understanding of what it means to become Christ-like, for the promises to the victor (along with the other transformations signaled in the book) lead us to reflect upon the conqueror's union with God in Christ and to situate that union within the larger dynamic of the mystery of the mutual indwelling of the three persons of the Blessed Trinity (Jn 17:21–24).[248] Complementing the Fourth Gospel's mystical language of "abiding" (Jn 6:56; 15:4–10), the Book of Revelation offers the faithful a celestial place to stand with the angels before the heavenly throne.

At the same time, it is clear that the glory given by the Father to Christ is in turn bestowed by Christ upon the victorious fourth Face depicted as enthroned at the table of the Trinity (Jn 17:23), recalling once more Paul's language of the "image of the Image." In the Book of Revelation, union with Christ begins in our earnest response to hearken to His voice and to open the door to Him. Within the circle of the life of the Blessed Trinity, alongside Christ, this union reaches its ultimate goal (*telos*) and completion. Therefore, the distasteful, lukewarm quality of an accommodated, self-satisfied, and ineffectual witness to the Gospel must be abandoned without delay, in favor of a powerful, prophetic witness that is able to confront and to confute the perennial cultural, social, and political countercurrents that demand acquiescence, accommodation, and compromise (Jn 4:10–14; 7:38). St. John reminds us of the power of an authentic public confession of belief as he challenges us to become "more marginalized, edgier disciples leading lives of costly testimony."[249] For as G. K. Chesterton observes, "it is the paradox of history that each generation is converted by the saint who contradicts it most."[250] He adds that the saint:

> will generally be found restoring the world to sanity by exaggerating whatever the world neglects, which is by no means always the same element in every age. Yet each generation seeks its saint by instinct.[251]

Ultimately, the saint is "not what the people want, but rather what the people need."[252] How best to chart a course through the dark forests of postmodernity toward the straight and narrow path of the Gospel in the era of the New Evangelization remains a topic for debate. What is needed to restore our own generation to the spiritual and religious well-being to which Chesterton alludes? The "Benedict Option" is not without its proponents.[253] At the same time, images of St. Patrick lighting the Easter fire that would come to replace the High King's fire, St. Boniface cutting down the sacred oak tree, St. Francis of Assisi responding to God's call to "rebuild my Church," or St. Gregory the Great—the monk who became Pope in a dark age—all remind us of the inspiring courage of the great saints of ages past. The Augustine Option invites us to take up the struggle against the barbarians—whether at the gate or reigning upon the emperor's throne—but not without first actively engaging in that spiritual struggle which unseats the dark powers within our own hearts that hinder the arrival of God's City within ourselves and the communities that the angelified Christ is calling us to build. Finally, St. Maximilian Kolbe's understanding of Marian consecration leads us to consider the "Woman Adorned with the Sun Option," and to look upon Mary the Mother of God as the model and "Star of the New Evangelization," as she challenges us to enter bravely into the spiritual struggle to bring forth the light of Christ into a postmodern world through our courageous witness to the "eternal Gospel" (Rev 14:6) that it may shine brightly for all to see.

The Conquering Victor

Looking beyond the content of the individual letters and considering them as a whole, John's overarching rhetorical goal has become more apparent:

> John wants "conquerors." He wants his hearers to "overcome" the challenges to faithful discipleship and the forces, social and spiritual, that conspire to defeat disciples in their contest to keep the commandments of God and to keep faith with Jesus. And for John, "overcoming" entails gaining critical distance from, and engaging in prophetic witness in the midst of, the domination systems of Roman Asia Minor.[254]

The Apocalypse calls forth in its audience a bold Christian witness as John deploys a rather audacious "hermeneutics of suspicion on the much-touted imperial propaganda of the *Pax Romana* and its claims of divine blessing,"[255] and seeks instead to remind those members of his audience who would "support the imperial economic order too enthusiastically of the blood and tears on which the Roman Empire is built."[256] John's message is still far ahead of its time in our own era of neo-liberal global capitalism. This journey from paradise lost to paradise regained, from the age of Adam to "asterified" co-regency with Christ, cannot occur, however, unless the soul first opens the door in response to the loving and merciful Christ who knocks, enters, dines with, and ultimately adorns the victor with *His own* spiritual beauty. Ultimately, it is He alone who decorates the soul with "the jewels of simplicity, and the flowers of temperance, gleaming chastity, shining charity and joyful almsgiving."[257] As Pseudo-Macarius reminds us:

> Thus the soul is completely illumined with the unspeakable beauty of the glory of the light of the face of Christ and is perfectly made a participator of the Holy Spirit. It is privileged to be the dwelling-place and the throne of God, all eye, all light, all face, all glory and all spirit, made so by Christ who drives, guides, carries and supports the soul about and adorns and decorates the soul with his spiritual beauty.[258]

Enthroned alongside Christ in the circle of the Blessed Trinity, the victorious conqueror and fourth Face of Christ thus reflects the glory of God (2 Cor 4:6), just as their suffering witness served to reflect Christ's own light before a darkened world (Mt 5:14). For ultimately, it is the gold tried by the fire of suffering witness and purchased from Christ Himself which adorns the New Jerusalem, as we are reminded in John's descriptions of the radiant aura of the City's jewel-studded foundations with its street of gold (21:19–21).

The Mysterium Lunae: *Reflecting the Light of the Sun*

St. John Paul II reminds us that while a new century and a new millennium have opened in the light of Christ, not everyone sees this light:

Ours is the wonderful and demanding task of becoming its "reflection." This is the *mysterium lunae [mystery of the moon]*, which was so much a part of the contemplation of the Fathers of the Church, who employed this image to show the Church's dependence on Christ, the Sun whose light she reflects. . . . This is a daunting task if we consider our human weakness, which so often renders us opaque and full of shadows. But it is a task which we can accomplish if we turn to the light of Christ and open ourselves to the grace which makes us a new creation.[259]

Opening ourselves up to the transforming graces that begin even now to make us this new creation is certainly the challenge that John's visions set before us. At the same time, St. Paul, Origen, Augustine, and other early Christian writers help us to see beyond the partitioning, either/or rhetoric of John's narrative world so as to be able to discern with greater clarity and precision the more subtle gradations of the both/and nature of the reality of the spiritual struggles of a fallen humanity (Rom 7:14ff), which are themselves a part of the process of the journey toward the New Jerusalem. In his reflections upon the mystery of "the 'intermingling' of the *civitas Dei* with the *civitas terrena* as the In-Between reality of history," Augustine (among others), provides us with a keen sense of the *in-between-ness* of human existence as we live, love, struggle, and discern within the context of the cosmic conflict between the spiritual forces that shape not only the external world, but the human heart.[260] These are, once again, the forces at work in the invisible, mortal combat that rages over the everlasting destiny of souls (Rev 12:7–12; Eph 6:11). Certainly the two cities can be seen as kingdoms or empires, but they speak as well—and most eloquently—of the trajectory of the soul on its journey toward God in between the already and the not yet of God's everlasting promise.

But how shall we begin to leave behind the age of sin, the age of Adam, the old order that is rapidly fading and hasten toward the New Jerusalem as victors? Once again, as St. Bonaventure reminds us, the heavenly Jerusalem must first descend into the heart by grace. How does the New Jerusalem begin its descent into our hearts? John the Baptist responds succinctly that the Kingdom of God is near, therefore we must "repent, and believe in the Gospel" (Mk 1:14–15). According to Augustine, it is the love of God which marks the beginning of our exodus from the earthly city, for one begins to leave behind the earthly city, "the pragmatic world of power,"[261] when one begins to love. Charity opens the gates to the New City at whose center stands the everlasting throne of God and the Lamb. St. Gregory of Nyssa reflects upon the importance of living a life of Christian virtue as we await and prepare for the arrival of God's new creation:

> For on this day God makes a new heaven and a new earth, as the prophet says. What heaven? The firmament of faith in Christ. What earth? I mean the good heart, as the Lord said, the earth which drinks the rain which comes on it and ripens plentiful grain. In this creation pure living is the sun, the virtues are stars, transparent conduct is the air, the depth of the riches of wisdom and knowledge is the sea, good teaching and divine doctrines

> are herbage and plants, which the people of his
> pasture, that is God's flock, graze on, the per-
> formance of the commandments is trees bearing
> fruit.[262]

John's visions inspire us to strive to become that temple
and well-ordered city at whose very center is God Almighty
and the Lamb (7:10; 22:1, 3). Here is a powerful vision for
the human journey between two worlds, as the road to the
New Jerusalem opens up before us—and within us—in the
present moment, with all of its grace, hope, and promise,
and with all of its sinfulness, brokenness, and imperfection.
Whatever the future may bring, Our Lord is calling us to
heed His voice, to repent and to leave Babylon far behind
(18:4) as we continue to share in the royal, priestly, and
prophetic ministry of preaching good news to the poor,
of proclaiming release to captives, the recovery of sight to
the blind, of freeing the oppressed, and proclaiming the
year of the Lord's favor, always speaking—and living—the
truth with love (Lk 4:18–19; Eph 4:15). God's promise to
make all things new will reach its ultimate fulfillment in
the restoration of the ancient ruins and the rebuilding of
the ruined cities symbolized in the arrival of the New Jerusalem (Amos 9:14; Is 61:4; Lk 4:16–21).

Reflecting the Light of the Divine in a Post-Secular Age

In a postmodern era when so many live as though God did
not exist (*etsi Deus non daretur*, in the words of Augustine),
the Book of Revelation challenges us to contemplate our
own search for the God who is in search of us. And we are

called to do so in light of these images of the victorious witness who is an image of both the divinized, Christified self, and the divinizing, Christifying light bearer of the Holy Trinity before the hostile powers of a darkened world. Certainly John's late first-century understanding of the human soul—created in God's image and likeness and called to reflect the divine—stands in stark contrast with that of the fragmented worldview of the postmodern self. A number of movements of thought figure in the gradual closing of the door of the soul to the transcendent world of vision and, with it, to the voice of Christ who stands and knocks at the door of the postmodern Laodicean (and awaits a reply). These include the gradual shift from the profound depths of the Christian vision of the human person in Christ and the richness of the interior life in the Spirit—characteristic of classical Jewish and Christian mysticism—to René Descartes' "theater of consciousness,"[263] the Kantian turn toward the self and, with it, the rise of a fragmented, narcissistic self-absorption that approaches solipsism. Yes, the truth dwells within, as Augustine writes in his *De vera religione* (39.72), but a careful study of these movements in the history of ideas reveals that the transcendent relationship with the living God of Abraham, Moses, Isaac, and Jacob has been severed, leaving the soul "entirely encapsulated in itself."[264] Here we are better able to arrive at a greater appreciation of the fragmented world of meaning, and the flattened perspectives and diminished horizons characteristic of the writings of the phenomenologists, psychologists, and postmodern philosophers. Finally, John's message is profoundly countercultural in a narcissistic era given more readily to self-deification than to crucifixion with Christ.

For it is He who calls us to strive toward that transformation and renewal that is otherwise impossible to attain except through God's grace and a committed life of faith in the Spirit.

In his letter to the Philippians, Paul underscores the importance of striving toward what lies ahead and pressing on "toward the goal for the prize of the heavenly call of God in Christ Jesus" (Phil 3:13–14). However, it is St. Gregory of Nyssa who reminds us we are to strive not for the possible, but rather what is "unattainable," for even if we attain a part of what is good by nature we "could yet gain a great deal."[265] The Psalmist invites us to aspire toward the spiritual heights, to "climb the mountain of the Lord," to stand upon that rock which is higher than we are through the life of faith (Ps 24; 61:1–2; cf. 1 Cor 10:4). John's victor strives both forward and upward toward what is impossible unaided by God's grace, on the journey between time's imposed limits, the dangers of public witness to the Gospel (with its threats of persecution and martyrdom), on the one hand, and the radiant promise of the newness of their ultimate transformation in Christ, on the other. The aspiring victor does so by reaching out constantly toward that infinite mystery which "transcends all grounds and limits."[266] Again, although John's language and conceptual world are quite distinct from Paul's, both the threats and the persistent calls which the Book of Revelation makes to "remember," to "repent," to be zealous and to "endure patiently" (alongside imagery drawn from the world of the athlete, such as the imperishable crown [cf. 1 Cor 9:25]) inspire the faithful to strive toward that newness of life which Christ is offering. Moreover, the aspiring victors are called to heightened constancy and vigilance concerning the quality of their witness. By striving toward the prizes articulated so compellingly in the narrative, the victor begins the journey toward realizing the ultimate goal and *telos* of the story told by John's reflections on Christ, namely, that of becoming a new creation and fourth Face of Christ.

Beyond the calls to endure patiently, John's message bids us today to be zealous (3:19) in responding to our preeminent calling in Christ. Nor should we dwell excessively upon our own sense of unworthiness. For according to the author of the *Cloud of Unknowing*, "It is not what you are nor what you have been that God looks at with His merciful eyes, but what you desire to be."[267] St. Clare of Assisi once wrote that Jesus Christ is the "radiance of everlasting light, and a mirror without tarnish," and so encouraged a religious sister to:

> Look into this mirror every day . . . and continually examine your face in it, so that in this way you may adorn yourself completely, inwardly and outwardly, clothed and covered in multicolored apparel, adorned in the same manner with flowers and garments made of all the virtues as is proper. . . . Moreover, in this mirror shine blessed poverty, holy humility, and charity beyond words, as you will be able, with God's grace, to contemplate throughout the entire mirror.[268]

Let us pray, then, for the grace to give powerful countercultural witness to that newness of life in Christ which is ours through our share in His own victory over the powers of sin and death. The portrait of a fourth Face of Christ that emerges in the narrative of the Book of Revelation is the victorious image of the Image and sparkling reflection of Christ's own light, like the moon reflecting the light of the sun. Knowing that God has revealed to the victor the light of the knowledge of His glory in the Face of Christ (2 Cor 4:6), let us "seek the face of the Lord" (Ps 27:8; cf. 2 Chron 7:14; Ps 24:6) and pray for the grace to become radiant reflections of the face of the Victorious Son of God before a darkened world, as we pray together with the Psalmist: "Let the light of your face shine on us, O Lord" (Ps 4:6, cf. Ps 31:16) "that we may be saved" (Ps 80:3, 7, 19; 119:135; Song 2:14).

Endnotes

1. Cf. comments in Ugo Vanni, *L'Uomo dell'Apocalisse* (Rome: Edizioni AdP, 2008), 20, n. 3 and literature cited.

2. Arthur W. Wainwright, *Mysterious Apocalypse: Interpreting the Book of Revelation* (repr. 1993; Eugene, OR: Wipf & Stock, 2001), 203.

3. Edward Edinger, *Archetype of the Apocalypse: Divine Vengeance, Terrorism, and the End of the World*, ed. George R. Elder (Chicago: Open Court, 1999), 16.

4. Cf. April DeConick, "What is Early Jewish and Christian Mysticism?" in *Paradise Now: Essays on Early Jewish and Christian Mysticism* (Atlanta: Society of Biblical Literature, 2006), 24.

5. Cf. George A. Maloney, S.J., ed., *Pseudo-Macarius: The Fifty Spiritual Homilies and the Great Letter* (New York: Paulist Press, 1992), Homily 43.7, 222.

6. Cf. *De Trinitate*, XIV, 11.

7. Cf. Henri de Lubac, *The Drama of Atheist Humanism*, trans. Edith M. Riley, et al. (San Francisco: Ignatius Press, 1995), 20–21.

8. Philip Blond, "Introduction: Theology Before Philosophy," in *Post-Secular Philosophy: Between Philosophy and Theology* (London: Routledge, 1998), 8.

9. Ellis Sandoz, *Political Apocalypse: A Study of Dostoevsky's Grand Inquisitor* (Baton Rouge, LA: Louisiana State University Press, 1971), 190.

10. Gil Bailie, "The Vine and Branches Discourse: The Gospel's Psychological Apocalypse," in *Contagion: Journal of Violence, Mimesis, and Culture* vol. 4 (1997): 129: "The issue at stake here has been cogently captured in what Henri de Lubac has referred to as the diminishing of 'ontological density' in the modern world, a remark echoed by Gabriel Marcel when he lamented the loss of 'ontological moorings.'"

11. DeConick, "What is Early Jewish and Christian Mysticism?", 24: "The cosmic had collapsed into the personal. The period-literature indicates that some Jews and Christians hoped to achieve *in the present* the eschatological dream, the restoration of God's Image *within themselves*—the resurrection and transformation of their bodies into the glorious bodies of angels and their minds into the mind of God."

12. Alexander Golitzin, "Earthly Angels and Heavenly Men: The Old Testament Pseudepigrapha, Niketas Stethatos, and the Tradition of Interiorized Apocalyptic in Eastern Christian Ascetical and Mystical Literature," in *Dumbarton Oaks Papers* 55 (2001): 141 and literature cited.

13. Cf. Dan 10:2f; Apocalypse of Abraham 9:7–10, 12:1f; Apocalypse of Elijah 1:15–22; Greek Apocalypse of Ezra 1:3f; and comments by Susan Niditch, "The Visionary," in *Ideal Figures in Ancient Judaism:*

Profiles and Paradigms, ed. John J. Collins and George W. E. Nickels-burg, Society of Biblical Literature Septuagint and Cognate Studies 12 (Atlanta: Scholars Press, 1980), 159–160.

[14] Murray Krieger, *A Window to Criticism: Shakespeare's Sonnets and Modern Poetics* (Princeton, NJ: Princeton University Press, 1964), 3–4; and the discussion of John's Gospel in R. Alan Culpepper, *Anatomy of the Fourth Gospel: A Study in Literary Design* (Philadelphia: Fortress, 1983), 3.

[15] David E. Aune, "The Apocalypse of John and the Problem of Genre," *Semeia* 36 (1986), 90.

[16] De Conick, "What is Early Jewish and Christian Mysticism?" 24.

[17] Barr, *Tales of the End,* 171.

[18] Aune, "The Apocalypse of John and the Problem of Genre," 89–90.

[19] Cf. St. Clement, "Epistle to the Corinthians," ch. 36, 1–2; and James A. Kleist, S.J., ed., *The Epistles of St. Clement of Rome and St. Ignatius of Antioch* (New York: Paulist Press, 1946), 31.

[20] Temple Chevallier, ed., *A Translation of the Epistles of Clement of Rome, Polycarp, and Ignatius, and of the Apologies of Justin Martyr and Tertullian* (Cambridge, UK: J. & J. J. Deighton; and London: J. G. & F. Rivington, 1833), 35.

[21] H. O. Maier, "Staging the Gaze: Early Christian Apocalypses and Narrative Self–Representation," *Harvard Theological Review* 90 (1997): 131–154. I am also grateful to Professor Ugo Vanni for his comments concerning the role of the Spirit in the Book of Revelation.

[22] As quoted in Andrew Louth, *Greek East and Latin West: The Church AD 681–1071,* The Church in History vol. III, idem., ed. (Crestwood, NY: St. Vladimir's Seminary Press, 2007), 59 and literature cited.

[23] Leonid Ouspensky, *Theology of the Icon,* trans. Elizabeth Meyendorff (Crestwood, NY: St. Vladimir's Seminary Press, 1978), 165.

[24] Eugene Trubetskoy, *Icons: Theology in Colour* (Crestwood, NY: St. Vladimir's Seminary Press, 1973).

[25] Ouspensky, *Theology of the Icon,* 164. See also 166: "For the Church, therefore, the icon is not an art illustrating Holy Scripture; it is a lan-guage which corresponds to Scripture. . . . "

[26] Ibid., 228.

[27] Ibid.

[28] Boring, *Revelation,* 52.

[29] Ibid., 52, 54 and literature cited.

[30] Ibid., 53.

[31] Boring, *Revelation,* 57.

[32] Ouspensky, *Theology of the Icon,* 225.

[33] Michel Quenot, *The Icon: Window on the Kingdom* (Crestwood, NY: St. Vladimir's Seminary Press, 1991), 31.

34 John Baggley, *Festival Icons for the Christian Year* (Crestwood, NY: St. Vladimir's Seminary Press, 2000), 148.

35 Boris Bobrinskoy, *The Mystery of the Trinity* (Crestwood, NY: St. Vladimir's Seminary Press, 1999), 141.

36 Maria Giovanna Muzj, *Transfiguration: Introduction to the Contemplation of Icons,* trans. Kenneth D. Whitehead (Boston: St. Paul Books & Media, 1991), 165.

37 Quenot, *The Icon,* 31.

38 Ouspensky, *Theology of the Icon,* 224.

39 Henri J. M. Nouwen, *Behold the Beauty of the Lord,* 1st rev. ed. (Notre Dame, IN: Ave Maria Press, 2007), 32.

40 Bobrinskoy, *The Mystery of the Trinity,* 141.

41 Nouwen, *Behold the Beauty of the Lord,* 33.

42 Quenot, *The Icon,* 106.

43 Susan G. Eastman, *Recovering Paul's Mother Tongue: Language and Theology in Galatians* (Grand Rapids: Eerdmans, 2007), 143, 151 and literature cited.

44 Ouspensky, *Theology of the Icon,* 225.

45 Ibid., 228.

46 St. John of the Cross, *The Spiritual Canticle,* Stanza 5.4, in E. Allison Peers, *The Spiritual Canticle and Poems: St. John of the Cross,* vol. 2 (London: Burns & Oates, 1978), 48.

47 Philip Schaff, ed., *Chrysostom: On the Priesthood, Ascetic Treatises, Select Homilies and Letters, Homilies on the Statutes,* in *Nicene and Post-Nicene Fathers: First Series,* vol. IX (New York: Cosimo Classics, 2007), 123–24.

48 Willem F. Smelik, "On Mystical Transformation of the Righteous into Light in Judaism," *Journal for the Study of Judaism* 26 (1995): 122 and literature cited.

49 For the expression "transformation soteriology," see: Seyoon Kim, *Paul and the New Perspective* (Grand Rapids, MI: Eerdmans, 2002), 173.

50 Cf. Rom 8:15, 23; 9:4; Gal 4:5; and Eph 1:5; and John's language of adoption in 1 Jn 3:1–3. See also Trevor J. Burke, *Adopted Into God's Family: Exploring a Pauline Metaphor,* New Studies in Biblical Theology, 22 (Downers Grove, IL: Apollos/InterVarsity Press, 2006). See also M. David Litwa, *We are Being Transformed: Deification in Paul's Soteriology* (Berlin: Walter de Gruyter, 2012), 31–34.

51 Cf. comments on the *Apocalypse of Zephaniah,* 5, by James H. Charlesworth, ed., *The Old Testament Pseudepigrapha: Apocalyptic Literature and Testaments* 1 (Peabody, MA: Hendrickson, 1983), 512 and notes. Does biblical and extra-biblical reflection concerning such figures as Enoch (Gen 5:24), Elijah (2 Kings 2:11), Moses (Ex 34:29), and the "transformed righteous" described by Daniel (Dan 12:3) suggest a *continuum*

between angels and transformed human beings? See 4 Ezra 7:97, 125; 2 Bar 51:3, 10; 1 Enoch 39:7; 104:2.

[52] Smelik, "On Mystical Transformation of the Righteous into Light in Judaism," 124.

[53] L. W. Hurtado, "Revelation 4–5 in the Light of Jewish Apocalyptic Analogies," *JSNT* 25 (1985) 108.

[54] Cf. comments in Aune, *Revelation 1–5*, 99.

[55] Cf. Pieter W. van der Horst, "Moses' Throne Vision in Ezekiel the Dramatist," *Journal of Jewish Studies* 34 (1983): 21–29; and comments in Aune, *Revelation 1–5*, 261–62.

[56] Cf. Litwa, *We are Being Transformed*, 106–109 and literature cited. See also Litwa, "The Deification of Moses in Philo," *The Studia Philonica Annual* 26 (2014): 1–27.

[57] Cf. M. David Litwa, *We are Being Transformed*, 24–25.

[58] Cf. Gregory E. Sterling, "'The Image of God': Becoming Like God in Philo, Paul, and Early Christianity," *Portraits of Jesus: Studies in Christology*, ed. Susan E. Myers WUNT 2, Reihe, 321 (Tübingen, Germany: Mohr Siebeck, 2012), 157–174.

[59] Beale, *We Become What We Worship*, 241–267.

[60] Cf. Peter Schäfer, *The Origins of Jewish Mysticism* (Tübingen, Germany: Mohr Siebeck, 2009; Princeton, NJ: Princeton University Press, 2011), 105, where he observes that the dividing lines between God and the Son of Man are blurred. See also 111. See Leonard L. Thompson, *The Book of Revelation*, 81, on the "soft boundaries" of the Book of Revelation's symbolism.

[61] Norman Russell, *The Doctrine of Deification in the Greek Patristic Tradition* (Oxford, UK: Oxford University Press, 2006), 11.

[62] Josephine Massyngbaerde Ford, "The Priestly People of God in the Apocalypse," *Listening* 28 (1993): 256.

[63] Carol Newsom, *Songs of the Sabbath Sacrifice*, 17–18, 61–72.

[64] Cf. David L. Barr, "The Apocalypse as a Symbolic Transformation of the World: A Literary Analysis" Interpretation 38 (1984): 47: "The eschatological world is realized in the cultic event." Aune, *The Cultic Setting of Realized Eschatology*, 141–42.

[65] Cf. Kyoung Shik Kim, *God Will Judge Each One According to Works: Judgment According to Works and Psalm 62 in Early Judaism and the New Testament* (Berlin: DeGruyter, 2011), 258–59.

[66] Cf. comments by Stephen S. Smalley, *The Revelation to John* (London: SPCK, 2005), 104–105, where he discusses four theological themes: judgment, love, conflict, and the need for steadfastness. See as well, Eugene M. Boring, *Revelation*, 91–97.

67 Are these angels supernatural beings (i.e., guardian angels)? Human beings (Christian prophets, emissaries, or Bishops)? See the discussion in: Aune, *Revelation 1–5*, 108–112.

68 Slater, *Christ and Community*, 149: "The letters were written primarily to strengthen the inner spiritual lives of the churches. A faithful witness would bring co-regency as priest-kings in the new age. This promise, an Exodus motif, is a maintenance strategy aimed at sustaining the union between Christ and community."

69 Pilchan Lee, *The New Jerusalem in the Book of Revelation: A Study of Revelation 21–22 in the Light of Its Background in Jewish Tradition* (Tübingen, Germany: Mohr Siebeck, 2001), 246.

70 Cf. Matthijs Den Dulk, "The Promises to the Conquerors in the Book of Revelation," *Biblica* 87 (2006): 516ff.

71 B. J. Oropeza, *Churches Under Siege of Persecution and Assimilation: The General Epistles and Revelation*, Apostasy and New Testament Communities, vol. 3 (Eugene, OR: Cascade Books, 2012), 193–94.

72 Caird, *The Revelation of St. John the Divine*, 33.

73 See comments by Aune, *Revelation 1–5*, 151.

74 Barr, "The Lamb Who Looks Like a Dragon?," 209.

75 DeSilva, *Seeing Things John's Way*, 107–108; and Johns, *The Lamb Christology of the Apocalypse of John*, 182.

76 Beasley-Murray, *The Book of Revelation*, 71.

77 Caird, *The Revelation of St. John the Divine*, 33.

78 Harrington, *The Apocalypse of St. John*, 102.

79 Aune, "Excursus 3A: The Sayings of Jesus in Revelation," in *Revelation 1–5*, 264–65 and literature cited.

80 DeSilva, *Seeing Things John's Way*, 228.

81 Swete, *Apocalypse*, 66.

82 Ouspensky, *Theology of the Icon*, 225.

83 Cf. Grant R. Osborne, *Revelation*, Baker Exegetical Commentary on the New Testament (Grand Rapids, MI: Baker Academic, 2002), 109; Robert H. Mounce, *The Book of Revelation*, rev. ed., The New International Commentary on the New Testament (Grand Rapids, MI: Eerdmans).

84 Cf. Aune, *Revelation 1–5*, 140–41 and literature cited; Gregory K. Beale, *The Book of Revelation: A Commentary on the Greek Text*, The New International Greek Testament Commentary (Grand Rapids, MI: Eerdmans, 1999), 228.

85 See Boring, *Revelation*, 89.

86 See comments by Barr, *Tales of the End*, 53.

87 Cf. Osborne, *Revelation*, 121. Robert H. Mounce, *The Book of Revelation*, 71.

[88] See comments in Robert H. Mounce, *The Book of Revelation*, 71.

[89] Osborne, *Revelation*, 125.

[90] Ibid., 117.

[91] Cf. Matthijs den Dulk, "The Promises to the Conquerors in the Book of Revelation," 516; Aune, *Revelation 1–5*, 152, as well as G. K. Beale, *The Book of Revelation*, 234–35 and literature cited.

[92] Cf. Mounce, *The Book of Revelation*, 72, n. 32 and literature cited. See especially, Hanns Lilje, *The Last Book of the Bible*, trans. Olive Wyon (Philadelphia: Muhlenberg, 1957), 72.

[93] Cf. Andrew of Caesarea, "Commentary on the Apocalypse," in *Greek Commentaries on Revelation: Oecumenius and Andrew of Caesarea*, trans. William C. Weinrich, ed. Thomas C. Oden, Ancient Christian Texts (Downers Grove, IL: InterVarsity Academic, 2011), 120.

[94] Aune, *Revelation 1–5*, 152.

[95] Ibid., 153

[96] Bede the Venerable, "Explanation of the Apocalypse," 2:7; as quoted in *Latin Commentaries on Revelation: Victorinus of Petovium, Apringius of Beja, Caesarius of Arles and Bede the Venerable*, trans. William C. Weinrich, Ancient Christian Texts (Downers Grove: IVP Academic, 2011), 118.

[97] Caesarius of Arles, *Exposition on the Apocalypse*, Homily 2, as quoted in *Latin Commentaries on Revelation*, 67.

[98] Tyconius, *Commentary on the Apocalypse*, 2.7, as quoted in *Revelation*, Ancient Christian Commentary on Scripture, New Testament, vol. XII, ed. William C. Weinrich (Downers Grove, IL: InterVarsity, 2005), 23.

[99] Osborne, *Revelation*, 124.

[100] Swete, *The Apocalypse of St. John*, 30.

[101] Colin J. Hemer, *The Letters to the Seven Churches of Asia in Their Local Setting* (Sheffield: University of Sheffield, 1986), 45.

[102] Cf. "Origen on Prayer," Chapter XV, "Thy Kingdom Come," *Christian Classics Ethereal Library*, trans. William A. Curtis (2015): 48.

[103] Cf. Aune, *Revelation 1–5*, 160.

[104] Ibid.

[105] Ibid.

[106] Hemer, *The Letters to the Seven Churches*, 62–63.

[107] Beale, *The Book of Revelation*, 241 and literature cited.

[108] Ibid.

[109] Cf. Tyconius, "Commentary on the Apocalypse," 2.9, as quoted in *Revelation*, Ancient Christian Commentary on Scripture, vol. XII, 25.

[110] Cf. Andrew of Caesarea, "Commentary on the Apocalypse," 2.9, as quoted in *Revelation*, Ancient Christian Commentary on Scripture vol. XII, 25.

[111] Barr, *Tales of the End*, 56.

[112] Cf. R. H. Charles, *Revelation*, vol. I, 58; Grant R. Osborne, *Revelation*, 135.

[113] Cf. Aune, "Excursus 2C: Ancient Wreath and Crown Imagery," in *Revelation 1–5*, 172–75.

[114] Cf. Greg M. Stevenson, "Conceptual Background to Golden Crown Imagery in the Apocalypse of John (4:4, 10; 14:14)," *Journal of Biblical Literature* 114 (1995): 257–272, especially 258.

[115] Cf. comments by G. R. Beasley-Murray, *Revelation*, 82–83; as well as Aune, in *Revelation 1–5*, 167.

[116] Brian E. Daley, *The Hope of the Early Church: A Handbook of Patristic Eschatology* (New York: Cambridge University Press, 1991), 14.

[117] Cf. Aune, *Revelation 1–5*, 167.

[118] Swete, *The Apocalypse of St. John*, 33.

[119] Cf. Jerusalem Targum on Deuteronomy, 33:6, as quoted in Aune, *Revelation 1–5*, 168.

[120] Beasley-Murray, *The Book of Revelation*, 83.

[121] Cf. Osborne, *Revelation*, 128; and comments in Hemer, *The Letters to the Seven Churches*, 62–63.

[122] St. Cyprian, "*To the Martyrs and Confessors*," Epistle VIII, *Christian Classics Ethereal Library: Anti-Nicene Fathers: Fathers of the Third Century: Hippolytus, Cyprian, Caius, Novatian, Appendix* vol. 5, trans. Philip Schaff (2015); originally published 1885, 717.

[123] St. Francis de Sales, *Introduction to the Devout Life*, trans. and ed. John K. Ryan (Garden City, NY: Image Books/Doubleday, 1972), 16.

[124] Anders Klostergaard Petersen, "Between Old and New: The Problem of Acculturation Illustrated by the Early Christian Use of the Phoenix Motif," in *Jerusalem, Alexandria, Rome: Studies in Ancient Cultural Interaction in Honour of A. Hilhorst*, ed., F. García Martínez and G. P. Luttikhuizen (Leiden, Netherlands: Brill, 2003), 147–164. Ernest Evans, *Tertullian's Treatise on the Resurrection* (orig. 1960; Eugene, OR: Wipf & Stock, 2016), 35.

[125] Peterson, "Between Old and New," 162–63.

[126] Fulgentius of Ruspe, "On the Forgiveness of Sins," 2.12.3–4, as quoted in *Ancient Christian Commentary on Scripture: New Testament XII: Revelation*, 28.

[127] Osborne, *Revelation*, 139.

[128] Cf. Hemer, *The Letters to the Seven Churches*, 244, n. 101.

[129] Cf. Aune, *Revelation 1–5*, 180.

[130] C. J. Hemer, *The Letters to the Seven Churches*, 85.

[131] Cf. Beale, *The Book of Revelation*, 248.

[132] Cf. David E. Aune, "The Form and Function of the Proclamations to the Seven Churches," *New Testament Studies* 36 (1990): 191–193.

[133] Aune, *Revelation 1–5,* 189; and *Genesis Rabbah,* 82.8 on Gen 35:17.

[134] Cf. Aune, *Revelation 1–5,* 189; H. B. Swete, *The Apocalypse of St. John,* 39.

[135] Ibid.

[136] Ibid.

[137] Oecumenius, "Commentary on the Apocalypse," in *Greek Commentaries on Revelation: Oecumenius and Andrew of Caesarea,* 13.

[138] Hemer, *The Letters to the Seven Churches,* 96 discusses seven options.

[139] Caird, *The Revelation of St. John the Divine,* 42.

[140] Grant R. Osborne, *Revelation,* 149.

[141] Hemer, *The Letters to the Seven Churches,* 96.

[142] Oecumenius, "Commentary on the Apocalypse," 2:12–17; as quoted in *Ancient Christian Commentary on Scripture: New Testament XII: Revelation,* 31.

[143] Victorinus, "Commentary on the Apocalypse," 2.3, as quoted in *Ancient Christian Commentary on Scripture: New Testament XII: Revelation,* 29.

[144] Bede the Venerable, "Explanation of the Apocalypse," 2:17, as quoted in *Latin Commentaries on Revelation: Victorinus of Petovium, Apringius of Beja, Caesarius of Arles and Bede the Venerable,* trans. William C. Weinrich, Ancient Christian Texts (Downers Grove, IL: InterVarsity Press Academic, 2011), 120.

[145] James A. Wiseman, O.S.B., ed., *John Ruusbroec: The Spiritual Espousals and Other Works* (New York: Paulist Press: 1985), 161.

[146] C. S. Lewis, *The Screwtape Letters, with Screwtape Proposes a Toast,* 75.

[147] St. Bernard, *Sermones De Diversis* as quoted in Mariano Magrassi, *Praying the Bible: An Introduction to Lectio Divina* (Collegeville, MN: Liturgical Press, 1998), 99.

[148] Swete, *The Apocalypse of St. John,* 39 and literature cited.

[149] Nikitas Stithatos, *On the Practice of the Virtues: One Hundred Texts,* n. 75, in *The Philokalia: the Complete Text* vol. 4, ed. G. E. H. Palmer, Philip Sherrard, and Kallistos Ware (London: Faber and Faber, 1995), 137–38.

[150] Primasius, "Commentary on the Apocalypse," 2.17, as quoted in *Ancient Christian Commentary on Scripture: New Testament XII: Revelation,* 32.

[151] James A. Wiseman, O.S.B., ed., *John Ruusbroec: The Spiritual Espousals and Other Works* (New York: Paulist Press, 1985), 160.

[152] Ibid., 160–161.

[153] Johannas Behm, *"kainos,"* in *Theological Dictionary of the New Testament,* vol. 3, ed. Gerhard Kittel and Gerhard Friedrich (Grand Rapids, MI: Eerdmans, 1964–76), 449. Swete, *The Apocalypse of St. John,* 41.

[154] Hemer, *The Letters to the Seven Churches,* 106.

[155] Aune, *Revelation 1–5,* 201; Osborne, *Revelation,* 151–52.

[156] Aune, *Revelation 1–5*, 201.

[157] Hemer, *The Letters to the Seven Churches*, 117.

[158] Osborne, *Revelation*, 157 and literature cited.

[159] Beale, *The Book of Revelation*, 261.

[160] Grant R. Osborne, *Revelation*, 151–52.

[161] Aune, *Revelation 1–5*, 211.

[162] DeSilva, *Seeing Things John's Way*, 228. See as well, Beasley-Murray, *Revelation*, 93, and Aune, *Revelation 1–5*, 210.

[163] E. Bernard Allo, *Apocalypse de Saint Jean*, 46 (author's translation).

[164] Beasley-Murray, *The Book of Revelation*, 93–94.

[165] Cf. Aune, *Revelation 1–5*, 212–13.

[166] Swete, *The Apocalypse of St. John*, 48.

[167] Cf. H. B. Swete, *The Apocalypse of St. John*, 47.

[168] See the discussion in Peter Schäfer, *The Origins of Jewish Mysticism* (Princeton & Oxford: Princeton University Press, 2011), 105

[169] Andrew of Caesarea, "Commentary on the Apocalypse," in *Greek Commentaries on Revelation: Oecumenius and Andrew of Caesarea*, 123.

[170] From the Latin, *"Iter tibi per aera ipsum et transitum pollicetur." Origen: Homilies on Joshua*, Homily 4, trans. Barbara J. Bruce (Washington, DC: Catholic University of America Press, 2002), 51–52, which renders "a passage for you through the air itself." Cf. Pliny, *Natura*, 2.102.

[171] Beale, *The Book of Revelation*, 260.

[172] Tyconius *Commentary on the Apocalypse*, 2.28 (CCL 92:36); as quoted in *Revelation, Ancient Christian Commentary on Scripture*, vol. 12, 38.

[173] St. Gregory the Great, "Moral Reflections on Job," XXIX, 2–4; PL 76, 478–480; as quoted in *Morals on The Book of Job by S. Gregory the Great*, 3 vols., 303–304.

[174] See comments in Hemer, *The Seven Churches of Asia Minor*, 131; as well as in Osborne, *Revelation*, 171.

[175] Aune, *Revelation 1–5*, 218.

[176] Hemer, *The Seven Churches of Asia Minor*, 129.

[177] Aune, *Revelation 1–5*, 219.

[178] Hemer, *The Seven Churches of Asia Minor*, 137; Osborne, *Revelation*, 172.

[179] Richard L. Jeske, "Spirit and Community in the Johannine Apocalypse," *New Testament Studies* 31 (1985): 462.

[180] Cf. G. B. Caird, *Revelation*, 48.

[181] Beale, *The Book of Revelation*, 272–73.

[182] Hemer, *The Seven Churches of Asia Minor*, 148–49.

[183] Aune, *Revelation 1–5*, 223.

[184] Grant R. Osborne, *Revelation*, 179 and literature cited.

[185] Osborne, *Revelation*, 179; Hemer, *The Letters to the Seven Churches*, 147.

186 Heinrich Kraft, *Die Offenbarung*, 78; E. B. Allo, *Apocalypse de Saint Jean*, 48.

187 Caird, *The Revelation of St. John the Divine*, 49.

188 Aune, *Revelation 1–5*, 224.

189 Hemer, *The Seven Churches of Asia Minor*, 149.

190 See the detailed discussion in Aune, *Revelation 1–5*, 224.

191 Ibid.

192 Hemer, *The Seven Churches of Asia Minor*, 149–50.

193 Andrew of Caesarea, "Commentary on the Apocalypse," 3.2, in *Greek Commentaries on Revelation: Oecumenius and Andrew of Caesarea*, 124.

194 St. John Paul II, *Reconciliatio et Paenitentia*, no. 28. See also *Novo Millennio Ineunte*, no. 37.

195 Pope Pius XII, Radio Message to Participants in the National Catechetical Congress of the United States in Boston, October 26, 1946.

196 Etienne Gilson, *The Breakdown of Morals and Christian Education* (New York: Doubleday, 1960), 2.

197 See Karl Menninger, *Whatever Became of Sin?* (New York: Hawthorn Books, 1973).

198 Christopher Lasch, *The Culture of Narcissism: American Life in an Age of Diminishing Expectations* (New York: W. W. Norton & Company, 1979), xvi.

199 Aune, *Revelation 1–5*, 222.

200 Andrew of Caesarea, "Commentary on the Apocalypse," 3.5–6, *Greek Commentaries on Revelation: Oecumenius and Andrew of Caesarea*, 125.

201 St. Cyprian, *"A Treatise on the Lord's Prayer,"* Nn. 11, in *The Fathers of the Church*, ed. Roy J. Deferrari et al., vol. 36, St. Cyprian Treatises (Washington, DC: Catholic University of America Press, 1956), 136.

202 Hemer, *The Letters to the Seven Churches*, 154; as well as comments in Osborne, *Revelation*, 184.

203 Osborne, *Revelation*, 184.

204 Hemer, *The Letters to the Seven Churches*, 158.

205 Aune, *Revelation 1–5*, 234.

206 Ibid., 235.

207 Slater, *Christ and Community*, 142.

208 Andrew of Caesarea, *Commentary on the Apocalypse*, 3.7; as quoted in *Ancient Christian Commentary on Scripture: New Testament XII: Revelation*, 44.

209 Slater, *Christ and Community*, 142–43.

210 Ibid., 142–43 and literature cited.

211 Primasius, *Commentary on the Apocalypse*, 3.8; as quoted in *Ancient Christian Commentary on Scripture: New Testament XII: Revelation*, 45.

212 Beale, *The Book of Revelation*, 289.

213 See the discussion in Osborne, *Revelation,* 194–195.

214 Hemer, *The Letters to the Seven Churches,* 166.

215 Grant Osborne, *Revelation,* 196–97 and literature cited.

216 Stephen S. Smalley, *The Revelation to John* (London: SPCK, 2005), 94; Beasley-Murray, *Revelation,* 101–102.

217 Cf. Harrington, *The Apocalypse of St. John,* 98.

218 See Hans Bietenhard, art. "Onoma," *Theological Dictionary of the New Testament,* Abridged in 1 vol., 1, ed. Geoffrey W. Bromiley (Grand Rapids, MI: Eerdmans, 1985), 696–699.

219 Beasley-Murray, *The Book of Revelation,* 103; as well as Aune, *Revelation 1–5,* 243 and literature cited.

220 Swete, *Apocalypse,* 58.

221 James L. Resseguie, *The Revelation of John: A Narrative Commentary* (Grand Rapids, MI: Baker Academic, 2009), 100.

222 Håkan Ulfgard, "The Songs of the Sabbath Sacrifice and the Heavenly Scene of the Book of Revelation," *Northern Lights on the Dead Sea Scrolls: Proceedings of the Nordic Qumran Network, 2003–2006,* ed. Anders Klostergaard Petersen, Torleif Elgvin, et. al. (Leiden, Netherlands: Brill, 2009), 261.

223 Dale Allison, "4Q403 Fragm. 1, Col. I, 38–46 and the Revelation of John," *Revue du Qumrân* 12 (1986): 413. See also Andrea Spatafora, *From the "Temple of God" to God as the Temple: A Biblical Theological Study of the Temple in the Book of Revelation* (Rome: Editrice Pontificia Universitá Gregoriana, 1997), 132–33.

224 Cf. Mt 22:30; Mk 12:25; 2 Baruch 51:5; Apoc; Zeph 8:1–5, 4Q 403 Fragm. 1; Col 1: 38–46, and comments by Dale Allison, ibid., 413.

225 George A. Maloney, S.J., ed., *Pseudo-Macarius: The Fifty Spiritual Homilies and the Great Letter* (New York: Paulist Press, 1992), Homily 1.7, 41.

226 Maloney, *Pseudo-Macarius,* Homily 25, 161.

227 Alexander Golitzin, "Earthly Angels and Heavenly Men," 146. See also Golitzin's, "'Suddenly, Christ': The Place of Negative Theology in the Mystagogy of Dionysius Areopagites" in *Mystics: Presence and Aporia,* ed. Michael Kessler and Christian Shepherd (Chicago: University of Chicago Press, 2003), 17–18.

228 Maloney, *Pseudo-Macarius,* 256.

229 Golitzin, "Earthly Angels and Heavenly Men," 146. Maloney, *Pseudo-Macarius,* Homily 32.6, 199, 256.

230 St. Leo the Great, *Sermo in Nativitate Domini,* 7.2.6; *PL* 54, 217–18; 220–21 (author's translation). The original reads: "Si enim templum Dei sumus, et Spiritus Dei habitat in nobis (I Cor. III, 16), plus est quod fidelis quisque in suo habet animo, quam quod miratur in coelo."

231 Hemer, *The Letters to the Seven Churches,* 180ff.

[232] Mounce, *The Book of Revelation*, 107.

[233] Aune, *Revelation 1–5*, 249–250.

[234] Smalley, *The Revelation to John*, 96–97; Beasley-Murray, 104; Aune, *Revelation 1–5*, 255. Osborne, *Revelation*, 203–204.

[235] Mounce, *The Book of Revelation*, 108.

[236] Ibid., 109.

[237] Pierre Prigent, *Commentary on the Apocalypse of St. John*, trans. Wendy Pradels (Tübingen, Germany: Mohr Siebeck, 2004), 212; and Ugo Vanni, *L'Apocalisse Ermeneutica, esegesi, teologia* (Bologna, Italy: Edizioni Dehoniane, 2005), 143.

[238] John Paul Heil, *The Book of Revelation: Worship for Life in the Spirit of Prophecy* (Eugene, OR: Cascade Books, 2014), 62. See as well: Craig R. Koester, "The Message to Laodicea and the Problem of Its Local Context: A Study of the Imagery in Rev 3:14–22," *New Testament Studies* (2003): 407–424.

[239] Hemer, *The Letters to the Seven Churches*, 201.

[240] A. Robert Nusca, "Apocalisse e Liturgia: Alcuni Aspetti della Questione," in *Apokalypsis: Percorsi nell'Apocalisse di Giovanni in Onore di Ugo Vanni*, trans. Elena Bosetti, ed. Elena Bosetti and Angelo Colacrai (Assisi: Cittadella Editrice, 2005), 467–472 and literature cited.

[241] Beasley-Murray, *The Book of Revelation*, 107.

[242] Ibid., 108 and literature cited.

[243] Aune, *Revelation 1–5*, 262–63.

[244] DeSilva, *Seeing Things John's Way*, 102.

[245] Craig R. Koester, *Revelation and the End of All Things* (Grand Rapids: Eerdmans, 2001), 51.

[246] Cf. comments on Psalm 118 by St. Ambrose, "Exposition on the Psalms," Nn. 12. 13–14: Corpus Scriptorum Ecclesiasticorum Latinorum 62, 258–59 (author's translation).

[247] Cf. St. Jerome, "Homily on the Psalms 9," as quoted in *Ancient Christian Commentary on Scripture: New Testament XII: Revelation*, 54.

[248] Cf. James D. Gifford, *Perichoretic Salvation: The Believer's Union with Christ as a Third Type of Perichoresis* (Eugene, OR: Wipf and Stock, 2011).

[249] Harry O. Maier, *Apocalypse Recalled: The Book of Revelation After Christendom* (Minneapolis: Augsburg Fortress Press, 2002), 29.

[250] G. K. Chesterton, *St. Thomas Aquinas*, in *The Collected Works of G. K. Chesterton*, vol. 2 (San Francisco: Ignatius, 1986), 424.

[251] Ibid.

[252] Ibid.

[253] Rod Dreher, *The Benedict Option: A Strategy for Christians in a Post-Christian Nation* (New York: Sentinel, 2017).

254 DeSilva, *Seeing Things God's Way*, 70.

255 Maier, *Apocalypse Recalled*, 20–21.

256 Ibid.

257 Caesarius of Arles, Sermon 187.3, as quoted in *Revelation, Ancient Christian Commentary on Scripture, New Testament*, vol. XII, 54.

258 Maloney, *Pseudo-Macarius*, Homily 1.2, 38.

259 *Novo Millennio Ineunte*, no. 54.

260 Eric Voegelin, *The Collected Works of Eric Voegelin, Volume 17: Order and History, Volume IV, The Ecumenic Age*, ed. Michael Franz (Columbia, MO: University of Missouri Press, 2000), 200.

261 Augustine, *Enarratio in Psalmos*, 64.2, and comments by Eric Voegelin in Ibid.

262 Cf. "On the Three-day Period of the Resurrection of Our Lord Jesus Christ," in *The Easter Sermons of Gregory of Nyssa: Translation and Commentary: Proceedings of the Fourth International Colloquium on Gregory of Nyssa; Cambridge, England, 11-15 September, 1978*, trans. S. G. Hall, ed. Andreas Spira and Christoph Klock (Cambridge, MA: Philadelphia Patristic Foundation, 1981), 34–35.

263 Kevin Hart, "God and the Sublime," in *God Out of Place?: A Symposium on L. P. Hemming's "Postmodernity's Transcending, Devaluing God,"* ed. Yves de Maeseneer (Utrecht, Netherlands: Ars Disputandi, 2005), 37.

264 See comments by Alexandra Pârvan, "Beyond the Books of Augustine into Modernity," in *Augustine Beyond the Book: Intermediality, Transmediality and Reception*, ed. Karla Pollmann and Meredith J. Gill (Leiden, Netherlands: Brill, 2012), 315 and literature cited. See as well Augustine's *De vera religione* 39.72; and Edmund Husserl's *The Paris Lectures*, trans. Peter Koestenbaum (The Hague: Martinus Nijhoff, 1975), 39. Husserl has quoted Augustine in a manner that is highly selective and in no way does justice to Augustine's thought in its original context.

265 See Gregory of Nyssa, *Life of Moses*, Preface, par. 8–10, *The Classics of Western Spirituality*, ed. John Meyendorff, et al. (Mahwah, NJ: Paulist Press, 1978), 31–32, and comments by Kevin Hart, "God and the Sublime," 33–38.

266 Frederick Copleston, *Religion and Philosophy* (Dublin: Macmillan, 1974), 12: "[T]he search for a metaphysical ultimate, for one ultimate ground of finite existence is based on an experience of limits, coupled with a reaching out towards that which transcends and grounds all limits."

267 J. Walsh, SJ, ed., *The Cloud of Unknowing* (Mahwah, NJ: Paulist Press, 1981), 265.

268 Joan Mueller, ed., *Clare of Assisi: The Letters to Agnes* (Collegeville, MN: Michael Glazier, 2003), 87.

CHAPTER SIX

Christian Hope in an Era of Posts

If the "death of God" in the developed West has long been the subject of philosophical reflection and cultural debate, too little acknowledged in our time has been the corresponding decline of atheism,[1] indeed, secularism's own "crisis of faith."[2] In a postmodern era, the compelling questions and profound existential concerns reflected in the writings of the architects of modern atheism (including Nietzsche, Feuerbach, Marx, Freud, Durkheim, Comte, and Weber) find a decidedly impoverished counterpart in the writings of the four horsemen of the new atheism, whose often caricatured and tiresome arguments against religion certainly lack any of the urbane and sophisticated wit of a Bertrand Russell, for example. At least Nietzsche's Madman was in search of his lost God. In a post-enlightenment era, contemporary secular atheism is for so many people, arguably, less a conscious, deliberate ideology of choice than the default position of modern culture, one that is "as non-optional in the contemporary West as a polytheist worldview was for the ancient Greeks."[3] The phenomenon of the collapse of the transcendent in our time reflects less a deliberate abandonment of the vertical or a defection from God characteristic of atheism's golden age, than an "apatheism,"[4] a practical indifference toward God.

In fact, some who in decades past had confidently predicted the arrival of a post-religious age have begun to reconsider whether rumors of God's demise have not been greatly exaggerated and whether His "obituary notice has been prematurely posted."[5] It is already more than twenty years since Harvey Cox—the prophet of the secular city—asserted that today "it is secularity, not spirituality, that may be headed for extinction," as he and others have spoken not merely of the return of religion to cultural, philosophical, and scientific discussion and debate, but of "a religious renaissance of sorts" across the globe.[6] For instance, although still officially an atheist state, in little more than forty years following the death of Chairman Mao, the number of Christians in China is set to exceed the number of those registered in the communist party. Indeed, one expert predicts that before 2030 China is set to become the largest Christian country in the world.[7]

The broader question of whether (and in what respects) secularism may be in the process of undergoing a cultural shift in the direction of a post-secular era is a topic for lively discussion and debate. Rabbi James Diamond leads us to consider the broader context for this turning of the cultural tides when he observes that we live in an age of "posts" (postmodern, post-colonial, post-Christian, and, more recently, post-truth), with the dominant sensibility in our time being that of "coming after."[8] Admittedly, the expression "post-secular" is itself in need of considerable clarification. Like the terms "postmodern" and "secular," "post-secular" admits of no comprehensive, categorical definition. Moreover, the notion that one can trace an

unambiguous line of development from the pre-secular
through a secular to a post-secular era is not without its
own difficulties.[9] In any event, what is clear is that an intelligent and constructive dialogue concerning our secular
age certainly invites greater nuance with regard to the
language employed in the discussion, as many have recognized the need to move beyond the strictures of an either/
or approach.[10]

Although there has been a trend in the developed
West—particularly since the 1960s—toward an increased
secularity (allowing for differences between Europe and
North America), many have never subscribed to secularism's practical atheism, its moral and ethical relativism,
nor to any social imperative that would exclude the voice
of religion from the public square. One is led to ask what
the term "post-secular" would mean for the many faithful adherents of Christianity or Judaism, or the followers
of Islam, or for many other individuals who live in the
secular world without ever having identified with and/
or subscribed to secularist ideology and beliefs. Moreover, does the expression "post-secular" really apply to the
many for whom secularism is much less an ideology of
choice than that immanentist "default option" from which
many people today experience the world?[11] Whether the
"twilight of atheism"[12] is now upon us and a renaissance of
religion and spirituality is dawning, the sun will no doubt
continue to rise on both believer and non-believer alike
(Mt 5:45).[13] Is the term "post-secular," then, a manner of
giving expression to the perception that religion appears to
be returning to prominence and becoming "de-privatized"
politically, socially, and/or culturally?[14] Does the post-secular signal the advent of an important cultural moment of

greater dialogue, as a secular culture in search of renewal looks to the great religious and spiritual traditions that have shaped the West as wellsprings of reflection?[15]

Whether and to what degree one may speak of ours as a post-secular age, the premise that the world, as it became more secularized, would as a matter of course become progressively less religious appears to be in need of re-appraisal. Moreover, it can be argued that the secularist ideology that is so prominent in our time clearly goes beyond "affirming the virtues of the ostensibly neutral," for the line of "demarcation between religion and the secular is made, not just found."[16] Indeed, contemporary sociologists challenge the prevailing wisdom (too often unquestioned by the mass media and cultural elites) that the steady progress of secularization leads to an inevitable decline of religious belief and practice. Marx and Freud together with the postmodernists appear to have seriously underestimated both the perennial need to address the ultimate questions of human life, as well as the manifest resilience, indeed, "staying power," of the major religions.[17] At the very least, the architects of modern/postmodern atheism appear to have undervalued what Viktor Frankl refers to as the human spirit's "will to meaning," as believer and non-believer alike continue to struggle with the great questions of human life and existence, of suffering and death, as well as with the question of how best to create communities and social spaces in which people with divergent views can live together in peace and harmony.[18] Even if God were dead, one contemporary philosopher comments that "the urgent issues which impelled us to make him up still stir and demand resolutions which do not go away when we have been nudged to perceive some scientific inaccuracies in the tale of the seven loaves and fishes."[19] Again, whether or not the heart is in search of God in a rationalist, post-religious era that is wont to speak of the "varieties of secularism,"[20] the human heart is—by nature—ever in search of itself on life's journey toward self-knowledge, self-discovery, and meaning. Genuine human maturity is not achieved "by outgrowing mystery, but by entering ever deeper into the mystery."[21]

John's visions set before the readers of every age an open door that leads ever deeper into the mystery, providing thereby an upward-, forward-, and inward-looking, divine, transcendent perspective whose sacred light has the power to inspire, to illuminate, and to inform the search for meaning in dialogue with that living Mystery (and "Eternal Thou") which initiates the dialogue and awaits our reply (Rev 3:20).[22] From among the varieties of secularism, there is none that lives in dialogue with the Transcendent Other who continues to create, bless, and consecrate (i.e., to set apart for God) while calling forth a rendering back of all that has been given. He does this along a trajectory of life and growth which extends and expands the horizons of the finite self toward the borderline of the infinite, and beyond ("Thy Will be done" [Mt 6:10]).

The Seer's Tale of Two Cities in a Secular Age

The Book of Revelation's tale of two cities, two thrones, two kings, queens, princes, and empires offers a coherent and compelling vision in a postmodern era. Admittedly, where God is dead the New Jerusalem finds neither a heaven from which to descend nor a ready heart into which it might first enter and take shape, to paraphrase Bonaventure. Over the centuries, visions of the open heaven in the writings of prophets and apocalyptic seers have certainly played an important role in sustaining the religious imagination and renewing the hope of the faithful in times of crisis.[23] But the postmodern Narcissus of the contemporary secularist era is left to contemplate the deformed image of the human person as reflected across the surface of the stagnant waters of a system of life which has renounced the divine image and is completely absorbed with itself. The question of Nietzsche's Madman—"Who gave us the sponge to wipe away the entire horizon?"—continues to echo and resonate in our postmodern era.[24] A post-Enlightenment humanity that has abandoned its lofty standing as a "frontier being"[25] situated between the Creator God and the animals, spirit and matter, time and eternity, has made itself absolutely self-reliant, but has lost something vital in the process. Karl Löwith evokes the image of the tightrope walker in the prologue to Nietzsche's *Thus Spoke Zarathustra* and speaks of humanity as having placed itself "upon a rope stretched over the abyss of nothingness, extended into emptiness," with "danger" becoming its vocation and destiny.[26] Whether one considers the biblical world's transcendent axis of life and vision to have been usurped by the human ego in a Promethean act of will to power or eclipsed by a post-enlightenment rationalist skepticism that dismisses it as a vestige of a bygone era of magic, myth, and superstition; or whether it has been quietly absorbed into the shifting sands of a postmodern world view that is simply incapable of offering it a more stable support, the Seer's open door and upward looking horizon confront the contemporary reader with a perspective that is indeed world-moving.

The Seer's Critique of the Seven Churches

At the same time, although Revelation offers a striking critique of the Roman Empire—its gods and cults of worship, its altars and economies of sacrifice—it is important to appreciate the way in which John, as we have already seen, effects a powerful, prophetic critique of the seven Churches of his time. The comments of the angelic Christ to the faithful in Revelation 2 and 3 confirm that the portrait of the Churches developed by the Seer is far from an idealized one. Once again, these communities represent an admixture of saints and sinners, of faithful witness and lukewarm adherence to the Gospel, of those who reject the values of empire and strive to live as a royal and priestly people, and of those who appear to be having difficulty (or perhaps no intention) of doing so. Again, the Seer's critique resonates with Augustine's in its realism. Both recognize that the Church is, again, essentially an admixture of positive and negative elements, of good and evil, of weeds and wheat, in a world in which the City of God (*civitas Dei*) and the earthly city (*civitas terrena*) intermingle. Augustine's observations serve as a solemn reminder to the faithful in every generation that the Church must strive for constant renewal and purification.

In their different—although complementary—ways of conceptualizing and speaking of the New City, both John and Augustine remind us of the truth concerning the Church's makeup and composition during the time of its journey between two worlds, the time in between the comings of Christ. The Christ who entered into history at the moment of the Incarnation and continues to be present in the post-Resurrection era in mystery, will return again at the end of time in glory. So it is that John calls us to recognize that it is by standing with Christ in the power of the Holy Spirit (the Advocate and Consoler) that one is properly equipped for the struggle to discern (and to choose between) these incompatible, opposing, intermingled elements—whether within the seven Churches, or within a human heart that (as St. Paul tells us) is engaged in a constant struggle between the grace that is within us, and that other power at work that endeavors to hinder us from carrying out the good (Rom 7:14–25). While the human heart may desire the good, too often it fails to choose and to act upon that good when put to the test (Lk 22:56–62). For as *corpus permixtum* the Church always lives in the same "precarious present as the human soul," it is "a mixture of otherworldly yearning (*caritas*) and carnal misdirection (*cupiditas*)."[27] Indeed, the heart is the place where "the boundaries meet and all contradictions exist side by side," as Dostoevsky observes.[28]

Philosophers and social critics are quick to enumerate the many—and at times terrible—failings of Christians throughout the centuries: from the inquisitions to anti-Semitism, to contemporary scandals. At the same time as the Church's critics perceive with such keen insight the shortcomings of Christians past and present, secularist culture appears unwilling to confront its own shadow self. Today's secularist *imperium* is not without its own dark side, as reflected clearly in its own conflicted, self-deceptive "Janus face."[29] The culture of death has evolved into what Pope Benedict XVI repeatedly referred to as a "dictatorship of relativism" whose soft totalitarian impulse is increasingly evident in its willingness to override both freedom of conscience and freedom of speech (with regard to such issues as abortion and euthanasia, now "medical assistance in dying"), despite its own ardent claims to be committed to the liberal values of freedom, openness, tolerance, and inclusion. Ultimately, the "ideal essence of religion" remains far beyond the reach of secularist atheism's critique of it (just as the depth of its mystery lies beyond institutional religion's own capacity to comprehend it entirely and to articulate it fully, as others have observed).[30]

The Seven Churches and the Rising Dawn

Again, the tensions between the light and darkness which are inherent in the Church's (indeed in the soul's) journey through this passing world lead St. Gregory the Great to compare the Church to the daybreak or advancing dawn. Gregory suggests that when St. Paul states that *"the night is nearly ended,"* he does not add that "the *day has come,"* but rather, that *"the day draws near"* (Rom 13:12, emphasis added).[31] While the light of the rising dawn dispels the darkness, the two remain intermingled, and indeed, "are contending one against the other."[32] Likewise, the Morning Star that sparkles on both the inner and outer— the spiritual and temporal horizons of a community of faith on its journey between two worlds—always appears at its brightest before the dawn, when the light and darkness remain intermingled in the already and not yet that characterize the Christian experience of time in this passing world. So it is that the Seer challenges the faithful in every generation to choose wisely, to exercise vigilance in their efforts to remain in the light, to strive unceasingly to discern the spiritual forces at work within, and to listen

to "what the Spirit is saying to the Churches." The Apocalypse issues the call to a spirit of vigilance, of watchfulness
and wakefulness (3:2, 3; Mt 24:42; 1 Thess 5:6) so as not to
be confounded by the spirit or spirits of the age.

Ultimately, the mirror into which we gaze (1 Cor
13:12) reflects back to us deformed and misshapen images
of the human person created in God's own image and likeness. That this spiritual dynamic is at work in the empires
of every age should never lead us to overlook that other
law or power at work in all of us, as Paul reminds us in
Romans 7:14–25. The Seer's Faces of Christ and the
promise of the deified, victorious witness offer the readers
a renewed perspective and help them to fix their gaze upon
the mystery of divine grace at work in the brokenness of
God's own image wherever it may be encountered in this
passing world of shadows: within ourselves, in the seven
Churches, in the sparkling images of a New Jerusalem
that has dawned upon the "already" of faith's ultimate
horizon, as well as in the "not yet" (or the "not at all") of
a world that includes so many cities of endless desire built
upon the shifting sands of subjectivism and relativism. For
as the commentators have long observed, the faithful are
encouraged not to despair despite the fact that the power
of earthly empire is great, that the image of the heavenly
city remains indistinct and remote, or that dark images of
a deformed and distorted humanity are reflected back to us
through the mirror of the book's story world. John's visions
through an open door into heaven encourage the faithful
to be joyful and to take hope, while challenging them not
only to witness to the Gospel in the light of the dawn that
is at hand (Rom 13:12), but to enter even now into the
process of *becoming* the light of the rising dawn in this world

of shadows, through lives of courageous witness. Again, this rising dawn is an ongoing process, as St. Gregory the Great reminds us in his *Moral Reflections on Job*:

> But the Church of the Elect will then be fully day, when the shade of sin will be no longer blended with it. It will then be fully day, when it has been brightened with the perfect warmth of the inward light. It will be then fully day, when tolerating no longer the seducing remembrance of its sins, it will conceal from itself even all the remains of darkness. . . . For what is the place of dawn but the perfect brightness of the eternal vision?[33]

Through the Glass of Contemporary Culture, Darkly

How then, can we speak to others of the Book of Revelation's "Eternal Gospel" (14:6) in a post-Christian era, when talk of God has too often come to be excluded from the public square of an empire whose ideology of openness and inclusiveness is experienced by so many as a dictatorship of relativism? When we enter the postmodern city square to address an intelligent if skeptical audience (Acts 17:18), how shall we begin to say something new (Acts 17:21) to so many for whom the God of Jesus Christ is not simply unknown, but is widely considered to be dead, indeed, whose murder was proclaimed by Nietzsche's Madman so long ago? How shall John's story be told in the city square of the postmodern era when the God of the Apocalypse has disappeared from sight and has been eclipsed in the West? How shall we begin to communicate to a postmodern Areopagus that the God of the Apocalypse is not the caricatured, murdered god of the philosophers (and psychoanalysts), but rather that voice which emerges from a "consuming fire" (Heb 12:29; Deut 4:24)[34] and which "may properly only be addressed and not expressed"?[35]

Moreover, how shall we begin the work of the New Evangelization in an era marked by scandals in the Church, when too often the faithful are offered little more than the "cheap grace"[36] of a deformed and misshapen Gospel that is scarcely distinguishable from the philosophy of the age,[37] when so many have abandoned their faith in God and with it the accompanying vision of the human person created in God's image and likeness, and when so many regard the Christian Churches to be the "tombs and sepulchers of God" of which Nietzsche wrote so long ago?[38] As the Madman observed so far ahead of his time, "lightning . . . thunder . . . [and] . . . the light of the stars," like the death of God, require time to make themselves known.[39] Parenthetically, in 1871—several years before Nietzsche published *The Gay Science* (which features the Madman's speech)—Dostoevsky warned that it was not God, but rather *the West* that was in the process of dying.[40] Western Christendom's own role in the death of God, the loss of Christ, and the rise of the secularization that it opposes remains a valid question.

The Eclipse of God

One psychologist speaks of contemporary society as having "lost the longitudes and latitudes of the soul."[41] Others speak of the sense of relativism and moral drift that mark the spirit of the age. In the words of Philip Blond, ours is a time of "failed conditions."[42] The secularized West, as many have observed, is a world with no moral compass.

The dawn of the Enlightenment, the death of God, and the rise to prominence of the immanent in its wake have left a profound void. As Blond suggests: "Reality is real, but if configured only within the secular or pagan rubric it is reality at its lowest power."[43] Ours is a world in which God has been "sidelined."[44] Pope Benedict XVI speaks (as did his predecessor, St. John Paul II) of the "eclipse of God"[45] in our time, echoing the words of Martin Buber: "Eclipse of the light of heaven, eclipse of God—such indeed is the character of the historic hour through which the world is now passing."[46] What are these sidelines of which Benedict speaks, and behind what clouds shall we search for God during this time of His eclipse? A number of possibilities figure in the discussion.

The Death of God and the Deification of the Self

According to C. G. Jung, when the gods left Mount Olympus they took up their abode in "the solar plexus."[47] Elsewhere he observes that "when Westerners fell off the roof of the medieval cathedral . . . they fell into the abyss of the Self."[48] Jung's statements concerning the disappearance of the gods into the abyss of the self are useful for trying to begin to conceptualize and to trace the intellectual and cultural roots of the broader phenomenon of an eclipse of God in our time, even if more could be said with regard to the role of human free will in the process. To speak of the "renunciation of vertical" (or other-worldly) transcendence[49] has the merit of recognizing the more deliberate, rebellious, indeed, Promethean dimension of the death of God, and the concomitant birth of the superman who stands in God's stead. For the death of God involves an act of free will, indeed, an abandonment or "defection from that which supremely is, to that which has less of being," as Augustine observes.[50] Here is a choice that, some would argue, sees not only the death of God, but the deification of the self as its final result (an act that is not devoid of far-reaching political and social consequences, as history has shown). Indeed, "the deicide of the gnostic theoreticians is followed by the homicide of the revolutionary practitioners ," as Eric Voegelin observes.[51] Ultimately, the death of God and the deification of the self are related.

What has been lost as a result? As many have pointed out, with the eclipse of God, the human person created in God's own image and likeness (Gen 1:26–27) comes in the process to abandon its ground of being and deepest identity, for "creation without the Creator fades into nothingness" (i.e., *Creatura enim sine Creatore evanescit*).[52] According to an earlier generation of scholars, the consequences are enormous. Karl Löwith suggests that "Happiness, reason, virtue, justice, civilization, compassion—the whole essence of traditional humanity is no longer relevant for Nietzsche's redefinition of man's destiny."[53] Eric Voegelin observes that "the new creature who committed the murder of God does not recognize its own death in what happened,"[54] while Nikolai Berdyaev's more terse and apophthegmatic phrase, "where there is no God, there is no man either,"[55] serves to accentuate further the eclipse of humanity which is the ultimate result of the death of God. However, if one were to attempt to delineate secular humanism's own salvation history, it might be better argued that this reversal of the vision of the Judeo-Christian understanding of the human person has its roots not in the Enlightenment but in the Garden of Eden (Gen 3:5). There is merit in the claim that "Humanism is not new. It is, in fact, man's second oldest faith. Its promise was whispered in the first days of Creation under the Tree of the knowledge of Good and Evil: 'Ye shall be as gods.'"[56] The living, personal God who addresses Moses from the midst of the fire on Mount Sinai (Ex 3:4) came to be absorbed into the abyss of a rebellious, Promethean, narcissistic, Gnostic self, whose ultimate goal is no longer eternal salvation in God, but self-realization.[57] Admittedly, one could argue that Gnosticism rather than atheism is the "real antagonist of the reality of faith"[58] in our time. Nevertheless, whether or not the former is ultimately more inimical to the faith than the latter, each represents, in its own distinctive way, an echo across the abyss created by God's eclipse.

The Book of Revelation's story world as mirror prompts a contemporary audience to contemplate images of cosmic destruction and of a renewed creation. At the same time, the book's rhetoric simultaneously sets before the postmodern seven Churches images of a humanity that is being angelified and even deified through its struggles to share in the victory of Christ and images of a humanity at its "lowest power"[59]—image without archetype, stream without source, a humanity that has renounced its transcendent origins (and divinely inspired purpose, or "telos"), and whose mystical oneness with creation has come to be unburdened by any sense of moral responsibility toward the Creator God. Ours is an era in which the Gospel's logic of reversal has itself been reversed. Or in the words of Hegel: "I have made my guiding-star the Biblical saying, the truth of which I have learnt by experience—'Seek ye first food and clothing and the kingdom of heaven shall be added unto you.'"[60] Dante's exalted vision of hope in God's promise of eternal salvation stands in stark contrast to this, while Jesus' golden rule, "Love God and your neighbor as yourself" (Mt 22:37–39) has too often been reduced to mere altruism. Or in the words of Eric Voegelin, altruism is the "secular-immanent substitute" for "love," which is associated with Christianity: altruism is the "basis of the conception of a brotherhood of man without a father."[61] Augustine's extended reflections on the spiritual struggle to build the *City of God* (itself inspired by the Book of Revelation) finds its antithesis in the effects of our contemporary secularist *imperium* to create a city of endless desire. The book has something to say to a society that highly esteems the value of choice, namely, that other, less obvious (indeed eclipsed) possibilities are not lacking in a postmodern humanity that is still very much in search of itself.

The Throne of Empire in the Era of the New Evangelization

Contemporary social democracy appears in so many respects to be at variance with the liberal democracy that is rooted in the British empirical philosophical tradition of Jeremy Bentham, John Locke, and John Stuart Mill. In its twenty-first century neo-Marxist, neo-Weberian, socialist, New Left iteration, democratic institutions can too easily acquire a totalitarian bent, as courts of law appear to be increasingly less reluctant to encroach upon the right to freedom of religion and conscience. Human rights commissions and tribunals increasingly suppress the free speech of Christians, while the secular state boldly redefines (and deforms) social institutions—including marriage and the family—that have provided the stable foundation for every *civilized* society throughout history (and prior to it). Critics argue that the secularist ideology of identity politics, with its understanding of rights, openness, and inclusion, are experienced too often by the faithful of today's seven Churches as expressions of the dictatorship of relativism. Admittedly, the soft dictatorship of the contemporary secularist *imperium* is more indebted to the cultural Marxism of Antonio Gramsci, Theodor Adorno, Max Horkheimer, and Herbert Marcuse, and to the ideas of the American cultural revolution of the 1960s and 1970s, than to the traditional economic Marxism-Leninism of the communist era. But, as many have observed, while the Berlin Wall may have fallen, the cultural Marxism inherent in such ideologies as political correctness and multiculturalism has successfully completed its "long march" through the institutions[62] of the West, "working against the established institutions while working in them," in the words of Herbert Marcuse.[63] And while Marx understood religion to be the opium of the people, so much has changed since the nineteenth century. In our own time, opium has become the opium of the people (even, as some have argued, that cultural Marxism has become the opiate of choice for enlightened intellectuals).[64]

Many of today's educated elites who are a driving force in our postmodern Mars Hill (Acts 17:18–34)—particularly within the media, the universities, and the courts—appear unable (or unwilling) to recognize society's profound indebtedness to the legacy of Judeo-Christian ethics and to the ideals and values born from it. The dignity of the human person (created in God's image and likeness) and "spirit, reason, liberty, truth, brotherhood, justice . . . quickly become unreal when no longer seen as a radiation from

God."[65] Disconnected from their transcendent source and origin, these ideals lose their "full strength" and "authentic integrity"[66] and, indeed, have come to be appropriated by the contemporary secularist empire in the service of its lexicon of anti-Christian rhetoric.[67] Admittedly, the ideas and principles that inspired the Enlightenment in the eighteenth century and played an important role in the rise of modernity are not at all devoid of their own nobility. Indeed, their emphasis upon reason, empiricism, and scientific rationalism led to the birth of the pure and applied sciences, political science, and economics, resulting in great advances during the centuries that followed. However, as de Lubac observes, without God even truth and justice are always idols, albeit "idols too pure and pale"[68] when compared with the magnificent bronze statues and marble altars consecrated to the worship of the gods and emperors of late first-century Greece and Rome. When viewed across the surface of the mirror of the Seer's symbolic universe, the exclusivist humanism of a secularist empire that lacks a transcendent axis too easily becomes inhuman, for "exclusive humanism is inhuman humanism."[69] Moreover, when politics is no longer guided by a vision of the transcendent God, it can come to function as a kind of "secular religion" which "operates under the illusion of creating a paradise in this world."[70] So it is that John's text, as mirror, can help the faithful today to discern not only something of the dynamics at work in the phenomenon of a self-deifying humanity, but the analogous dynamics at work in the politics of a self-deifying state. It has been argued that the choice in our time is not between the religious and the secular, between Church and State, "religion and no religion," but involves a choice "between true religion and false religion."[71] Some have spoken in this regard about "atheist theocracy."[72] Jacques Maritain uses the expression "theocratic atheism," while more recently others have spoken of "secular fundamentalism."[73] At the very least, the world of the biblical story helps one to perceive more acutely the ways in which the contemporary secular humanist imperium is not free of its own agendas, fundamental presuppositions, ideologies, and dogmatic absolutes.

Revelation's Political Theology and the Messianisms of the Age

John's prophetic message reveals to its audience "the beast behind the beauty of Greco-Roman culture," even as the Churches of Asia Minor discern their own deficiencies.[74] The visions are spiritual, but at the same time quite political, as they parody and invert the power symbolisms of the Roman Empire. How can Revelation's political theology help the modern-day Churches to discern more clearly the beasts behind the beauty of the contemporary secularist imperium, to live out their own prophetic call to unmask the powers behind the thrones, to be able to name the gods adored in their pantheon, and so to begin to understand more fully the nature and cost of the sacrifices that are being demanded upon postmodernity's altars? At the very least, the story world of the Apocalypse has the power to remind us of the nature of our Christian hope, a Jewish-Christian, apocalyptic hope in God's unilateral power to renew a faltering world, as the Seer's visions of a new heaven and new earth serve to illustrate. The audience is reminded that the glory of the human person created in the image and likeness of God consists in the fact that we are "born from above" (Jn 3:3), indeed, from the "highest actuality and it is this and our participation in it that alone allows human beings to transfigure themselves and their world."[75]

The prophet calls us to recognize and to reject not only the devolved and deformed symbolisms of an immanentist world empire, but the displaced messianic aspirations of humanity at its "lowest power." The book's story world serves as a mirror in which the seven Churches of the twenty-first century may distinguish their own hope in Christ their Messiah (King of kings, Lord of lords) and the approaching Kingdom of God from hope in a globalist messianism that would create a utopian paradise on earth; from secular-humanist messianic efforts to construct a Promethean, immanentist city of endless desire; and finally, from a scientific messianism that would place its hope in the specters of the trans-human and the post-human in the era of bio-engineering at the dawn of the fourth industrial revolution.[76] Finally, the biblical story world reveals the ways in which contemporary nationalist movements may be seen to be "copies of religious movements" and their longings for liberation as "secular reprints of longings for redemption."[77] So too, it challenges us to consider the ways in which contemporary neo-Marxist, materialist accounts of history are ultimately "guided by theological narratives of salvation."[78] Erasmus attributed to the Spartans the expression "whether called or not called, God is present."[79] The deep wellsprings of Judeo-Christian reflection concerning what is human have much substance to offer contemporary secularist culture. What remains to be seen is whether in an era of failed conditions, the architects of postmodern culture will turn to "draw sustenance now as in the past"[80] from the boundless depths of these lines of reflection—both "ever ancient and ever new," in the words of Augustine. Hopeful signs of intelligent dialogue are not lacking.[81]

The Search for Meaning

Even in a world in which God has been eclipsed, "the sacred cannot *by-pass the material world.*"[82] A secularist humanity that is no longer in search of God is still actively in search of itself, as it struggles with the basic questions that are a part of the perennial search for meaning: "Who am I? Where have I come from and where am I going? Why is there evil? What is there after this life?"[83] To the great questions of life and meaning, postmodern reflection appears incapable of offering answers of any depth and substance. The human heart—by its nature—strives to find meaning. Indeed, the human heart is "restless until it rests in" God (*Confessions,* I.1). Although written in the fourth century, Augustine's observation addresses the restlessness and longing which are characteristic of every age. The human heart is indeed wired for God, as the idea has come to be expressed in our digital (indeed, wireless) age. The Seer's exhortation to render worship to God (19:10; 22:9)—and God alone—guides the book's rhetorical strategy and reflects a larger, ongoing polemic against every form of immorality, idolatry, apostasy, and false prophecy, whether religious or secularist. For John, nothing else is capable of filling the vast expanse of a human heart that has been created to know, love, and worship God (and to do so standing alongside the angels). Christian tradition throughout the centuries attests to the basic truth that the human heart, in the words of St. Maximilian Kolbe, "is too big to be filled with money, sensuality, or the deceptive but intoxicating smoke of fame," for the heart "desires a higher good, without bounds and lasting eternally. Only God is such a good."[84] Indeed, the human heart is too big to find lasting fulfillment in any other manifestation of "the derangement of loves,"[85] with its love of self and contempt for God that constitutes the earthly city's founding principle and the motor of its history (as Augustine argues so compellingly in the *City of God*).

The ultimate choice set before the audience in the book's narrative world is between true worship and false worship, between God and idols. For humanity "always has God or an idol," as Martin Luther once observed.[86] For John it is axiomatic that one's everlasting destiny is inextricably linked with the object of one's worship in the present life. Notwithstanding the epic, cosmic magnitude of the canvas upon which John paints his masterpiece, the audience must never lose sight of the fact that, ultimately, the human heart remains the final battlefield wherein the heavenly armies of God and the forces of evil engage in mortal combat over the everlasting destiny of souls (12:7–12; Eph 6:11).[87] The Book of Revelation reminds the faithful that God is very near to them in their struggles in the here and now.

An Apocalyptic Archimedean Point in a Postmodern Era

Kierkegaard inspires us to ask: "Where in the vulgar sphere of reasoning am I to find a foothold" in a postmodern age?[88] Is the Book of Revelation capable of offering to a postmodern world such an Archimedean point? Rooted in the world of Jewish apocalyptic vision rather than Greek philosophical reflection (and certainly not German Idealism), John's visions are not the final result of a process of intellectual enquiry, but have been received "in the Spirit" (1:10; 4:2; 17:3; 21:10). So it is that he explains spiritual realities not in the language of human wisdom, but in words taught by the Spirit, to paraphrase St. Paul (cf. 1 Cor 2:13). Again, with the aim of moving the audience's world in the direction of God's everlasting Kingdom (cf. 2:5), John invites the seven Churches to begin to look for themselves in the mirror of the book's unfolding story and Sacred Scripture's overarching meta-narrative, and so to find a place to stand among the expanding circles of angels and transfigured victors before the throne of God and of the Lamb (Rev 7:9, 11; cf. 2 Chron 29:11; Ps 24:3).

While postmodern atheism tends to avoid the more acerbic tones characteristic of the classic "God is dead" atheism of Nietzsche, Marx, and Freud, it draws from the same streams of reflection and is ultimately no less inimical to faith. The postmodern world is post-God, post-Christian, post-religion, post-truth, and post-virtue. Deconstructionist faith is faith without hope, hope against hope, as John D. Caputo suggests: "For we do not know who we are, and we have no such determinate Archimedean point, for the name of God is endlessly substitutable."[89] The deconstructionist speaks of God without God, of faith without faith, religion without religion, of "apocalypse without apocalypse."[90] If postmodernism offers a place to stand, it remains a place without place. The radical subjectivism, pluralism, and anti-metaphysical stance that figure among the marks of postmodernist thought combine with an inherent inconsistency, one that risks creating a "new kind of cultural apocalypse."[91] Here is a contemporary breed of "monster that swallows every earlier expression of cultural patrimony, thumbing its nose at reason and readying itself for the final sublime ecstasy of devouring itself."[92]

The throne-centered universe onto which John's visions open beyond the door to heaven challenges a postmodern audience with the message that the ultimate meaning of our human existence awaits discovery in conversation with the Eternal. The transcendent perspective into which the audience is invited can still serve today to situate, inform, and shape the search for meaning along the everyday world's horizontal axis of time and space, in the here and now. St. John Paul II reminds us of our great need for the transcendent.[93] John's apocalyptic door to heaven is opened through the power of the Spirit and the eyes of faith, not through a process of abstract reasoning, and it waits to be discovered in conversation with the fire of the divine (Ex 3:4), that encounter with the sacred by which "the human substance is melted by the spiritual fire which visits it."[94] At the same time, discernment is always necessary, as each of us must determine for ourselves whether it is our own voice and inner processes that are echoing back from the abyss, or whether it is the Transcendent Other who replies. For "the abyss of God calls to the abyss" as John Ruusbroec reminds us.[95] God calls and never ceases to call.

The Book of Revelation is capable of offering now— just as in first century Rome—a renewed perspective, indeed, a place to stand in an "expanded world."[96] This place to stand is ultimately a place in the presence of the living God and His multi-dimensional Christ (Rev 4–5) in whom (and through whom) the axes of divine transcendence and human immanence meet, as past, eternal present, and future coalesce in the oscillating Faces of Christ. The light shining through the open door to heaven challenges the audience to live courageously a life of faithful witness to the Gospel in a dangerous time so as to be able to purchase the "gold tried by fire" (Rev 3:18) in the form of the Christ-like fourth Face promised to the victors.

Mircea Eliade reminds us that "if Abraham's faith can be defined as 'for God everything is possible,' the faith of Christianity implies that everything is also possible for man."[97] What Christ does by *nature,* His followers—the asterified, shining righteous (Dan 12:3; Zech 9:16)—are called to do by *participation.* In this way they continue the mystery of the Incarnation in every age. Today there is a greater need than ever "to rediscover the dimensions of the heart,"[98]—that interior, spiritual dimension of our lives where we encounter the living God. Thus the Book of Revelation challenges its postmodern audience to shift their coordinates beyond the fruit of reason that grows on the tree of knowledge (without ever diminishing its importance in any way), to that fullness of human life and experience which blossoms in our encounter with the divine at the tree of life (Rev 2:7; 22:2, 14, 19; Jn 19:26–27).

A Prophetic People Proclaims the Twilight of the Idols

Whether one understands the term "post-secular era" to signify the de-privatization of religion and a more prominent role for religion in the public square, or an increasing indifference toward the ideas of the sacred and the transcendent, or the arrival of a cosmic-humanist secular spirituality which is divorced from religion, or finally, the dawn of a renaissance of religion and spirituality, the Book of Revelation calls the seven Churches living in a post-secular world to integrity of life in its proclamation of the Gospel both in season and out of season (3:8). John issues a clarion call to the faithful—in this era of the New Evangelization—to hear "what the Spirit is saying to the churches" and to discern the spirits of the age, so as to be able to proclaim the twilight of the idols to both a post-secular world (2:10) and a lukewarm faithful drawn to its allure (3:15).

The seven Churches are called to proclaim the redeeming power of God's love, whether by rejecting the merging of politics and religion, the use of religiously motivated violence in any form, or the idols of religious extremism, fanaticism, and fundamentalism (1:5). They must give witness to the reversal of human power signified in the apocalyptic Lion/Lamb whose victory has been won through the self-emptying powerlessness of the Cross (5:6, 9). A prophetic people (11:18) must announce bravely the twilight of the idol of a lukewarm Gospel accommodated to the values of the world (3:15). The Church must "continuously purify its own perception of truth by the vision of the utterly Holy One, the Sovereign Creator, who shares His throne with the slaughtered Lamb."[99] It must give credible, authentic witness to the Eternal Gospel (14:6) by its integrity of life (3:4; 19:8), by speaking the truth of the Gospel courageously and with love (Eph 4:15), and by witnessing to the virtues of faith, hope, and charity, as expressed concretely in love for the poor, the marginalized and suffering, and all who live in what Pope Francis refers to as "the peripheries" of our world.

A priestly people (Rev 1:6; 5:10; 20:6) declares the twilight of the idols: of a humanity at its lowest power; of the
idol of the autonomous self and its radical freedom that
acts apart from the source of all life (3:14); of morality
and ethics divorced from revealed truth and the ground
of being; of reason divorced from faith. The faithful are
called to proclaim the twilight of the idol of a dictatorship
of relativism that would constrain the legitimate expression of religious belief as it seeks to compel the voice of
conscience—that inner tribunal in which the soul con-
verses with God. A people transformed by the fire of the
Spirit (3:18) boldly proclaims the twilight of the idol of an
aggressive secularist ideology that presents itself as "the
true voice of reason when, in fact, it is only the expression of a certain type of rationalism,"[100] and of the idol
of any choice that would take a human life in the process
(12:4–5). Finally, the unbridled growth of materialism
and consumerism presage the wholesale reduction of the
human person (including human organs), human labor,
relationships, knowledge, education, natural resources,
along with culture and the arts into commodities governed
by and subject to the logic and rules of free trade and
the marketplace. In the era of global capitalism, John's
visions serve as an ominous warning to Babylon's merchants—"the magnates of the earth" (18:23)—that among
the many goods that constitute their precious cargo, some
things must never be reduced to mere exchange, "com-
modified," or offered for sale (18:13).[101]

Contrary to these contemporary idols, the seven
Churches are called to proclaim the liberating power of
God's Holy Spirit and a generous, self-sacrificing love
as the road to authentic selfhood and transformation

(2:28; 3:18). Or, as St. Paul proclaims in 2 Corinthians
3:17: "Where the Spirit of the Lord is, there is freedom."
True freedom—human freedom in its fullness—is both
a freedom *from* the powers of sin and death, just as it is
freedom *for* life in the Spirit. In the face of a world that
lives as though God did not exist, a people whose eyes
remain fixed upon God—and who have a genuine appreciation of the greatness of the human person created in
God's image and likeness—is called, above all, to strive "to
make God credible"[102] through lives of patient endurance
and faithful witness to the Gospel and its values of faith,
hope, and charity (2:3, 19; 3:10). For ours is a God who is
not only present in our human struggles, but struggles with
us, indeed *within us* (cf. Gal 2:20). Again, as St. Cyprian
reminds the aspiring victor, Christ not only crowns but is
crowned in the conflict of our struggles.[103]

Spiritual Struggle in the Apocalypse:
To Be Transformed by Either Fire or Fire

Revelation's black-and-white, either/or rhetoric represents
an imposing challenge to the modern reader. Its clash of
images and its often violent language (cf. 2:16, 23) represent an even greater challenge to the commentator, even if
subtlety, nuance, and gradations of meaning are not lacking
(as we saw earlier, in chapter 4 for example, with regard to
the book's portrait of Christ as Lion, conqueror, messianic
ruler, and as Lamb, child, and the angelic "one like a Son
of Man"). Again, the narrative is guided by an urgent—
indeed apocalyptic—logic and rhetoric that call the reader
to choose: God or Satan, Christ or Antichrist, Heaven or
Hell, the New Jerusalem or Babylon in smoking ruins.

John's art of persuasion involves the filtering out of most shades of grey, as he tells his tale of two cities and of the invisible, spiritual struggle that rages between the armies of angels and the forces of darkness (12:7). In a manner reminiscent of the choice set before the people of Israel in Deuteronomy 30 and in the early Christian treatise *The Teaching of the Twelve Apostles* (or Didache), John calls the Churches of Asia Minor to choose between the two ways: of "life and death," of "blessing and curses" (Deut 30:11–20; cf. Didache 1:1); the ways of light and darkness (cf. The Epistle of Barnabas 18–20). They are exhorted to worship God and God alone (19:10; 22:9), to choose sides in the struggle between good and evil, and so to seek entrance into the new creation as the old order rapidly fades. At the same time, the audience is placed between two fires and is called to choose between the angelic Christ's offer to become "gold refined by fire" (3:18) or to face being cast into the "burning lake of fire'" (20:14–15).

The Image of Fire in the Bible

Scholars refer to the "ambiguous character" of fire in the writings of the Old Testament where it is associated with the glory of God, His "actions and presence," and "functions as an instrument of purification, ordeal, destruction, or punishment."[104] It is from the fire that the voice of God addresses Moses (Ex 3:2; Deut 4:12, 36; 5:4; cf. Jer 23:29).[105] God is a consuming fire (Ex 24:17; Deut 4:24; 9:3; Heb 12:29) who leads His people through the wilderness under the appearance of a pillar of cloud and fire (Ex 13:21; Neh 9:19). It is from the fire that the golden calf emerges (Ex 32:24), just as it is into the fire that the idols are thrown in order to be destroyed (Deut 7:5; 2 Kings 19:18; Is 37:19). The sacred fire of the altar of sacrifice is not to be confused with "strange fire" derived from elsewhere (Lev 10:1–2; Num 3:4). God is a wall of fire around Jerusalem and the glory within it (Zech 2:5). God's holy ones walk unscathed in the fiery furnace (Dan 3:25; cf. Is 43:2). Fire tries, purifies, and refines the elect (Ps 66:12; Mal 3:3; Zech 13:9; 1 Pet 1:7), accompanies the transformation of the prophet (2 Kings 2:11; Sir 48:1), just as it exacts retribution upon God's enemies (Gen 19:24; Mt 3:10–12; Rev 8:7). The prophet Malachi speaks of the Day of the Lord as a "refiner's fire" (Mal 3:2), while the Second Letter of Peter envisions the fiery dissolution of the elements at the close of the age (2 Pet 3:7, 10). The fire that purifies the gold (Zech 13:9) burns the chaff (Mt 3:12). Isaiah warns against walking in the flames of one's own fire and by its light (cf. Is 50:11), suggesting that the fire which people ignite "is also the fire that will consume them" (cf. Gal 6:7–8).[106]

In the Christian symbolic universe, however, the fire that addressed Moses from the burning bush and etched the Ten Commandments onto tablets of stone (cf. Deut 10:4) descends from atop Mount Sinai in search of a place to rest in the human heart, as the soul itself is transformed by the Holy Spirit (the Paraclete or Advocate; cf. Jn 14:16, 26; 15:26) into a mountaintop of the encounter with the God who continually purifies, illumines, and transforms the faithful with new fire from heaven (Acts 2:3). The writings of fourth-century monk and ascetic Evagrius Ponticus help us to reflect on the interiorization of the theophany of Sinai.[107] At the center of Revelation's seven Churches, flames of fire burn atop the golden lampstands (1:12). In their midst an angelic Christ, with eyes "like a flame of fire" (1:14) again, encourages, consoles, admonishes, threatens, and invites them to purchase from Him that gold which alone will make them rich (3:18). And just as it is from a fiery, apocalyptic process of cosmic transformation that the New Jerusalem will emerge, so it is through the fire of faithful witness that the victor must journey on the road toward the transformations signaled in the book. As indicated earlier, the reader must choose between the Spirit's consuming fire and the everlasting flames (19:20; 20:10, 14–15), and so be transformed by "either fire or fire," indeed by "pyre or pyre" (in the words of T. S. Eliot).[108] According to Origen:

> "God is spirit, and those who worship him should worship in spirit and truth." Our God is also "a consuming fire." Therefore God is called by two names: "spirit" and "fire." To the just he is spirit; to sinners he is fire.[109]

Not unlike St. Paul in 1 Corinthians 3:12–13, who suggests that we must be prepared to pass through that living fire which reveals our motives and tests our works, the Apocalypse invites the reader to "move in measure"[110] with the living, transforming fire of God's Spirit and the multidimensional Christ before whom "all falsehood melts away."[111] So it is that St. Gregory of Nazianzus cautions:

> Let us not walk in the light of our own fire and in the very flame we have kindled. For I know of a cleansing fire that Christ came to send on the earth, and that he himself is anagogically called

a fire. This Fire takes away whatever is material and of evil habit. This he desires to kindle with all speed, for he longs for speed in doing us good, since he gives us even coals of fire to help us.[112]

Just as Moses led God's people through the waters of the Red Sea, John's apocalyptic Christ leads His victorious witnesses over the surface of the "sea of glass mixed with fire" (15:2). The waters that God separated for Moses and the people of Israel have now solidified and turned to "crystal" (4:6; cf. 22:1) through the victory of the apocalyptic Lion/Lamb. While the waters are made solid through an unwavering faith in Christ (cf. the figure of Peter in Mt 14:29–31), this sea of glass is, however, mixed with fire (cf. Rev 15:2). Indeed, "the gate is narrow and the road is hard that leads to life, and there are few who find it" (Mt 7:14). And just as the Red Sea represented the last obstacle for the people of Israel on their journey through the desert sands to the land of everlasting promise, the sea of crystal mixed with fire stands before the victors as the last obstacle to personal transformation on their exodus through the desert of the earthly city to the Heavenly Jerusalem. It is through the way of the Cross, the renunciation of the self, and a life of "dangerous witness" against the values of the world that the victor overcomes this last obstacle to paradise. And as the victors, "who have overcome the lures of the beast," stand transformed before the throne—"on God's side of the sea" of glass mixed with fire—they join the company of the angels and saints to sing the Song of Moses and of the Lamb (Rev 15:3–4).[113]

The Journey toward the Far Side of the Sea of Glass Mixed with Fire

It is by accepting to follow the way of the Cross that the faithful are led to victory on the far side of the sea of glass mixed with fire. The reversal of the ego at work in the spirituality of the Cross constitutes as powerful a challenge to a postmodern era as it did during the time of Nero. For Christ's "Thy will be done" on the Mount of Olives (Mt 26:42; cf. 6:10) is the only way to transform the self-deifying "stance of Adam" (Gen 3:5–6).[114] Against the spirit of the age, the Apocalypse challenges the narcissism that marks the secularist culture of illusions. Marx's statement that religion "is only the illusory sun about which man revolves so long as he does not revolve about himself" gives voice most eloquently to the spirit of an age that can no longer distinguish creature from Creator, the vine from its branches (Jn 15:5), image from Archetype, Sun from satellite.[115] The resulting sense of loss, indeed peril, is implicit in Nietzsche's observation that "the ice that still supports us has become thin . . . where we still walk, soon no one will be able to walk."[116] The Enlightenment (and postmodern) motif of "deifying mystically the instincts instead of hallowing them in faith" invites comparisons, according to Martin Buber, with analogous trends in ancient Gnosticism.[117] Many centuries ago St. Gregory of Nyssa spoke of "the obscuring of the divine image" through original sin, indeed of exchanging "the image for a mask,"[118] underscoring—in the best tradition of the Patristic writers—the need for the human person to continually strive to grow in the life of the Spirit. His comments serve to emphasize the importance of consecrating the self, one's intellect, volition, and energies to the divine and—striving to move beyond image to likeness—to become a mirror and living icon of Christ.

Certainly, the Seer's apocalyptic, fiery place to stand on the journey across the sea of glass calls for faithful endurance and is not without its own dangers (1:9; 2:2, 10, 19; 14:12; cf. 2 Cor 11:23–28). And yet this image is capable of speaking directly to the narcissism and relativism that are among the marks of our postmodern age. When considered through the lens of Revelation's story world, Marx, Nietzsche, and the Enlightenment architects of contemporary thought chart a perilous journey tending toward nothing for the human person divorced from God. So it is that the Seer calls his audience to choose between the City of God and the city of endless desire, between the way of the Cross and the way of the autonomous self, the divine image and the self-deifying mask, the sea of glass mixed with fire and the fiery lake of burning sulphur (19:20; 20:10, 14–15), the solid foundations of the Gospel and the shifting sands of narcissism (Mt 7:24–25), the glory of the human person transformed by grace and the specter of the cyborg/golem that looms large at the dawn of the era of the post-human and trans-human. It is true that we are "dust and unto dust we shall return" (Gen 3:19), but in the Apocalypse—as throughout the biblical universe—this dust is joined to "the breath of God,"[119] indeed, to the fire of the God who strengthens, transforms, renews, illuminates, and guides the victors on their dangerous journey to the far side of the sea of glass mixed with fire (cf. 1 Cor 15:47f).

Hope in God, Hope in Crisis: The Fire, the Flood, and Becoming the Twice Born

While every age has its doomsayers, one contemporary scholar observes that it is a peculiar fact of our own time that we hear too much talk of endings without beginnings—for "earlier generations of doomsayers," he adds, "had tended to retain something of the messianic or millennial hope that out of the ruins would come regeneration."[120] Amid the decay of a passing world empire, John offers a people in crisis the opportunity to experience in the reading aloud of his Apocalypse, within the eternal present of the Lord's Day (1:10), that spiritual regeneration symbolized in his visions of the new heavens and a new earth. The Seer calls out to the community that strives to hear Christ's voice and so discern God's will in the midst of crisis, to consider the world anew through the light of the open door to heaven, to listen to the Spirit, to leave behind the order that is rapidly fading (18:4) and so to be transformed by the God who makes *all things new* (cf. 21:5).[121]

Whether or not the end of the world is near, Christians are living in the "final hour" (cf. 1 Jn 2:18), and, indeed, have been since the time of the Ascension of Our Lord. As a people of joy and hope in a time of danger, the seven Churches are called to live this hour in the *light* of Christ's return at the end of time rather than in the *shadow* of apocalypse (Lk 21:28). They seek a new beginning amid signs of the end—the falling stars, the earthquakes, and convulsions of a cosmic order that is rapidly passing away (Ps 102:25–26). As Aquinas reminds us, "The name of being wise is reserved to him alone whose consideration is about the end of the universe, which end is also the beginning of the universe."[122] Or as the celebrated Jesus of the "secret" Gospel of Thomas says: "Come into being as you are passing away."[123] Jürgen Moltmann does well to observe that God's final word in Sacred Scripture is not one of destruction and judgment but of regeneration and renewal (Rev 21:5), one that serves as a powerful corrective against the prophets of doom in every generation.[124]

The Book of Revelation's fiery river of apocalyptic transformation sets before the reader the challenge to appropriate with courage the struggle to enter—even now—into the new heaven and new earth, and so to emerge from the storms of time as the twice-born (Jn 3:3; 1 Pet 1:23). Or as an American psychologist writing in the 1940s reminds us:

> The flood comes at the moment of crisis. To the majority it spells destruction, to the hero rebirth. Which it shall be depends upon whether the spark of divine wisdom within him enables a man to orient himself positively to the experience of the waters, accepting them as a suprapersonal reality capable of bringing renewal. Such an orientation or adaptation is symbolized by the ark or chest or boat. In this he may ride out the deluge and emerge to a new heaven and a new earth. Thus he becomes the twice-born.[125]

Worship God, and God Alone: The Ark in the Flood

The ark that provides safe passage through the fiery transformations of the Apocalypse is found in the power of the

Holy Spirit at work in the liturgical life of the Church. Indeed, as Augustine reminds us, even though this ark may be "tossed about and battered by the storms of temptations and trials," it "alone carries the disciples and receives Christ on board" (cf. Mt 28:20).[126] On their perilous journey across the sea of glass mixed with fire toward "that shore to which all our hope belongs," a pilgrim people is offered new fire from heaven through the life of the Spirit in prayer and the liturgical life of the faith community.[127] It is in sacred time and space that the angelified Jesus is present through the power of the Spirit and continues to call forth wisdom and discernment (Rev 2:7). In the eternal present of the liturgy the victors are drawn—here and now—into the circles of heavenly praise surrounding (and extending outward from) the throne of God and the Lamb. For the world that lies beyond the prophet's open door to heaven (4:1) is always open to the faithful on earth through the life of the Spirit. In the liturgical life of the faith communities, the fire of the Holy Spirit is received and appropriated, contained and distributed. Once again, the prayers of the saints play an important role within the divine economy of salvation, as they are gathered together and applied directly upon the events of time and history and help direct the process of apocalyptic change leading to the New Jerusalem (5:8; 8:3–5). Syriac Christianity's spiritual tradition of reflection on the three Churches discussed earlier (i.e., the celestial Church "on high," the Church on earth with its sacramental economy, and the "little Church" of the heart), leads us to consider once more the vital role and significance of the second Church, namely, the Church on earth.

And from the fire out of which the voice of God

addressed Moses on the top of Mount Sinai (Ex 3:4f) to the pillar of cloud and fire that accompanied a priestly people through the desert (Ex 19:6) to the new fire of Pentecost (Acts 2:1f) that came to alight within the hearts of the faithful, the Holy Spirit continues to fire the religious imagination of God's people on their journey in a strange land. And as the faithful of the seven Churches "move in measure"[128] with God's refining fire, St. John bids them to ascend the mountaintop of the encounter with God, to be transformed by that encounter and so to become bearers of the divine fire to a darkened world. The angelified Christ grants the Churches a genuine share in the radiance of His own life and being, as He calls the victors to be transformed into the fire that He, the Morning Star, already is (2:28; 22:16).

John's spectacular visions of renewal can provide joyful reassurance in times of crisis and upheaval. But neither does he lack any of the somber realism of Isaiah's watchman who reminds us that "morning comes, and also the night" (Is 21:12). The New Jerusalem has appeared on the horizon, but the "sea of glass mixed with fire," with its dangers and trials, remains before us. From the watchtower of the prophet's Spirit-inspired perspective, both Isaiah and John remind us that empires fall, and with them their altars and the images of their gods. As one world comes to an end and the New City looms ever larger upon the horizon of the Spirit, John calls us to seek the Face of God through the Faces of Christ and so begin to recover the image of humanity's highest self—the goal and end for which humanity was created—as we strive to see with the eyes of Christ. It is in this way, we can discover that new beginning which is already taking shape in the midst of this world's chaos, suffering, impurity, and death, and so become even now, a new creation in Christ (2 Cor 5:17).

In response to those who would argue that religion is dead, Revelation's Jewish-Christian apocalyptic hope beckons us to look for the light amid the passing shadows of time and to make room for the God who is the source of all light. Beyond the intellectual clouds, philosophical stars, and ideological constellations, behind which God has been eclipsed in our time—from Adam's spirit of rebellion to the "apatheism" that marks the present age— let us, as Rabbi Abraham Isaac Kook invites us, look for a new beginning precisely in the shadows that are stirring to make way for the light:

> People believe that religion is dying, that the world is being overturned. In truth, however, the shadows are stirring, they are in flight in order to make room for the light. If religious faith is to be revitalized, a great effort is needed to deepen the knowledge of God, to follow the most subtle paths of mystical thinking through which one rises above every kind of limitation in God.[129]

So it is that Rabbi Kook inspires us strive to look beyond "the letters, the words," and "the vessels" of the light, to the Light itself.[130] While it may not be given to us to change the world, we have no excuse for not changing ourselves by entering ever more deeply into the mysteries of God and the soul, as Augustine reminds us (*Soliloquies* I.4). As one modern theologian comments, "the Christian of the future will be a mystic or he will not exist at all."[131] Dogmatic formulations, Codes of Canon law, and beautiful art and architecture all have their place. But in the New Jerusalem, John sees neither sun nor moon, nor temple, as a priestly and prophetic people encounters the glory of God's presence *without mediation* (22:4–5; cf. 1:7), for God and the Lamb are themselves the City's temple and its everlasting Light (21:22–23). Amid the sorrows and disorders of this passing life of shadows, St. John calls us to strive to become that well-ordered city whose temple is God Almighty and the Lamb (21:22). Here, amid the visions of the end of the world John opens for the Churches the door to the most profound mysticism in the eternal now of the worship life of a community of faith "poised on the boundary between earth and heaven."[132] Cardinal Jean Daniélou offers insights on how we are to live in two worlds at the same time. He writes:

> We must not be without a country on our arrival in heaven. Our Life is an apprenticeship. It is a matter of learning the rudiments of what we shall have one day to do. So let us already try in prayer to stammer what will later be the "conversation in heaven" with God and his angels; so we must try to make less crude this intellect of ours, which is so immersed in the world of time and space, and to acclimatize it gradually to heavenly things through the action of the gifts of the Holy Spirit. Thus charity itself is the clumsy beginning of that complete communion which will embrace all the saints. [133]

Like Ezekiel's visions of God's celestial throne (cf. Ezek 1 and 10), John's Christianized apocalyptic recreation of the heavenly world sets before the religious imagination of the Churches of Asia Minor the sparkling throne of God and the Lamb that stands forever beyond the power of the Roman Emperor and remains "inaccessible" to any military force.[134] Where the Temple no longer stands, where the community of faith walks in exile by the waters of the river Chebar (cf. Ezek 1:1), God's glory moves with His people, shining forth through the voice and Spirit-inspired vision of the prophet. John's visions of the Faces of Christ do not merely point to future salvation; they convey in the present time the divine call to participate actively in the vital process of the world's re-creation, and so strive to rebuild the ancient ruins and renew the ruined cities (cf. Is 61:4; 44:26).[135] The audience is called to that newness of life which God and the Lamb are bringing about in the midst of opposition to the arrival of the Kingdom. As faithful witnesses, they participate—even now—in the cosmic transformation elaborated so compellingly in John's visions of a new heaven and a new earth in Revelation 21–22.

With St. Ephrem of Syria, let us pray that as we journey toward the everlasting city we may "see it now in a vision, like Moses on the mountaintop."[136]

Solemnity of Our Lord Jesus Christ,
King of the Universe,
November 26, 2017

Endnotes

[1] Cf. Alister McGrath, *The Twilight of Atheism: The Rise and Fall of Disbelief in the Modern World* (New York: Doubleday, 2006); Robert B. Stewart, *The Future of Atheism: Alister McGrath & Daniel Dennett in Dialogue* (Minneapolis: Fortress, 2008).

[2] Cf. Jürgen Habermas, "Secularism's Crisis of Faith: Notes on Post-Secular Society," *New Perspectives Quarterly* 25 (2008): 17–29.

[3] Wendy Brown, "The Sacred, the Secular, and the Profane: Charles Taylor and Karl Marx," in *Varieties of Secularism in a Secular Age*, ed. Michael Warner, Jonathan VanAntwerpen, and Craig Calhoun (Cambridge, MA: Harvard University Press, 2010), 87.

[4] Jonathan Rauch, "Let It Be: Three Cheers for Apatheism," *The Atlantic*, May 2003; Ingolf U. Dalferth, "Post-secular Society: Christianity & the Dialectics of the Secular," *Journal of the American Academy of Religion* 78 (2010): 324.

[5] See Terry Eagleton, in *Culture and the Death of God* (New Haven, CT: Yale University Press, 2014), 199.

[6] Cf. *Fire From Heaven: The Rise of Pentecostal Spirituality and the Reshaping of Religion in the Twenty-First Century* (Cambridge, MA: DaCapo Press, 1995), xv–xvi.

[7] Cf. Fenggang Yang, *Religion in China: Survival and Revival Under Communist Rule* (New York: Oxford University Press, 2012).

[8] James S. Diamond, "The Post-Secular: A Jewish Perspective," *Cross Currents* 53 (2004): 580.

[9] Ingolf U. Dalferth, "Post-secular Society," 323.

[10] Cf. Eoin Cassidy, "'Transcending Human Flourishing': Is There a Need for a Subtler Language?," in Ian Leask, et al., eds., *The Taylor Effect: Responding to a Secular Age* (Newcastle upon Tyne, UK: Cambridge Scholars Publishing, 2010), 26–38. Iain T. Benson, "Seeing Through the Secular Illusion," NGTT Deel 54 *Supplementum* 4 (2013): 24.

[11] José Casanova, "The Secular, Secularizations, Secularisms," in *Rethinking Secularism*, ed. Craig Calhoun, et al. (New York: Oxford University Press, 2011), 58.

[12] Cf. Alister McGrath, *The Twilight of Atheism*.

[13] Keith M. Parsons, "Atheism: Twilight or Dawn?" in *The Future of Atheism*, 65.

[14] Cf. José Casanova, *Public Religions in the Modern World* (Chicago: University of Chicago Press, 1994), 5. See also Charles Taylor, *A Secular Age* (Cambridge, MA & London: The Belknap Press of Harvard University Press, 2007), 426.

[15] Giancarlo Bosetti and Klaus Eder, "Post-Secularism: A Return to the

Public Sphere," *Eurozine,* Aug. 17, 2006, 1–3.

[16] Craig Calhoun, "Time, World, and Secularism," in *The Post-Secular in Question: Religion in Contemporary Society,* ed. Philip S. Gorski, David Kyuman Kim, John Torpey, and Jonathan VanAntwerpen (New York: New York University Press, 2012), 361.

[17] Cf. Reginald W. Bibby, *Restless Churches* (Toronto: Novalis, 2004), 8: "[T]here is very good reason to believe that 'the wise men were wrong'—that people such as Marx and Freud overestimated people's ability to set aside so-called ultimate questions about the meaning of life, suffering, and death, while Durkheim badly underestimated the staying power of well-established religious groups, notably the Roman Catholic Church."

[18] Viktor Frankl, *The Will to Meaning: Foundations and Applications of Logotherapy* (New York: A Meridian Book, 1988).

[19] Alain de Botton, *Religion for Atheists: A Non-believer's Guide to the Uses of Religion* (New York: Pantheon Books, 2012), 12.

[20] Michael Warner, et al., *Varieties of Secularism in a Secular Age.*

[21] Richard John Neuhaus, "Moral Leadership in Post-Secular America," *Imprimis,* 2:7 (July 1982), 3.

[22] Martin Buber, *I and Thou,* trans. Walter Kaufmann (New York: Simon and Schuster, 1996).

[23] Cf. See also Jon D. Levenson, "The Jerusalem Temple in Devotional and Visionary Experience," in ed., Arthur Green, *Jewish Spirituality: From the Bible Through the Middle Ages* vol.1 (New York: Crossroad, 1986), 32–61.

[24] Friedrich Nietzsche, *The Gay Science,* section 125, in *The Portable Nietzsche,* trans. Walter Kaufmann (New York: Penguin Books, 1976), 96.

[25] Cf. W. Norris Clarke, S.J., "Living on the Edge: The Human Person as 'Frontier Being' and Microcosm," in *The Creative Retrieval of St. Thomas Aquinas: Essays in Thomistic Philosophy New and Old* (New York: Fordham University Press, 2009), 132–151.

[26] Karl Löwith, *From Hegel to Nietzsche: The Revolution in Nineteenth-Century Thought* (New York: Columbia University Press, 1964), 322.

[27] Ann R. Meyer, *Medieval Allegory and the Building of the New Jerusalem* (Bury St. Edmunds, Suffolk, UK: St. Edmundsbury Press, 2003), 62.

[28] Fyodor Dostoevsky, *The Brothers Karamazov,* trans. Constance Garnett (London: Wordsworth Editions, 2007), 114.

[29] Parsons, "Atheism: Twilight or Dawn?", in *The Future of Atheism,* 65.

[30] Cf. Abraham Isaac Kook, "The Pangs of Cleansing," in *The Lights of Penitence, the Moral Principles, Lights of Holiness, Essays, Letters, and Poems,* compiled and trans. Ben Zion Bokser (New York: Paulist Press, 1978), 267.

[31] Cf. St. Gregory the Great, "Moral Reflections on Job," XXIX, 3–4, in

Morals on The Book of Job by S. Gregory the Great, 303–04.

[32] Ibid., 304.

[33] Cf. St. Gregory the Great, "Moral Reflections on Job," XXIX, 4, in *Morals on The Book of Job by S. Gregory the Great,* 304.

[34] Blaise Pascal, as quoted in *Pascal: The Man and His Two Loves,* ed. John R. Cole (New York: NYU Press, 1996), 106: "Fire. God of Abraham, God of Isaac, God of Jacob, not of the philosophers and the learned."

[35] Cf. Martin Buber, *I and Thou,* as quoted in *Philosophical and Religious Issues: Classical and Contemporary Statements,* ed. L. Miller (Encino & Belmont, CA: Dickinson, 1971), 144.

[36] Dietrich Bonhoeffer, *The Cost of Discipleship* (London: SMC, 2006), 3ff.

[37] Edward Norman, *Secularisation* (New York: Continuum, 2002), 156–57: "The Church in the Western world is rapidly reinventing itself as the ethicising handmaiden of the aspirations of secular Humanism . . ."

[38] Friedrich Nietzsche, *The Gay Science,* trans. Walter Kaufmann (New York: Vintage Books, 1974), 182.

[39] Ibid.

[40] Cf. de Lubac, *The Drama of Atheist Humanism,* 304; and Sister Joan Gormley, "The Christian Response to Atheism: Dostoevsky" *The Fellowship of Catholic Scholars Newsletter* 19, no. 3 (Summer 1996): 43–44: "The West has lost Christ and that is why it is dying; that is the only reason. Those who 'kill' God also kill man."

[41] James Hollis, *Tracking the Gods: The Place of Myth in Modern Life* (Toronto: Inner City, 1995), 8.

[42] Blond, *Post-Secular Philosophy: Between Philosophy and Theology,* 1.

[43] Ibid., 27.

[44] Cardinal Joseph Ratzinger, *La Repubblica,* November 19, 2004.

[45] Angelus Message for the First Sunday of Lent, March 13, 2011.

[46] Martin Buber, *The Eclipse of God: Studies in the Relation Between Religion and Philosophy* (New York: Harper & Row, 1952), 23.

[47] Cf. Hollis, *Tracking the Gods,* 28.

[48] Cf. Carl Jung, "Letter to Olga Fröbe-Kapteyn," as quoted in Hollis, *Tracking the Gods,* 28, n. 18.

[49] Cf. Ellis Sandoz, in his Introduction to Eric Voegelin's, *Science, Politics, and Gnosticism* (orig. 1968; Wilmington, DE: ISI Books, 2004), xiv.

[50] See Augustine, *The City of God,* XII, 7, trans. Marcus Dods (New York: Modern Library, 1950), 387.

[51] Eric Voegelin, *Science, Politics, and Gnosticism,* 48: "Historically, the murder of God is not followed by the superman, but by the murder of man: the deicide of the gnostic theoreticians is followed by the homicide of the revolutionary practitioners."

52 Cf. *Gaudium et Spes,* no. 36.

53 Karl Löwith, *From Hegel to Nietzsche: The Revolution in Nineteenth-century Thought* (New York: Columbia University Press, 1964), 322.

54 Voegelin, *Science, Politics, and Gnosticism,* 46.

55 As quoted in deLubac, *The Drama of Atheist Humanism,* 65, cf., note 152 and literature cited.

56 Whittaker Chambers, as quoted in *Cheque Mate: The Game of Princes,* Jeffrey A. Baker (Springdale, PA: Whittaker House, 1993), 206.

57 Hollis, *Tracking the Gods,* 28.

58 Cf. Buber, *Eclipse of God,* 136.

59 Blond, *Post-Secular Philosophy,* 27.

60 As quoted in *Walter Benjamin: Selected Writings, vol. 4: 1938–1940,* ed. Michael William Jennings (New York: Harvard University Press, 2003), 390 and note 5, 398.

61 Eric Voegelin, *Science, Politics, and Gnosticism,* 63.

62 Cf. Roger Kimball, *The Long March: How the Cultural Revolution of the 1960s Changed America* (San Francisco: Encounter Books, 2000), xvi–xvii: "The phrase, popularized by the German New Leftist Rudi Dutschke, is often attributed to the Italian Marxist philosopher Antonio Gramsci—an unimpeachable authority for countercultural standard-bearers. But of course the phrase also carries the aura of an even higher authority: that of Mao Tse-Tung and *his* long march and cultural revolution. . . . It was primarily by this means—by insinuation and infiltration rather than confrontation—that the countercultural dreams of radicals like Marcuse have triumphed."

63 Ibid., xvii; and Herbert Marcuse, *Counter-Revolution and Revolt* (Boston: Beacons Press, 1972), 55.

64 Cf. Raymond Aron, *The Opium of the Intellectuals* (orig. 1955; New Brunswick, NJ: Transaction Publishers, 2001).

65 de Lubac, *The Drama of Atheist Humanism,* 70.

66 Ibid., 70.

67 Rene Girard, *I See Satan Fall Like Lightning,* 179. "Neo-paganism would like to turn the Ten Commandments and all of Judeo-Christian morality into some alleged intolerable violence, and indeed its primary objective is their complete abolition" (181).

68 De Lubac, *The Drama of Atheist Humanism,* 71.

69 Ibid., 14.

70 *Centesimus Annus,* no. 25.

71 Etienne Gilson, *The Breakdown of Morals and Christian Education* (Toronto: St. Michael's College, 1952), 6.

72 Cf. Eduard Heimann, "Atheist Theocracy," *Social Research* 20 (1953): 311–331. On 311: "The Soviet form of government is most easily

understood as a kind of theocracy resting on the atheist religion of salvation which is Marxism."

[73] Cf. Iain T. Benson, "Notes Toward A (Re)Definition of the 'Secular'", *University of British Columbia Law Review,* 33 (2000): 541 and note 57. Jacques Maritain, *The Social and Political Philosophy of Jacques Maritain: Selected Readings,* ed. Joseph W. Evans and Leo R. Ward (New York: Charles Scribner & Sons, 1955), 248. Lois Sweet, *God in the Classroom* (Toronto: McClelland and Stewart, 1997), 211 for the expression "secular fundamentalism."

[74] Barr, *Tales of the End,* 180.

[75] Blond, *Post-Secular Philosophy,* 28.

[76] Concerning the term "transhuman," cf. Dante's use of the term *"trasumanar,"* in *Paradiso,* Par. 1.70; and the discussion in Peter Harrison and Joseph Wolyniak, "The History of 'Transhumanism,'" *Notes and Queries* 62, issue 3 (2015): 465–467. See as well 1 Cor 2:9; 2 Cor 12:4.

[77] See Martin Buber, *Selected Writings on Judaism and Jewish Affairs,* vol. 2. Jerusalem: The Zionist Library, 243–244 [In Hebrew], as quoted in David Ohana, "Ambiguous Messianism: The Political Theology of Martin Buber," *Religion Compass* 5/1 (2011): 55.

[78] Daniel Worden, "Killing the Big Other," *Postmodern Culture,* 14 (2004): 2.

[79] *"Vocatus atque non vocatus, Deus aderit."* Cf. *Collected Works of Erasmus: Adages, Volume 4, II i l to II vi 100,* ed. R. A. B. Mynors (Toronto: University of Toronto Press, 1991), 146 and comments.

[80] Cf. Jürgen Habermas, *Religion and Rationality: Essays on Reason, God, and Modernity,* ed. Eduardo Mendieta (Cambridge, MA: MIT Press, 2002), 148–149: "Universalistic egalitarianism, from which sprang the ideals of freedom and a collective life in solidarity, the autonomous conduct of life and emancipation, the individual morality of conscience, human rights and democracy, is the direct legacy of the Judaic ethic of justice and the Christian ethic of love. This legacy, substantially unchanged, has been the object of a continual critical reappropriation and reinterpretation. Up to this very day there is no alternative to it. And in light of the current challenges of a post-national constellation, we must draw sustenance now, as in the past, from this substance. Everything else is idle postmodern talk."

[81] Jürgen Habermas and Joseph Ratzinger, *The Dialectics of Secularization: Reason and Religion* (San Francisco: Ignatius Press, 2006). Pope Francis, "Letter to a Non-Believer," *Vatican,* September 4, 2013, which responds to Eugenio Scalfari of the Italian Newspaper: "La Repubblica." Accessed at http://w2.vatican.va/content/francesco/en/letters/2013/documents/papa-francesco_20130911_eugenio-scalfari.html.

⁸² M. E. Williams, "Apocalypse Now," in *Is the World Ending?* Concilium 4, 9.

⁸³ Cf. St. John Paul II, *Fides et Ratio*, Introduction, nos. 1 and 2.

⁸⁴ Cf. Dominic Wisz, O.F.M. Conv., *Aim Higher: Spiritual and Marian reflections of St. Maximilian Kolbe* (Chicago: Marytown Press, 2007), 121.

⁸⁵ James J. O'Donnell, "Augustine, *City of God*," (unpublished paper) accessed at http://www9.georgetown.edu/faculty/jod/augustine/civ.html.

⁸⁶ "Der Mensch hat immer Gott oder Abgott." Cf. Ellis Sandoz, *Political Apocalypse*, 177 and literature cited.

⁸⁷ F. Dostoeveky, *The Brothers Karamazov*, ET, C. Garnett (New York: Modern Library, 1996; orig. 1880), 117–118: ". . . Yes, man is broad, too broad, indeed. I'd have him narrower . . . God and the devil are fighting there and the battlefield is the heart of man."

⁸⁸ Ed. Bruce H. Kirmmse, Niels Jørgen Cappelørn, and Alastair Hannay, *Kierkegaard's Journals and Notebooks 1, AA-DD* (Princeton: Princeton University Press, 2007), Journal DD: 208, 1837, 280.

⁸⁹ John D. Caputo, "Either-Or, Undecidability, and Two Concepts of Irony: Kierkegaard and Derrida," in *The New Kierkegaard*, ed. Elsebet Jegstrup (Bloomington, IN: Indiana University Press, 2004), 36.

⁹⁰ Jacques Derrida, "On a Newly Arisen Apocalyptic Tone in Philosophy," in *Raising the Tone of Philosophy: Late Essays by Immanuel Kant, Transformative Critique by Jacques Derrida*, ed. Peter Fenves (Baltimore: John Hopkins University Press, 1993), 167.

⁹¹ Edmondo F. Lupieri, *A Commentary on the Apocalypse of John* (Grand Rapids, MI: William B. Eerdmans Publishing Company, 2006), viii.

⁹² Ibid.

⁹³ St. John Paul II, *Agenda for the Third Millennium* (London: Harper Collins, 1996), 123.

⁹⁴ Buber, *Eclipse of God*, 135.

⁹⁵ John Ruusbroec, *The Adornment of the Spiritual Marriage*, ch. LXIV in *The Adornment of the Spiritual Marriage, The Sparkling Stone & The Book of Supreme Truth*, trans. C. A. Wynschenk Dom (orig. 1916; New York: Cosimo, 2007), 149.

⁹⁶ Cf. Thompson, *The Book of Revelation: Apocalypse and Empire*, 32.

⁹⁷ Mircea Eliade, *The Myth of the Eternal Return* (New York: Pantheon, 1954), 160.

⁹⁸ St. John Paul II, Angelus Message, September 29, 1996.

⁹⁹ Bauckham, *Theology of the Book of Revelation*, 162–163.

¹⁰⁰ Cardinal Joseph Ratzinger, *"La Repubblica,"* Nov. 19, 2004.

[101] Cf. Walter L. Adamson, *Embattled Avant-Gardes: Modernism's Resistance to Commodity Culture in Europe* (Berkeley and Los Angeles: University of California Press, 2007), 35.

[102] Pope Benedict XVI, *Christianity and the Crisis of Cultures,* trans. Brian McNeil (San Francisco: Ignatius Press, 2005), 52.

[103] St. Cyprian, *To Martyrs and Confessors,* Epistle, VII. Craig Calhoun, "Time, World, and Secularism," in, *The Post-Secular in Question,* 359: "We might engage God less as the Absolute or the One at the center of the Neoplatonic order and more as being 'in the struggle with us.'"

[104] Carl-Martin Edsman, art., "Fire," in *The Encyclopedia of Religion,* vol. 5, ed. Mircea Eliade (New York: Macmillan, 1987), 342.

[105] Cf. F. Lang, art. "pýr," in ed., G. W. Bromiley, *Theological Dictionary of the New Testament* (Grand Rapids, MI: Wm. B. Eerdmans, Paternoster Press, 1985), 975ff.

[106] Joseph Blenkinsopp, *Isaiah 40–55,* Anchor Bible, vol. 19A (New York: Doubleday, 2002), 322.

[107] See comments by Alexander Golitzin, "Earthly Angels, Heavenly Men," 149 and literature cited.

[108] T. S. Eliot, *Four Quartets,* "Little Gidding" (London: Faber and Faber, 1946), 42.

[109] Origen, Homilies on the Gospels of Luke, 26.1 (FC, 94: 109), as quoted in *Exodus, Leviticus, Numbers, and Deuteronomy,* ed. Joseph T. Lienhard, S.J. (Ancient Christian Commentary on Scripture, OT, III; Downers Grove: InterVarsity, 2001), 278.

[110] T. S. Eliot, *Four Quartets,* "Little Gidding," 40.

[111] Pope Benedict XVI, *Spe Salvi,* art. 47.

[112] St. Gregory Nazianzus, "On Holy Baptism, as quoted in *Isaiah 40–66,* ed. Mark W. Elliott (Ancient Christian Commentary on Scripture, OT, XI; Downers Grove, IL: InterVarsity, 2007), 135.

[113] C. Rowland, Open Heaven, 422.

[114] Cf. Benedict XVI, Homily for Holy Thursday "Mass of the Lord's Supper," April 5, 2012.

[115] Cf. A Contribution to the Critique of Hegel's Philosophy of Right, in *The Marx-Engels Reader,* ed. Robert C. Tucker, 2nd ed. (New York: W.W. Norton & Co., 1978), 54.

[116] *The Will to Power,* Ed. and Trans. W. Kaufmann and R. J. Hollingdale (New York: Vintage, 1968), 40.

[117] Buber, *Eclipse of God,* 137.

[118] Cf. Constantine Scouteris, "Never As Gods: Icons and Their Veneration," *Sobornost,* 6 (1984): 10; and St. Gregory of Nyssa, Patrologia Graeca, 44, 193C.

[119] Cf. comments by Rabbi Jonathan Sacks, *To Heal a Fractured World: the Ethics of Responsibility* (New York: Shocken Books, 2005), 47.

[120] Krishan Kumar, "Apocalypse, Millennium and Utopia Today," in *Apocalypse Theory and the Ends of the World,* ed. Malcolm Bull (Oxford: Blackwell, 1995), 204ff.

[121] Cf. Ugo Vanni, "La Chiesa in preghiera discerne la storia. Lettura del libro dell'Apocalisse," *Horeb* 16 (1997), 34–47.

[122] St. Thomas Aquinas, *Summa Contra Gentiles,* I.1, as quoted in Joseph Campbell, *The Hero With a Thousand Faces,* Bollingen Series, XVII (Princeton, NJ: Princeton University Press, 1973), 269.

[123] Cf. Marvin Meyer, *The Gospel of Thomas: The Hidden Sayings of Jesus* (San Francisco: Harper Collins, 1992), Saying 42, 87. The original is more often translated "become passersby."

[124] Moltmann, "In the End—God," 123.

[125] Eleanor Bertine, "The Great Flood," in *Jung's Contribution to Our Time: The Collected Papers of Eleanor Bertine* (New York: C. J. Jung Foundation, 1967), 203–204. The essay was first published in 1944.

[126] St. Augustine, Sermon 75, 3: PL 38, 475; *The Works of Saint Augustine: A Translation for the 21st Century,* Part III, Sermons, Vol. III, Sermons 51–94, trans. Edmund Hill, O.P. (Brooklyn, NY: New City Press, 1991), 305. The original reads: "Quia etsi turbatur navis, navis est tamen. Sola portat discipulos et recipit Christum. Periclitatur quidem in mari, sed sine illa statim peritur."

[127] Cf. Adapted from a letter from St. Aloysius Gonzaga to his mother (dated June 10, 1591, shortly before his death), as quoted in: F. Olgiati, "L'epistolario di S. Luigi," *Vita e Pensiero: Rivista culturale dell'Università Cattolica del Sacro Cuore* 13 (1927), 345. The original text reads: "Con la sua materna benedizione mi accompagni ed aiuti a passare questo golfo, ed a giungere a riva di tutte le mie speranze" (author's translation).

[128] T. S. Eliot, *Four Quartets: Little Gidding,* 40.

[129] Cf. Abraham Isaac Kook, "The Pangs of Cleansing," in *The Lights of Penitence, the Moral Principles, Lights of Holiness, Essays, Letters, and Poems,* trans. Ben Zion Bokser (New York: Paulist Press, 1978), 268.

[130] Ibid., 268–69.

[131] Karl Rahner, "The Spirituality of the Church of the Future," in *Theological Investigations* 20, *Concern For the Church,* trans. Edward Quinn (London: Darton, Longman & Todd, 1981), 149.

[132] Josephine M. Ford, "The Priestly People of God in the Apocalypse," 256.

[133] Jean Daniélou, "The Sign of the Temple: A Meditation," in *Letter and Spirit: Temple and Contemplation,* ed. Scott Hahn (Steubenville, OH: St. Paul Center for Biblical Theology, 2008), 287.

[134] Samson H. Levey, ed., *The Targum of Ezekiel* Aramaic Bible, 13 (Wilmington, DA: Michael Glazier, 1987), 3.

[135] Susan Niditch, "Ezekiel 40–48 in a Visionary Context," *Catholic Biblical Quarterly*, 48 (1986): 215–17.

[136] As quoted in *Awakening Faith: Daily Devotions from the Early Church*, ed. James Stuart Bell with Patrick J. Kelly (Grand Rapids: Zondervan, 2013), 3.